The asses and angels in Gail Black's title are people. They are the men who have used and abused her -- and all those folks who have supported and helped. Gail's book reads like a sexy novel. Reading it, I laughed out loud and cried. Gail's grit, creativity and humor shine through. "Asses and Angels" is a fast-moving and gripping read.

Daniel O'Rourke, author of *The Spirit at Your Back*
and *The Living Spirit*.

How does one woman pack so much into her life? Journey with Gail as she grows up in post WW II America, falls in love, experiences not one but three abusive husbands, and emerges into her own as a successful, spirited agri-entrepreneur. My hat is off to this spunky, never-say-die woman.

Bobbi Montgomery, co-author of *Across America By Bicycle*

Asses and Angels

A Journey from Abuse to Achievement

To Ella M. Williams
5-20-2013

Gail L. Black

GAIL L. BLACK

iUniverse, Inc.
Bloomington

Asses and Angels
A Journey from Abuse to Achievement

iUniverse books may be ordered through booksellers or by contacting:

iUniverse
1663 Liberty Drive
Bloomington, IN 47403
www.iuniverse.com
1-800-Authors (1-800-288-4677)

Because of the dynamic nature of the Internet, any web addresses or links contained in this book may have changed since publication and may no longer be valid. The views expressed in this work are solely those of the author and do not necessarily reflect the views of the publisher, and the publisher hereby disclaims any responsibility for them.

Any people depicted in stock imagery provided by Thinkstock are models, and such images are being used for illustrative purposes only.

Certain stock imagery © Thinkstock.

ISBN: 978-1-4759-4046-6 (sc)
ISBN: 978-1-4759-4048-0 (e)
ISBN: 978-1-4759-4047-3 (dj)

Library of Congress Control Number: 2012913908

Printed in the United States of America

iUniverse rev. date: 8/21/2012

DEDICATION

To Bruce Bradford who picked me up in a bar even though neither of us drinks, took me to Europe, then to his lovely home in Sun City, Georgetown, Texas where he provided me with an office and encouraged me to write this book.

He has read the manuscript numerous times, critiqued and reread, always with positive support for this project.

Throughout summers spent on my farm, Bruce has picked fruit, waited on my customers, conducted farm tours and encouraged everyone he encounters to read this book.

His help and loving belief in me is over the top, way past the cliché "talk the talk and walk the walk."

Acknowledgements

Never having written a book before, I required a lot of help, direction and instruction. Any credit for this book should be shared with an army of people, all of whom I hope I remember to thank by name:

Bruce Bradford, to whom I dedicate this book, has laughed, cried and sworn he could not read it again. The pain I have endured is painful to him because of his tender heart and his love for me. Yet, he reads it again and again, with wonderful insight and positive feedback.

Bobbi Montgomery who rode down my driveway on a bicycle, insisted I write the story behind the creation of my farm gift shop, offered her knowledge and expertise, guided me though every sentence and chapter and repeatedly told me I could and should keep going.

I want to especially thank my three sons, Andy Putnam, Larry Putnam and Rob Black, for allowing me to share the painful personal details about our lives and our journey to now. I am so proud of each of them and their accomplishments, thankful they survived their upbringing, have become great parents, and that they live close by, visit often and help me continuously with the farming, computer snares, product creation, brainstorming, and more.

My three daughter's in law, Cindy, Jill and Christina, for sharing their husbands, giving support, and for mothering my nine beautiful grandchildren.

Special thanks to Christina Black for the back cover photo and her genius at including Iwannago.

I will be forever grateful to those I view as angels who have been with me though laughter, pain, uncertainty, loneliness, success and who have listened endlessly: Peg Beckman, Dick Davies, Carol Baumet, Sherry Simons, Lori Rhoden, Betty Teran and Linda Koenig.

I also wish to thank additional angels who appear when a need arises, hover briefly, and administer their love, blessings and help. Among them, but not limited to, are Charlotte Morse, Daniel O'Rourke, Phyllis Moses, Jana Monroe. Mary Ann Eidemiller and the list continues.

A very special thank you to Iwannago, my faithful cocker spaniel, who never leaves my side whether I am greeting customers, picking fruit or spending endless hours writing.

Thank you.

Contents

Preface

UNRAVELING LIFE IS LIKE dissecting a nightmare or a complicated dream. Life's successes and failures are woven together like the tangled brambles, stick tights and rose bushes in a thicket of wild berries. My personal path meandered through the briar covered, seemingly impenetrable fields of good and evil.

Every day, as I walked across the lawn to the rustic little shop where I sold my jams, jellies, syrup, homemade pot holders, and gift bags, a customer would ask me why I didn't write a book about my journey through life, culminating in the creation of my gift shop, which is nestled in the woods and vines of the farm I call home. I told customers my life stories often, and with each rendition, I daydreamed about writing such a book. I always concluded that it would be a waste of time and that no one would read it.

Mirror didn't agree with that conclusion and led me to reconsider. I thought about procrastination and uncertainty as it reflected a shrug of my shoulder and a tilt of my head.

The old mirror hung in the front hall, just inside the front door of my old farmhouse. It had seen abuse, kindness, trouble, jubilation, grief, disbelief, and a whole lot of love. It had witnessed over a hundred years of my family's history, since my paternal grandfather had manufactured it in his factory in Bradford, Pennsylvania, in the mid-1800s. Mirror, with its ornate, Victorian-style frame made of mahogany and black teak, had also graced the living-room wall in my childhood home. It bore witness to my young learning experiences and indiscretions. My mother nicknamed it the "silent chaperone," because she could stand in the kitchen and use it to see what was happening on the living-room couch. I called it Mirror, because it made me reflect on lots of things.

Mirror had appointed itself my guardian and had advised me often throughout my life. I couldn't part with Mirror when I moved into the farmhouse, so it hung by the front door for forty years, passing judgment on all who came and went. Mirror eavesdropped on conversations that took place on my wide, shady front porch and on the lawn. Mirror's opinions were not always like mine, but when I thought them over, I found I usually agreed. Sometimes years passed and Mirror's only job was to cover the piece of torn wallpaper behind it, but I could depend on its interference and opinions whenever I was embarking on a new adventure. Mirror didn't disappoint me when I contemplated writing my book. When I looked at my eyes in Mirror, I realized that I could share my strength and determination with many discouraged souls by writing a book about my journey. I could describe difficult times, my leap into entrepreneurship, and the creation of my successful and rewarding agritourism business.

Mirror said, "There was a time when you thought nobody would come down that long gravel driveway to visit your gift shop and buy your homemade fruit syrups, but they came. They'll read your book, too."

I sat in the living room of my one-hundred-and-fifty-year-old farmhouse, situated between the vineyard and the cliff edge of Lake Erie, listening to the wind, some recorded fiddle music and the crackle of the fire in the fireplace I built the fourth year I lived there. I had a few stories typed into my computer, but

I had so little time to write because of the vineyard work and the gift shop.

Suddenly, above those comforting, homey sounds, I thought I heard Mirror speak again: "It may take years, but it's important to write this book. Look at yourself. You're just one tiny, hundred-pound senior citizen. How long do you think you can maintain your workload? You don't jog across the lawn to your gift shop as fast as you did a few years ago. Writing a book is mental work, and it would be easier than growing, picking, cooking, bottling, and selling your crops as fruit syrups."

The day was cold and blustery along the shores of Lake Erie. The wind had been howling steadily for forty-eight hours, while the temperature dropped to near zero. The old house creaked and moaned, snapped and groaned under the assault.

Thanks to the hours I'd spent tucking insulation into all the cracks and spaces between hand-sawed boards, the house had a few warm corners where I could cuddle up with my cozy blanket. The heat of my laptop on the squeaky joints of my aging knees added to my comfort. No loud music blared through the old place, just the soft sound of bluegrass fiddle tunes and the crackle of a fire. Memories whirled in my head. I stared into the fire, my fingers poised over the keyboard, and I remembered the family from Texas who came to western New York in 1999 to experience a snowy Christmas. They asked, "Is this your family farm? Did your grandparents and parents live here? Did you grow up here and learn to make maple syrup from your parents?"

I knew I should be spending my time making pot holders, gift bags, wreaths, and wall hangings to sell in my gift shop next year, instead of writing about the past; but I had a compelling desire to share my stories. I remembered thinking about how hard I had struggled to find, buy, pay for, and improve the land those Texans were standing on. I was almost insulted by the idea that I had inherited it. "No, no. I bought it in 1969, and it was pretty much a dump," I told them.

WordPerfect popped up on the screen, bright and blank. I began to record how I arrived at this moment, in this living room. My life experiences confirmed my belief that I was predestined to share my journey from a horrific and hellacious life to a serene and successful one. My life has taught me that we all have the power to change awful to awesome. I did. Anyone can.

Chapter One: Background: Family Fun to Forgotten, 1939-1947

As I was often told, my sister was almost seven years old when Mom confronted her at lunch one day to prepare her for my arrival. "I have something interesting to tell you," she said. "We are going to have a new baby, so you will have a little brother or sister to play with."

Sis said, "Okay, but what were you going to tell me that was interesting, Mommy?"

I was born in western New York in 1939, just as World War II was about to intensify.

Our family was always just a little more exciting and independent than anyone else's. Some said my dad was a self-made man. Dad said he didn't owe anybody anything; by that he meant that he had no political debts or obligations. He was an entrepreneur in an unusual occupation—a mink rancher who raised thousands of beautiful animals to produce furs for coats. Dad's furs were sold at the Hudson Bay Company in New York City. His business was unique, and it set us apart from our neighbors and didn't require much interaction with the community.

My father was the primary sculptor of my personality and character. Dad was the final decision maker and the family's financial support. He determined and administered all discipline. Once in a while, when Mom complained about not having some luxury, Dad would say, "As the mink eat, so will we." Business came first, and the necessities for family life followed. He was a moderate risk taker and enjoyed successful returns on his optimistic business decisions.

My mother was the family anchor, and her primary job was to keep our house in order. She was the social and financial director, but she deferred to Dad's opinion, which was normal behavior in the 1940s. Mom was a pessimist and hated risk of any kind. Love, mutual respect and their differences gave balance to their marriage.

My parents believed that a united front was essential on all things child-related. If they had differing opinions on issues relating to my sister and me, we never knew it.

Mothers stayed home, hung the laundry in the backyard, cleaned, cooked, and never missed a PTA meeting, church on Sunday, or a neighborhood picnic in somebody's pasture. Life was slow; friends were more intimate; troubles were shared; and nobody had a credit card, a television, or a computer.

During World War II, my family, like millions of others, lived in the country, and we found ways to help ourselves. We cut firewood by hand, walked whenever we could to conserve gasoline, grew a victory garden using instructions and seeds provided by the federal government, and then preserved the produce for winter.

We traded maple syrup, fruit, and vegetables for eggs, milk, and meat if we didn't have our own farm animals. Eggs were plentiful at certain times, and we would store them in a solution of water glass. Water glass is a glasslike industrial adhesive and, chemically, is sodium silicate. We mixed eleven parts water to one part water-glass adhesive, forming a pastelike liquid that filled the pores and sealed the air out of the eggs. Eggs were taken directly from the chickens and dropped into the crock of thick goop unwashed, where they stayed fresh for a year or more. They were best used in baking or for scrambled eggs.

It was my job to retrieve vegetables and fruits from the root cellar and the slimy eggs from the cool, dark cellar where the dirt floor kept everything cold. We drank homemade wild-blackberry wine, hard cider, and fruit juice made from wild berries and fruits that we squeezed, canned, or fermented ourselves.

Nobody had any money, but we knew how to have fun when we had neighborhood corn roasts. Everyone saved a few tablespoons of coffee so we could put a graniteware coffee pot over the wood fire to boil delicious-smelling fresh coffee. We brought coffee cups, dishes, and silverware from our own kitchens.

We brought corn and potatoes from our gardens and hand-churned butter for the homemade bread.

The children played softball and hide-and-seek, fell in the creek, and occasionally stepped in a fresh cow pie. The men smoked their own hand-rolled cigarettes, and the women gossiped. The picnic cost nothing, provided fun, and was anticipated for months in advance.

I remember when the sirens would blow for a blackout test and my dad would take his flashlight and walk around the neighborhood checking windows for leaking light. The enemy could not bomb as easily if they couldn't see lights, and preparing for blackouts was a way that citizens participated in keeping America safe. We felt so much pride in being Americans.

My mother was a firm believer in education. She was the first in her family to graduate from high school, and she insisted that Sis and I take learning seriously. She thought that religious education was a good place to start, so when I was three, she enrolled me in Sunday school, left me in a nursery class, and went off to her own adult class. When it was time to go home, she came back and discovered me sitting alone in the middle of the room in an empty sandbox.

I had thrown great mountains of sand on the floor, and the teacher and other children were huddled at a table in a corner. The teacher sternly said, "Take her home, and don't ever bring her back to this Sunday school. She obviously doesn't like Sunday school, the other children, or me."

My mother continued to hone my social skills by inviting her childhood friend, who had a son my age, to our home for tea. I took the little boy by the hand, and we played quietly together until our mothers got involved in conversation. Then I told him I had a delightful game we could play as I took him into my parents' bedroom. I got him to take off his clothes and lie on the floor under my daddy's side of the bed. Just as I was about to take my clothes off, his mother heard us giggle, looked under the bed, and discovered her naked four-year-old little darling. They never came back to visit.

Mom sewed doll clothes out of old feed bags and scrap materials. She rolled up the old rugs in our living room and dining room, pushed the furniture aside, and put clamp-on roller skates on my shoes in an effort to tire me out. I learned to skate and spent hours rolling back and forth, polishing a path on the hardwood floors.

Mom taught us to play games, and Dad made stilts and taught us to walk on them. They read to us every night before bedtime, and we had a close, happy family.

When I got restless in the winter, sometimes my mother would send me outdoors to play in the snow while my dad worked in the mink yard. He was busy carrying out the breeding program, and I was supposed to play in the snow in the fenced-in area and get myself tired out. My mother told me that one day I wasn't out there long when Dad stomped through the kitchen door, shouting, "Here's your kid. Keep her in the house.

I asked her what she was doing rolling around in the snow and jumping up and down. She said, 'Oh, I'm playing that I'm a female mink. Shall I fight or let 'em do it?' You need to keep her in this house—I don't care how wild she is." He set my snow-covered butt down on the clean kitchen floor.

Finally I went to kindergarten and fell in love with a little boy named Donny. He seemed to like me, too, and gave me a hard rubber horseshoe for Christmas. It seemed that I fell in love every year with a different boy; they were all so cute, and it seemed a shame not to.

In first grade, I had a strict teacher who enforced a clean-your-plate rule. I was a stubborn, not-to-be-told-what-to-do, defiant child who had been allowed to be a unique individual. We had no cafeteria, so hot lunches were delivered to our room, and we ate at our desks. The trouble started when I decided the food smelled terrible; my kindergarten crush, Donny, didn't like it, either, so we both refused to eat it. One day, we combined our stinking food, poured our chocolate milk into it, and began grunting like pigs. "Oink, oink, snort, snort. Here piggy, here piggy, it's time for pig slop," we both chanted, giggling. The whole class began to chant along with us.

The episode struck terror into the teacher's heart. She must have imagined thirty-two boys and girls mixing huge batches of pig slop while they all oinked and snorted. She stormed down the row to our desks and then stood with her hands on her hips, her face puckered like a frosty thorn bush, and screamed, "Be quiet right now or you'll march straight to the principal's office." She pounded her fist on Donny's desk, and the tray of pig slop slid to the floor. Donny and I carried our own paper-bag lunches from then on and had no recess for two weeks. Mom was appalled at my behavior, and things got worse when we got unexpected company from out of town.

In the summer of 1948, I was playing with my dolls in the backyard when a car drove onto the cinder driveway. I ran to see who it might be, and a medium-height, severe-looking lady with a wrinkled face and gray hair secured with curved brown combs stepped from the car. She said, "You must be Gail. Where's your daddy?"

I said, "He's in the mink yard, feeding his mink."

A kindly-looking old man climbed out of the passenger side of the green 1946 Coupe and said with a pleasant smile, "Don't you know who she is?"

I answered, "No, but I'll take you both to the mink yard to see my daddy."

The woman said, "I'm your grandmother, your father's mother. You don't know me because a daughter is a daughter all her life and a son's a son 'til he gets him a wife. I'm sure you know your other grandparents."

It was the beginning of the great conflict between her and me and between her and my mother, who overheard the remark.

On the way to the mink yard, she spotted the outhouse used primarily by the hired men. It was a normal "two holer," unpainted and clean, but it definitely smelled like an outhouse in the summer heat. Grapevines wound around it, concealing its ugliness. The grapes grew big and luscious in the fertile environment, and the vines provided a wonderful hiding place for Sis and me. There was a knothole in the back, just above the seat; for us, it was a window into the secrets of maleness. When a hired man's duties required him to sit down, we had a stick just the right size to fit the knothole. We'd give one quick poke, and then we would run and hide before he got his pants up.

The day Grandma Bertha spied the outhouse, she had been traveling for several hours, and the urge was indeed strong. "Just a minute, young lady. You wait right there with Grandpa David," she commanded as she tried to disappear into the humid, smelly, vine-covered environment.

I learned to adore Grandpa David, my step-grandfather. He made faces at Grandma Bertha when she wasn't looking, and throughout the summer he took me for long walks when she was bitchy and mean. His hugs and snuggles were the good and safe kind. My mother liked him, too.

Grandpa David and I stopped on the edge of the lawn and watched Grandma Bertha take a shortcut through blackberry bushes to the outhouse door. She tried to get in, but the grapevines had fallen down and grasped the door tightly. She tore at them as she stomped and snorted and tried to wrestle with them. Finally she screamed, "David, you get over here and get this door open for me, right now!"

Grandpa David tried, but he was a bit frail. Meanwhile, my dad was close by, feeding the mink. When he heard the yelling, he recognized the voice and met his mother face to face at the outhouse door for the first time in twenty years. He broke the vines loose, and she disappeared into the almost-private world. Dad went back to work, and I introduced Grandpa David to the fun in my private world behind the outhouse. I even loaned him my stick and showed him how to use it just before we heard a terrible scream. It was the beginning of a war of will between her and me.

Mom was doing up the lunch dishes and heard the commotion. I heard the slam of the screen door on the back porch, and down the steps she came, wiping her clean hands on her flowered cotton apron. She always wore a full bib apron, one with bias binding or rickrack all around the edges. She was a pleasingly plump little woman with smooth pink skin; thin, curly, ash-blond hair; and pretty green eyes.

After introductions all around, sleeping arrangements were made. Grandma Bertha settled into my room, while I moved my pillow and blanket to the back porch.

Mom hollered up the stairs, "Coffee's ready. My folks are here, and they brought a sweet roll. Come on down and meet them."

My maternal grandparents visited nearly every day. I spent weekends with them in the city of Jamestown, and they spoiled me. I knew there was no question that they loved me, and I was glad to see them.

Grandpa David patted Grandma Bertha's shoulder and whispered in her ear as they passed me at the foot of the stairs, "Now, Mum, don't scrap before the fight starts."

Grandma Bertha ignored him and began to recite her original comment, "A son is a son...," but Mom interrupted her.

"I heard you say that the first time when you got out of your car and said it to Gail. I thought you must be kidding," she said. Then she made proper introductions, and everyone shook hands and sat down around the dining-room table. They all seemed congenial enough. The grown-up talk was boring, so I spent the time planning more ways to get myself in trouble. To think of a prank was to do it. I always weighed the consequences to see if the fun I planned was worth the punishment I knew I would get.

Grandma Bertha forbade me to go into my old room to get my dolls and toys, and she hated when I played records on the old wind-up record player in the living room, so I played it often. She threw the crank in the garbage, but Dad found it.

We had only one bathroom in the 1940s, and it was downstairs, next to my parents' bedroom. Grandma Bertha kept a chamber pot by the bed upstairs, which she emptied every morning. After I lost access to my dolls and the old record player, the war between us escalated. I observed her making her way to our one bathroom with the full chamber pot each morning. I timed her and knew exactly when she would show up with her prize in the pot.

I ran ahead of her into the bathroom, locked the door, and retrieved my stash of coloring supplies from under the pile of clean towels. I got comfortable on the floor while I colored.

Sure enough, Grandma Bertha was on her way to the bathroom. I could visualize her with her white china chamber pot in one hand, a towel discreetly covering it, trying the door handle. The door was locked, so she knocked and tried the handle again. "Damned spoiled little bitch," I heard her whisper as she banged harder on the door. I didn't answer, but I grunted really loudly.

"Irene, that kid is in this bathroom again. She does it every time I bring my toiletries down here to use the facility," she shrieked at my mother. I could imagine the pot sloshing and Grandma Bertha standing in the little dark hallway, hunched toward the door, trying to hide it. She thought we didn't know what her "toiletries" were, but we all knew.

I grunted again. She hissed so only I could hear, "You inconsiderate little bitch. This isn't over yet. I'll show you a thing or two."

I slowly put my crayons away under the towels, flushed the toilet, and ran the water in the sink. I unbuttoned my slacks and pulled out my shirt, opened the door, and blocked the doorway while I took my time getting out of her way.

I yawned and stretched as I said, "Oh, Grandma, I didn't know you were out here. I waited until late so I wouldn't be in your way, but I guess you slept in."

Grandma Bertha finally went home, right after she gave each of her other grandchildren beautiful pencil boxes full of crayons, paints, colored pencils, rubber stamps, stencils, rulers, and more. I got an insignificant little piece of clothesline with three clothespins on it.

My favorite grandparent was my maternal grandfather, who was president of a life insurance company. He was six feet tall, had a thin build and flaming red hair, and he had a wood shop in his basement, where he made doll furniture for me. He took pride in my grandma's African violets, because he mixed a special blend of potting soil for her that included some dark humus dirt from a patch of woods owned by the principal of our city school system. The land had "No Trespassing" signs all around it. One day, Grandpa invited me to accompany him while he sneaked into the woods to get a couple of metal pails full of that rich dirt.

"Gail, there are rules and procedures for this trip," he instructed me as he loaded his pails and tools into the trunk of his brand-new 1951 Pontiac. "Silence is essential. You must not talk or make noise of any kind. And we have to wait until the principal drives by on his way to school so that we don't get caught. Do you understand me?" I nodded, quietly acknowledging his instructions. It was an honor to be his assistant.

Finally we coasted up to the special patch of woods, and Grandpa started to hand me the equipment from the trunk. The metal pails were first. I set them on the ground and suddenly remembered the fire crackers our hired man had given me. They were in my pocket with a packet of matches. Grandpa was leaning into the trunk, sorting out his tools, and I lit a firecracker and put it in the metal pail. "Boom!" Grandpa was so startled that he landed head first into the trunk. He came out with a raging explosion of his own. He grabbed me by the seat of my jeans and my shirt collar, threw me into the backseat, threw the buckets and other stuff back into the trunk, and spun gravel on the country roads all the way home.

He told my mother, "She is incorrigible." Then, as was always the case when I was about to get spanked, he said to my grandmother, "C'mon, Mother. It's time to go home." He knew I needed to be punished, but he couldn't stand to see it done.

My behavior didn't improve, so Mother decided I needed more structured activities.

I joined 4-H and learned to sew, cook, iron, and raise rabbits. I planted evergreen trees, tended a garden, and got blue ribbons at the county fair. Mom sent me away to 4-H camp for three weeks so she could have a rest, but when I returned, the escapades continued.

A boy named Billy sometimes came to stay with his grandparents, who lived a quarter mile away, across a big, open field. He played the saxophone, and I was taking flute lessons. Each time he arrived for an extended visit, winter or summer, he would play, "Can She Bake a Cherry Pie, Billy Boy" on his saxophone. I would hear that, run for my flute, and answer with, "She Can Bake a Cherry Pie, Quick's a Cat Can Wink Its Eye." It was a signal for a game of croquet in the summer or skiing in the pasture in the winter. One snowy, windy day when I was eight, I fell at the bottom of the hill. Billy picked me up and kissed me on the mouth. I was overwhelmed with passion, so I kicked off my skis, took him by the hand, and pulled him into the frozen culvert under a nearby road, where we kissed again and again. I discovered that I loved kissing.

In 1948, when Sis was sixteen, she met a boy named Bernie at a 4-H meeting. His main project was chicken farming. After they dated for a while, his regular donations of fresh eggs to our family were always welcome. Sis got blue ribbons in 4-H and graduated from high school at the head of her class. She was accepted at Buffalo State Teacher's College, where she wanted to study to become a home-economics teacher.

I remember Bernie and Sis had their first date on a Saturday night, and he was nervous when he came to meet us that first time. A dozen paper airplanes were on the coffee table, and an old 78 record was spinning on the turntable. He sat down after the introductions, picked up one of airplanes I had made, and mutilated it while he answered polite questions about his family. When Dad asked him if he had a job, he destroyed three more airplanes during the answer. By the time he and Sis left on their date, all the airplanes had been destroyed, and I decided I didn't like Bernie at all.

The mink business was thriving, so Dad bought the first TV in our neighborhood and a new car. One night, Mom and Dad wanted to go out for a while to enjoy their new 1950 Mercury, so I was sent to bed around 9:00. Sis turned on my bedside radio to my favorite station, Cincinnati One, Ohio, so I could listen to Gene Autry and some old-time country music. She kissed me goodnight and tucked me in. I lay there and imagined her and Bernie watching television on our new TV set. Somehow I knew she would be back to check on me and to turn the radio off, so I waited quietly. Sure enough, she tiptoed in, pulled the covers over my pretend sleep, turned off the music, and tiptoed down the stairs.

After waiting about fifteen minutes, I slipped out of bed, stayed close to the walls where the floorboards didn't squeak, floated down the stairs, dropped to all fours, and crawled around the corner to the end of the davenport. The TV was playing, and I jumped up and yelled, "Surprise!"

Sis screamed. "You're supposed to be asleep! Get back upstairs and get in bed. I'm going to tell Mom!" she yelled. Bernie was frantically trying to extricate his hand from the front of her bra, but it was stuck in there. I thought he was scratching her tummy, because she was slapping at his hand and trying to pull her sweater down over it.

"Not if I tell her first," I said. "What's his hand doing in your blouse, Sis?"

"I thought you checked on her and she was asleep," Bernie grumbled.

Soon after that Sis got special permission to see a drive-in movie with Bernie. The drive-in theater was twenty-five miles from home, so her curfew was moved from midnight to 1:00

a.m. A lot of planning was involved. She put some lemonade in a thermos, made tuna-salad sandwiches, and took cookies along for Bernie. A blanket and pillows were added to the supplies in case there was an "evening chill."

Finally everything was ready, and Bernie arrived. It was summertime, and it didn't get dark until 9:30, so if they thought of me at all, they assumed that I was in bed. I watched from my bedroom window as the provisions were loaded into his two-door Coupe. They went back into the house to make sure Mom and Dad knew they would be late. Down the stairs and out the back door I snuck, quiet as a thistle seed on the wind. I crept quickly into the backseat, behind the driver, and hid under the pillow and blanket.

Pretty soon the engine purred to life, and the wheels rolled. I counted the turns and stops and knew exactly where we were. They talked softly, cooed, and got all mushy in the front seat. I waited until we were almost there and they were completely immersed in each other. Then I jumped from under the blanket and yelled, "Surprise!"

I nearly flew through the windshield when Bernie slammed on the brakes. "What the hell?" he screamed. "How'd you get in here?" Sis scooted to her own side of the front seat while she buttoned her blouse up crookedly. They frantically searched for a telephone booth and called Mother. Life imprisonment and a death sentence were imposed on me without the benefit of a trial or even a fair hearing. There was no reasoning, no common sense, and no sense of humor. They obviously couldn't think clearly in the face of the unexpected. Bernie was completely out of control and out of character, sputtering and muttering all kinds of threats. He slammed on the brakes and turned corners so sharply that I couldn't stay on the seat. Then he stopped the car in the middle of a town, dragged me out of the car in my red and white pajamas, stood me squarely on the corner, jumped back in the car, and drove off. I was terrified. I was just a spirited little girl, and they had abandoned me. Well, not quite. They drove around the block, and Sis jerked me back into the car before we went home to face my punishment.

One evening, Sis presented Bernie as her fiancé and announced they wanted to get married immediately. His parents, our parents, and all the grandparents voiced concern. The Korean War was raging, Bernie was due to be drafted, and Sis was just out of high school. The adults held family meetings, conferences, and consultations; they had arguments and frantic fights.

Finally it was agreed that they would go their separate ways while engaged. Bernie would enlist in the air force; Sis would go to college and become a teacher. If they felt the same in four years, the family would give their blessings to the union.

I filled the days with school, farm work, 4-H projects, and roller skating at a local rink. I helped with chores in the mink yard after school and on weekends to earn money to buy precision roller skates and pay for private roller-skating lessons.

However, when I went to bed in one of the two upstairs bedrooms, the other one, Sis's room, was empty. I missed her and couldn't wait for Thanksgiving weekend, when she was coming home. It was so lonely without her. There was no one to pick on and follow around and no one to play the silly word games we made up before we drifted off to sleep.

———

On Thanksgiving morning in 1950, Mom had the turkey in the oven. There were pies on the kitchen counter, and she was cutting up a squash to cook for the big family party. Sis was in the breakfast nook with toast and orange juice, and she kept making a funny noise in her throat. She would talk a little bit, and then a croak and squeak would come out of her. I thought she was doing something funny that she learned in college.

Finally Mom said, "Sis, cut that out."

"I can't," she replied, gasping for breath between the strange noises.

"That's not funny, Sis. You quit it right now. I mean it."

"But Mom, I can't help it. I do it all the time at school," Sis said.

The argument went on the whole time Sis was home for the holiday. Finally she went back to college, and the funny noises were forgotten. But I overheard my parents discussing the matter one evening after I went to bed. They said that she was making the noises because she missed Bernie and that she would get over it. They thought it was just a way for Sis to get some extra attention.

A week later, the college dean called and said Sis was really sick. She couldn't walk from one class to the next without sitting down in the hallway to rest. He suggested that Sis should come home until she got stronger.

It was raining the day we went after her, and the atmosphere in the car was as dark and gloomy as the weather. She cried because she couldn't stop the involuntary noises in her throat, and her head kept jerking to one side. She couldn't carry her suitcase or make it all the way to the car, and we had to help her. Laughter died in our family that day.

When we got home, Mom called the family doctor, who made a phone diagnosis. He said it was the beginning of a nervous breakdown caused by Sis and Bernie's separation. Within a month, Sis was flat on her back and couldn't hold her head up or feed herself. The food would spill on her clothes when her head and shoulder twisted and jerked all over the place. Mom was frantic, and Dad spent more time in the barn and mink yard.

Just before Christmas, my parents took her to Buffalo General Hospital for tests. After examining her, the doctors suggested she see a psychiatrist, which made Sis livid, because there was nothing wrong with her mind or her thinking process;

she just couldn't control the involuntary movements and noises in her throat. Finally, the doctors called our parents in for a conference. A week had gone by, and everybody was speculating on what was wrong. The doctor said that it was a rare and incurable disease that was so new it had no name. They advised Mom and Dad to take her home, make her comfortable, and quit wasting their money on doctors. They said Sis would be dead before she was twenty-five years old.

Things were never the same at our house again. Mom hid in the breakfast nook and cried. She went to her bedroom and sobbed. She made a bedroom out of our dining room and Sis took up residence there. At eleven years old, I suddenly inherited all the cooking, dish washing, cleaning, and ironing. Mom spent all her waking moments taking care of Sis, because she had to be fed, bathed, turned over, and strapped onto the bed so she wouldn't throw herself onto the floor. She made peculiar noises all the time. I was terrified and would wake up frozen in fear, thinking she might be dead in the morning. Winter was harsh; we all felt hopeless and isolated.

One day, Sis, Mom, and I were riding in the car. Sis had been sick for about a year, and she was bedridden. It was a herculean effort to take her out in the car.

"Mommy," I remember asking, "if we were out in a boat and the boat capsized, would you save Sis or me first?"

"Your sister, of course," Mom stated matter-of-factly. I knew life would never be the same. I had lost my mom's unconditional love; she would not save me first and probably wouldn't save me at all. I was devastated.

Neighbors brought our groceries, and grandparents visited when they could manage the snowy roads. Finally, a trip to the Cleveland Clinic was arranged.

Great aunt Nellie, my good grandma's sister, was summoned to look after me, and it was such a relief. Great aunt Nellie liked to play checkers and dominoes, and she liked to sew and knit.

She watched our brand-new TV, cooked for me, and did the washing and ironing for two whole weeks while I was in school. She hugged me, talked to me, played with me, and taught me to embroider. I felt her unconditional love.

When Sis came home, my mom's secret sobbing and wailing began all over again.

Dad thought he could help by making Sis feel useful, so he mixed up nuts, bolts and screws and told Sis they needed to be sorted. It would take her all day to sort a cup full, and then he would pay her. She used the money to buy stamps to send letters to Bernie, who sent a daily letter to her from an air-force base in England. Sis would tell Mom what to write back to him, because she couldn't hold a pen. Her voice was ebbing away; she grew weaker and wouldn't eat.

One morning in mid-February, Mom woke up angry. She said, "Sis is just getting worse and I am not going to have any part of it. I have waited on her enough and it isn't helping. I am not going to watch her lie in bed and get weaker. I'm going to make her help herself whether she likes it or not."

She called a chiropractor and tried to make an appointment, but after she told him about Sis, he refused to treat her. He referred her to an osteopath instead. Mom made the appointment and Sis started on a program of treatment and Mom's medicine of "self-help."

I came home from school one day to find Sis's bed empty. I heard her wailing in her peculiar, slurred way. "You're mean. You hate me. I can't do this," she said. Then there was a thud. The noise was coming from our bathroom, and I hurried in that direction, only to find Mom bent over Sis. She had fallen and was lying on her side, with her top half twisted as she tried to get up. Both Sis and Mom were crying. Mom was saying, "You can get up by yourself; you got this far. Of course you're going to fall. I don't hate you; I love you, Sis, so I have to make you try. Otherwise you'll wither up and die."

This went on daily. However, Sis progressed, and over the next two months she struggled to put her own clothes on. At first, it took her all morning, and many times she didn't finish dressing until after lunch. Each day, Mom would make her lurch and lumber the twenty feet from her bed to the bathroom, and the rest of the day was spent washing her face and combing her hair. Mom refused to help her, and she would retreat to the breakfast nook, out of Sis's sight, and sob from deep within. I don't know who suffered more, Mom or Sis.

After several weeks, Sis was able to walk out the front door and stagger along to the mailbox. She was motivated because Mom refused to bring in Bernie's letters.

Dad and I were quite amazed when Sis began sitting at the supper table with us. She spilled a lot of food down her front, but she got some of it in her mouth between the spasms. The struggle was all-consuming and I felt old and invisible. Nobody seemed to notice that I was alive, and I desperately missed the attention I was accustomed to receiving.

———————

Dad hired a high-school boy to help with most of my animal chores, because I was busy doing the housework. I made friends with him when I had time to help in the mink yard. He was a quiet, tall, athletic, blond boy by the name of Deet, and he was four years older than me. I sort of knew him because he rode the school bus with me; he lived around the corner, about a mile away. I began to tag along after him when he was working, and soon he was talking to me. He had to make several trips to the hay mow each day to get bedding for the animals, and I always volunteered to help him.

One rainy afternoon, it was tense in the house. Deet was working for Dad, so I escaped the misery and found him in the hay mow. I grabbed his cap and threw it across the hay.

"Hey, kid, what'd you do that for?" he asked.

"I don't know, just for something to do," I replied.

"Well, go get it. You threw it. "

"Make me."

"You think I can't?"

"Can't catch me," I yelled as I scooted across the loose hay.

He was after me in a second, and when he caught me he pushed me down and lay on top of me with my hands pinned above my head. My little seventy-pound body was quivering. Our eyes were locked, and his lips were only an inch from mine.

"Brat," he whispered.

"Let me up or I'll scream."

"I bet you won't. This is what you want, isn't it?"

"No. No, it isn't. I just wanted to tease you," I panted. His weight was on my chest, and I couldn't breathe. His body fit so perfectly on mine. He had protrusions where I had indentations. Then his first two fingers were unzipping the breast pocket of my old jean jacket.

"What's this?" he asked as those fingers dipped into the pocket. The rough fabric of the jacket was between his fingers and my flesh, but the sensation took my breath away. "There's something hard right here," he said as he continued to rub my chest.

"Stop it." I was so tense. I was sure Dad would come up into the hay mow, looking for us. "I have to get out of here now, right now." I wiggled and twisted until I was out from under him.

He laughed and said, "Okay, kid, but you can help me get hay any time you want to. You can steal my hat, too."

I ran out of the barn and looked around frantically to see if anyone had discovered where I was, but nobody had seen me. Nobody had time to care.

The next day at school, while I was in my fifth-grade class, I happened to look up at the door, whose window was all frosted glass except for one little panel in the middle. There in that one clear glass pane was Deet. He was smiling, winking and waving, and I couldn't concentrate anymore.

He sat behind me on the school bus every day after that. He would poke me when nobody was looking, and he was always in that window of the door of my fifth-grade class. I couldn't believe he liked me. I named my new puppy after him.

Afternoons and Saturdays, I met him in the hay. My family just thought I liked to work, and they thought it was good for me to escape from my sister's sickness and the worry and stress. I fell in love with Deet.

I slipped and fell one day, and Deet caught me. When he lifted me up, he made sure he slid my body up the length of his, and when I was on my feet, he kissed me. It was not at all like the kisses my parents gave me or even the ones with Billy in the culvert in the winter. It lingered and explored as his tongue tickled my tonsils and made me feel all warm and snuggly. Dad had taken Mom and Sis into town, and nobody was home except us. Deet picked me up, carried me to the hay mow and gently laid me down. He stretched out beside me, unbuttoned my jeans and began to play with my belly button, making my head all dizzy and slow.

Deet whispered, "I'm glad it's an inny." Then he bent down and stuck his tongue in it, slobbering all over my tummy. One of his hands was under my butt, and the other gently explored my body. I didn't understand my quivering, shivering feelings. The sensation was overpowering.

Then the dog barked, and we jumped. I zipped up my jeans and got busy with the hay just before Dad came in, asking if anyone had called or stopped by. The situation grew more and more intense.

One night after I went to bed, my mother came into my room. "You know, honey, I feel bad that we can't spend more time together. Is there anything you want to talk about, anything special? Maybe you and I could have a whole day to go shopping and exploring." She sounded guilty and concerned.

"Would you like to hear my prayers?" I asked.

"Sure. Go ahead," she replied.

As I began, she squeezed my hand and told me she loved me. I finished saying, "Now I lay me down to sleep," and, as usual, I ended with "God bless..." and then listed everyone in my family, starting with my sister. That night, I included Deet.

Mom asked, "Why did you include Deet? Do you like him a lot?"

"Oh, yes, I do. In fact, I love him. You know, Mommy, he kisses me right on the mouth, and he puts his hands inside my clothes."

"Oh, my God," she gasped. Her hand flew to cover her mouth. "Does he take his clothes off?"

"No, Mommy, he just runs his hands all over me. Is that all right?"

"It is not all right. I have to go tell your father now. Go to sleep. We'll talk about it in the morning." I was surprised and wondered if I had made her mad as I listened to her race down the stairs.

The next day was Saturday, and Deet didn't come to work. I watched and watched for him, but he never showed up. Finally I asked Dad where he was. Dad said, "Deet won't be working here anymore. His family is moving."

On Monday, Deet was not on the school bus. I watched the pane of glass in my classroom door, but it was always empty. I never saw Deet again.

I found lots of boys at the roller-skating rink, in school and working at neighboring farms. None of them were Deet, and none of them kissed me or took me to the hay mow like he did.

Life was lonely again as my parents helped Sis get better. Time passed, and the family fell into a routine that centered on her and her recovery.

Bernie returned from the service, and one day he came to see Sis for the first time since he'd left. Mom sternly said, "Gail. Go to your room. We don't need you and your pranks right now. Bernie is probably just coming by to be polite. We expect that he will break up with your sister because of her illness. He's been gone for over three years, and he's not prepared for how twisted and crippled she is. Find something quiet to do, and stay out of sight, because it's going to be an awful night."

From my window, I could see Bernie get out of his car. He had a dozen long-stemmed red roses. I thought about the roses, and I knew Sis was going to be brokenhearted when he walked away. I was surprised by the tears that trickled down my cheeks, but I kept watching. To my amazement, the next thing I saw was Bernie helping Sis into his car. When they came home, Sis was wearing a diamond engagement ring and announced plans for a September wedding. Everyone was elated, surprised and making plans to hold bridal showers and reserve the church and fire hall for the special day.

Mom and Dad took Bernie aside and explained that Sis would never be well and whole again. They told him that his life would be hard as he would have to take care of Sis and do most of the housework and that she probably could never have children.

Bernie said, "I don't care. I loved her before she got sick and I love her still. It doesn't change who she is or the fact that I love her."

Mom spent her spare time crying, incapacitated with grief and fear for Sis's future, even though she had a happy wedding to think about.

I didn't understand any of it. I just knew that Mom spoke to me only when she needed me to clean the bathroom, help with supper, do the ironing, or take on some other chore. We didn't play games or go for hikes in the woods or laugh anymore. Planning the wedding added to the time and support the family already gave Sis. I was happy for her, but I felt despair and filled my time working or roller skating and feeling lonely.

Chapter Two: Plans, Actions, Consequences, and Solutions, 1954-1958

An unusual invitation came for a family and friends picnic. The day of the event I said, "I'd rather go roller skating, so I'm not going."

Mom joked, "Who knows? Maybe you'll meet your future husband." That was a pretty stupid thing to say to a boy-crazy fifteen-year-old, but she was too involved with Sis to notice my infatuation with boys. My grandmother had always told her that I was born talking and that the first word I ever said was "boy."

I was forced to go, and I met the most handsome guy I had ever encountered. He was three years my senior, a college man, and almost six feet tall, with curly black hair and blue eyes. He had broad shoulders and a cute butt, and we went roller skating and dancing and hiking. He taught me to drive his car, and we couldn't keep our hands off each other. The young hormones were raging.

Summer turned to winter and then spring. My parents were cautious about allowing me to date a guy with his own car, but over the winter, they discovered family connections and many common acquaintances. Mom and Dad learned that Special Boy (or SB, as I called him) was an Eagle Scout and had received the Order of the Arrow. They trusted him to obey their rules.

At the Spring Fling sock hop, I wore a poodle skirt, bobby socks and penny loafers. The skirt was slate-gray felt with black poodles linked by little chains marching across the bottom. The poodles had red noses and little red plastic collars. Special Boy picked me up in his '49 Ford. I was the envy of all the other girls, because my mother didn't have to drive me to the school gymnasium. The dance was fun, even though the music was just records.

About half an hour before the dance was officially over, Special Boy whispered in my ear as we danced close, "Let's leave and get a milkshake at City View dairy bar."

The moon was bright on that warm spring night, and the air was clean and fresh and smelled like rain, new grass and flowers. SB rolled down the windows and drove slowly. He held me tightly as we kissed at red lights and stop signs, giggling with each smooch. The kisses deepened. He caught his breath as his hands cupped my face and his tongue explored my lips. I kept my eyes open, searching his face for some indication of pain, because he was moaning softly.

He drove onto a country road, pulled over and switched the engine and lights off. Quickly his tongue slipped inside my mouth. Pure fire ran directly to the pit of my stomach, where it caught my bowels on fire. A spot inside me ached—no, it throbbed, painfully deep. I squirmed and wiggled, but the intensity increased, and I wanted to go further. I needed to feel skin against skin. I needed to press my body against his. I had never seen or touched a boy's private parts, but I needed to, wanted to, had to. He slid his hands down my hips, and when he touched me, the heat was unbearable. My head whirled and spun. I was dizzy. The front seat ratcheted backward. I couldn't take my eyes or hands off his penis.

It ended with bloodstains and sobs and the reality that my innocence was gone forever. The white-hot heat of the moment gave way to a cold sweat when I understood what I had done.

"Oh, my God, what would my mother say?" I moaned.

"You're so young. If you were just older…" He was whispering, even though no one else was in the car. "I don't know what you'd say. I love you so much," he continued.

"What do you mean, you don't know what I'd say? You can ask me anything. I love you, too," I murmured tearfully. I was trembling, cold, and almost sick with a dark cloud of—what? Was it doom? Was it finality or fright? I didn't know then, but I know now that the terrible, dark feeling of the moment was guilt.

"You're only fifteen. Would you, will you, would your parents let you—marry me?" he asked, holding me closely.

I didn't answer, but I still remember the racking sobs, deep shudders, chattering teeth and shivers that overpowered me.

"Get dressed. I'll take you home. Will you be all right?" he asked tenderly.

When we turned into the driveway at my house, the porch light was on, and my parents were up. I knew they would see the whole episode in my lying eyes.

The TV was on, and they were watching the local news. They barely looked up when I came in. At the door, Special Boy kissed me lightly on the tip of my nose and whispered, "I love you," but he didn't come in. He disappeared into the night, and I went straight to bed. No one even noticed that I was home, before my midnight curfew.

The next day was April 2, and I was certain that the young man I had given my all to the night before would greet me with a sarcastic grin and say, "April fool's." But he didn't. He walked in the door that Sunday afternoon with a bunch of roadside wildflowers—the most beautiful ones I'd ever seen—and said "I love you" with a question in his eyes. He was only eighteen, a tall, handsome college freshman, a working man with a part-time job. To me, he had no faults at all.

I stretched my four-foot-eleven, ninety-pound body up to kiss him and said, "Yes, I will marry you."

Later that night, I whispered to Happy, my Airedale dog, who slept at the foot of my single four-poster bed, "What if I'm pregnant?" I shivered again and again in the cocoon of safety I had enjoyed throughout my childhood.

My parents trusted me to go out with Special Boy. They reminded one another of his accomplishments. Their confidence and trust in SB made me want him even more. I was glad they liked him, but I wondered why they didn't feel proud of me.

What was it Mom always said when I was going out? "If you act as good as you look, you'll pass." I thought it meant that I was just passable, not great, not pretty or cute—I would just squeak by. Mom called my hair color mousey brown. At last I had someone who loved me the way I was. SB loved me unconditionally. I was so happy when I was with him.

Why had they been so negative about me? Did they really favor my sister? Sis was sick—no, she was gravely ill. Sis was suffering, and watching a child suffer is one of the hardest things a parent has to do. My parents forgot that she was my sister, my best friend, and my mentor and that I worried about her, too. I missed our family life; I missed the way we had once been.

I filled the need for family closeness by spending more time with SB. Every date we had in the '49 Ford was a replay: sex, raw, frantic, and demanding, an itch in my gut that had to be scratched. No, it was like an itch on my back that I couldn't reach, and the door casing wouldn't satisfy. It was insanity, wonderful and guilt-ridden, a hunger I couldn't fulfill. I wanted to get married and spend all my time with SB.

Almost a year had passed since I'd met SB. Five weeks had flown by since I'd given my all, and it was another bright, moonlit night and the evening of my sixteenth birthday. Although we'd been invited to a couples party for Sis and Bernie, we decided to talk to Mom and Dad instead so that SB could declare his love for me and reveal our desire to get married.

Neither one of us knew what would happen when Special Boy asked my dad if he could marry me. We had imagined all kinds of scenes, but we were totally unprepared for the brutal response we received.

"What the hell do you mean, you want to get married? For Christ's sake, she's only fifteen—no, sixteen today. She's too young. No, you can't marry her, and what's more, I'll have you arrested if you so much as touch her. If she gets pregnant, I'll put her in a home and I'll put you in jail. Do you understand? Now, get out and don't come back," Dad screamed. Even though Dad was several inches shorter, thirty years older, and thirty pounds lighter, he lunged at Special Boy, pinning him against the living room wall while choking him with both hands.

"Stop it, Larry! You can't stop the feelings. You can't stop the love. Use your head. Let him go, now," Mom commanded.

SB freed himself and shot out the front door. His car roared out of the driveway amid a hailstorm of gravel.

I ran up the stairs to my room, shut the door, and barred it with a chair. I scrunched up in a fetal position under the covers, but I couldn't shut out the screaming.

"I tell you, Irene, I'll kill the fucking little bastard if he touches our daughter. Do you understand that?" my dad yelled.

"No, you won't. I know you're mad, but when you get control of yourself, you'll do the sensible thing like you always do. I'm shocked, too. We don't need this on top of Sis's problems and the wedding planning. Do you think they've had sex?" Mom finally asked as her mouth caught up with her brain.

I started to shake, and I was cold even though the bed was cozy and warm. I thought SB would never come back.

"Hell, yes, I think they're having sex. They're human beings, and humans are just a higher order of animals. Where's your brain? Do you think they'd be talking marriage if they weren't screwing?" Dad ranted.

"Do you think she's pregnant? Oh, God, I just thought of that. Do you think she is? What if she is? She's only sixteen years old," Mom cried.

I was trembling so violently the bed was shaking. Even my teeth were chattering. I cried and wondered the same thing as my mother.

"So help me God if she is. I'll send her to a home for unwed mothers, and I'll see that he goes to jail just like I threatened. If she's not pregnant, I'll send her away to a private school, where they can control her," Dad said.

I was so miserable. I cried endlessly, hopelessly, helplessly, until I fell asleep from exhaustion. I woke up crying the next morning. I ran downstairs and didn't stop in the kitchen, even though Mom called out to me. I ran outside and down the road. There was no love in that house, no love in our family, and now they wouldn't let me have any love anywhere. Sis was getting married, and it was okay for her to find love but not okay for me. Despair and desolation filled my heart. I was so alone. I was so cold. I heard a crunch on the gravel road and looked up. There was SB. He was out of his car in a second and had me in his arms, smothering me with kisses.

"Come on. Let's go right back and confront your dad again. He's had time to sleep on it and get used to it. Maybe he'll change his mind," SB said.

"Are you completely crazy? He'll kill you—maybe both of us. It's risky," I said. But I got into his car.

When we walked into the house, Mom and Dad were drinking coffee and trying to eat breakfast. Immediately Dad was on his feet with fisted hands, aggressive posture, and thunderous anger in his eyes. "What the fuck are you doing here? I threw you out last night. Don't you understand you're not wanted here?" Dad said, glaring at Special Boy.

"You can't scare me away, even though I know you want to," SB said, holding his ground. "I love your daughter, and I wouldn't do anything to hurt her. She loves me the same. All we want is to get married and be together forever. We know we're young, but we also know that her favorite grandparents were only seventeen and twenty when they were married, and that worked out okay."

I was shaking again. Mom was glaring at my tummy, and I knew she was trying to decide if I was pregnant. She said, "There must be some middle ground here. Sit down, and let's try to work this out."

My parents laid down the law. We were allowed to see each other on weekends in a limited way, with a curfew of five o'clock, but we were to have no contact during the week.

"Well, that's better than never seeing each other, isn't it?" SB said.

"Yeah, I guess," I replied.

Spring turned into summer, and the rules relaxed a bit when school was out. SB formulated a plan. He took me for a meeting with his mother in the summer of 1955.

Special Boy's mother was a big woman, with extra-thick hair and a narrow forehead. She wore loud colors, short skirts and lots of makeup. She had an underslung jaw and close-set, beady eyes, but she was so nice to me that I thought she liked me and that this was why she was going to help us. She told us that she had a plan, but I learned it was really an agenda. She didn't say anything positive about my parents; instead, she said that when she met my mother, she couldn't understand how a wonderful man like my father could ever have chosen her. Then she frowned hard and raised her eyebrows disparagingly while clearing her throat.

"I'll go to Sears Roebuck and buy a set of suitcases that are on sale for $29.99. I'll bring them here, and Gail, you can smuggle your things out of the house a little at a time and pack the suitcases here. You can get married in Georgia at sixteen with no parental consent. I checked it all out. Eventually your parents will forgive you, but they'll be really mad right now. If you love my son, you'll go along with this plan," she said.

I was young, and my mind was foggy with lust. If I thought at all, I thought she was brilliant. I started wearing extra layers of clothes and leaving them in the suitcases. Special Boy's mother bought me a white nightgown and robe and little white slippers for my wedding night. She said she loved me and that I could sleep with Special Boy in her bedroom for afternoon naps. She even covered us up with a blanket and shut the door. On one of those afternoons, I found it difficult to fall asleep, and I was thirsty. I opened the door quietly. At sixteen years old, I didn't fully understand when I saw her and her chiropractor entwined on the couch. SB's dad was away, working. Years later, I realized she wanted to get her son out of her way.

Our departure date was Labor Day, just two weeks before my sister's wedding, in which I was supposed to be the maid of honor. I'd smuggled out all my clothes, and I had stashed some money from my allowance and my job at the mink farm in one of the suitcases. SB's mother advised me to walk across all state lines so Special Boy could not be arrested for kidnapping in case we got caught.

My favorite grandpa, my best buddy and gardening partner, was hoeing the sweet corn on the departure day. I made my way out to the garden to see him one last time and to sweet-talk him out of a ripe musk melon. I hugged him, kissed his weathered, wrinkled cheek and watched his blue eyes twinkle as he pretended to refuse me the melon. Then he laughed, threw the melon to me, and said, "Go on, have a good time, young one."

Tears spilled down my cheeks as I turned away; I knew it might be the last time I would see my grandpa. Then I ran to the car, where Special Boy was waiting to take me to Georgia to become his wife. If Grandpa had known what kind of good time I was planning, he would not have wished me well.

We picked up the suitcases and the lunch Special Boy's mom had packed. She gave us a hundred dollars for good luck and said she would handle everything. As planned, we had told my parents that we were attending a picnic with Special Boy's family, going to church services with his father, and then going to the drive-in theater, which—with special permission to stay out late—gave us until two o'clock in the morning before anyone would miss us. We had earned my mom and dad's trust, and we were in Maryland by that time, sleeping in the car on a country lane under an apple tree.

Morning dawned with bright sunshine and birds singing in the apple orchard where we were parked. I couldn't stop crying. We drove into Cumberland and found a little restaurant. The waitress seated us at a window table, and the sunshine streamed in over the bacon and eggs. I cried even harder, because it was just like the sunshine on the kitchen table at home. "I want to call home," I sobbed. Special Boy got out some change and spotted a pay phone. We dialed the number, and it hardly rang before Mom said "Hello?" and then realized it was me. She screamed for my dad and asked, "Where are you?"

Before I could answer, Dad came on the line. "You tell me where you are right now, and then you come home. Your mother is beside herself with worry. She thought you were dead and never coming home." In the same breath, he informed me that he had the police looking for me in three states and he threatened Special Boy's life a couple of times.

I nearly hung up, but then I got a word in and told him that I was not going to tell him where I was. "I made a mistake. I want to come home," I said.

He started the threats and yelling all over again.

"Dad, I'll come home if you call off the cops, but if I see that you haven't, I will not come home, and I will not stay home."

He started to yell again, so I said, "I'm coming home. I'll be there tonight." I hung up.

Special Boy was also crying. He said, "We can't do this. You're right; we have to go home now." We paid for our uneaten breakfast and started the long ride. Two-lane highways went through every little town, and the trip took us all day. We were afraid of the consequences of our actions, so we traded locks of hair and made plans to meet when I turned twenty-one at the restaurant where we'd left our breakfast uneaten.

Finally we were on the road where my parents lived. The two miles to their house felt like two hundred miles.

By the time we turned into my parents' driveway, flashing lights and sirens were following us. We were surrounded by sheriff's cars. In an instant, we were pulled from the car, pushed over the hood, and searched. We were questioned repeatedly about where we'd gone and how many state lines we'd crossed. I insisted that I'd walked across every one, stuck out my thumb, and hitchhiked before Special Boy let me back into the car. The interrogation went on for an hour.

At last, Mother came out of the house like a mad bull and yelled at the police, "Stop. That's enough. There won't be any more questions. You can leave now." She crossed her arms over her chest and planted her short, stocky self in front of me. She then repeated in a no-nonsense voice, "I said, leave now."

The police backed off, got in their cars, and sped out of the driveway. Mom announced that supper was ready. Solemn-faced, with heads hanging, we marched single-file to the dining-room table. When I saw supper waiting there, I knew just how upset she was. Mom was an excellent and extravagant cook, but supper that night was only a bowl of chicken-noodle soup. Nobody complained. We just slurped soup, heads hung low. Finally Mom spoke. "I'm going to tell you how it will be. There will be a compromise of my choosing or nothing at all. There is only one choice here, and I have made it."

We were all frozen statues, our spoons in different positions between bowl and mouth. Dad looked murderous, but Mom was calm and firm. "Young lady, you will finish high school, one way or another. You will go to the principal tomorrow morning and ask him if you can finish your senior year as a married student. If he agrees, you will start your junior year this week, pass all subjects, cooperate, take part in school activities, and finish eleventh grade in June. SB, you will go to town tomorrow as soon as she is finished at school. If she gets the okay from the principal, you will buy her an engagement ring, and the two of you will announce your engagement at Sis's wedding. Gail, you *will* be her maid of honor. As soon as school is out next spring, you will have the wedding of your choice, just as nice as Sis's will be next week."

She paused. No one moved their spoons. No one broke eye contact with her. Dad's grim face remained frozen. I could hear the air come out of SB's lungs as he went limp. His spoon clattered into the bowl.

My cheeks and chin were dripping with tears of relief and happiness. I ran around the table to her side and threw myself into her arms, sobbing, "Thank you, thank you, Mom. I love you so much. Thank you." She held me tightly, and her love poured forth to me as we clung to each other. I knew it had been worth the pain and hardship of the drive home. I knew she loved me.

Supper was over. SB and I cleared the table. He put his hand out to shake hands with my father, and for an awkward moment I thought there would be a fight. Then Dad relaxed, took the hand that was offered, and reached out to hug SB. We said goodnight, and the following day we initiated Mom's new plan.

The principal agreed to let me finish high school as long as I promised not to get pregnant. We bought the ring—the only one in the jewelry case that fit my finger—and the clerk put it in a box, which SB put in his pocket. When we got to the house, my mom asked to see the ring. He took it out and showed it to her. She said, "Well, aren't you going to put it on her finger?" So he did.

Sis's wedding was lovely. It was the first day of a fifty-five-year marriage, throughout which Special Man loved her unconditionally and cared for her with every ounce of his strength. The school year progressed; SB worked every day, and we saw each other on evenings and weekends. When we were alone, the passion was unbearable. When we rode in the car, the neighbors said they could never tell if there was one person or two in the front seat, because we sat so close together.

Mom and I planned my wedding. We shopped for a dress and found the perfect one. My band director agreed to sing at my wedding, and the home-economics class catered the reception as a project, under the direction of the teacher. Some of my friends' mothers forbade them to talk to me; they said I was a terrible example and that my mother should have spanked me for the whole episode.

There were bridal showers and couples parties. The mountain of gifts took up all of Sis's old room and the upstairs hallway. I was busy writing thank-you notes and keeping lists of who gave me what. Every time SB and I could get away in his car, we would park on the back road, neck and kiss, and make love in the backseat. I couldn't stand it if more than a day went by and we didn't get a chance to be alone. My aching need for sex was all-consuming. SB said he was the same. Winter became spring, and June finally arrived.

On the morning of our wedding, which was scheduled for one o'clock, I got up, dressed in jeans, and climbed to the top of the old oak tree. It was my favorite spot in the whole world, because I could see for miles and hear the church bells in town about two miles away. The birds were used to me being up there and would sit close to me and sing or chirp. Nobody else was up; the sun was just rising, and dew was still on the grass. The mock-orange bush was in full bloom just under my bedroom window, below the old oak tree. Its white flowers were perfect for a wedding morning and made me think of the inappropriate virgin white of the wedding dress waiting in my bedroom. I was no virgin, and I was glad of it. As I sat up there on top of the world on my wedding day, I reminisced about all the incredible, erotic sex I had experienced with SB. This marriage was going to be a lot of fun. We wouldn't have to sneak around anymore, and we could do it as much as we wanted, whenever we felt like it.

A car drove onto the driveway. It was my dad's best friend, who was going to take the wedding pictures. I had overheard them talking about him sneaking up to my bedroom and taking pictures of me before I got up. That was why I was in the tree. I just sat up there and waited. He got out his gear and went into the house, and I could hear my parents and him talking quietly. After a few minutes, I heard him holler, "She isn't here. She's not in her bed. Where the hell is she?"

There was pandemonium in the house. Everyone thought I had run away. They got a little tense and panicky while I took my time climbing down from the tree. Eventually I strolled in the back door and asked, "What's going on? Why is he here so early with all his cameras?"

Their relief was so great that they all just started to laugh, and Mom announced that breakfast was ready. It was only six o'clock. I took my food and went to eat it on the back porch. Happy, my Airedale dog and best friend in the world, sat down beside me. He put his chin on my knee and rolled his big brown eyes up to my mouth as I ate. Now and then he would slap my knee with his big brown paw so that I would remember to leave a little for him to lick out of the bowl.

I patted his curly, furry head and said, "Happy boy, you and I have had some real good times. Remember when I shot my first woodchuck? And when I was sad or frightened of fighting with Mom and Dad, I would go over to the evergreen thicket, and you would always find me and sit right beside me while I cried. Do you remember when my girlfriends would have a sleepover and you'd get right in the middle of the group and lie on your back and expose your privates? You were such a naughty dog."

Happy sat so still that morning while I reminisced about the times I'd saved my toast and slipped it to him as I went out the front door to meet the school bus, and all the days that he'd waited on the road bank for the bus to bring me home so that he could leap and jump with glee at the sight of me. We used to race to the door, but he would always stop and lick my free hand while I opened it. He slept beside my bed in the summer, even though it was hot upstairs in my room. In the winter, he slept on my bed. He got up when I did, accompanied me to bed, and lay by my chair while I ate or did homework. He'd rarely left my side for eight years except when I was with SB. Happy seemed to have reservations about SB and never connected with him. On this wedding morning, he was sure sticking close to me. He had been at the base of the oak tree the whole time I was up there, and now, as I ate my cereal, he just sat there, staring up at me.

"What's with you, Happy?" I asked him as I set the nearly empty dish on the floor for him to lick.

He wasn't interested. He ignored the milk. He wouldn't take his chin off my knee. Finally, I wiggled out from under his head, picked up the dish and started into the kitchen. He got up really slowly, head low, tail down, and bumped the screen door open as he went out into the yard. I thought it was strange and wondered if he had eaten something that didn't agree with him. I had put my dish in the sink and started out the back door after him when I heard truck brakes screech. There was a sickening, hollow thump, and then I heard his shriek of pain and a shrill half-bark, half-scream that would not stop. I raced to the road ditch just as the truck driver ran back, saying, "I never saw anything like it. That dog just stood at the end of the driveway and waited until I was just about to him. Then he ran right in front of me. He didn't chase the truck—he just ran right in front of me."

Dad arrived on the scene and told me to get back. He tried to get near Happy, but Happy just snarled, bared his teeth and tried to bite him. Mom had called a veterinarian, who arrived with Dad. He tried to move in on Happy but had no more success. I said, "He wants me, only me." I was sobbing. I knelt down in the ditch and lifted the curly brown head I had just stroked as it rested on my knee. Happy rolled his eyes up to meet mine. They were full of pain, but he did not snarl or cry; he just let himself rest in my arms. The vet moved in and gave him a shot to quiet him. I held Happy, letting my tears fall on his face. The vet got a canvas, and he and Dad gently lifted Happy onto it as I caressed his head and whispered to him that I loved him and that I would always love him. They took him away to the veterinary hospital. I sobbed as I lay on the ground, in the ditch, in a pool of his blood, on my wedding morning.

I don't remember how I got back to the house or to the church, or how I got into my wedding dress. It was a good thing I had a veil, because my eyes were red and swollen nearly shut when I walked down that church aisle. I didn't see the ribbons or flowers on the ends of the pews. I didn't see all the friends and family who had gathered to watch me wed. All I could think about was my dear best friend bleeding in the ditch after being hit by a delivery truck. At the altar, I looked up into SB's loving eyes and whispered, "Happy got killed today."

The wedding reception and honeymoon anesthetized the grief over the loss of my best friend, Happy.

Our first apartment was a three-room affair, with a bedroom, living room, kitchen and bath. Money was tight, but we were able to buy some furniture, and I enjoyed settling in with my bridal shower and wedding gifts.

SB graduated from a two-year college and landed a good job at a local factory as a time-study man, where he walked around all day with a stopwatch in his hand and wrote down how long each movement took an employee, later suggesting ways to save movement and time.

I went back to high school in September as a married student and walked into the school office with a note in my hand.

"Good morning," I said to the school secretary. "I have a note here for you, and I'd like a set of permits for the contents."

The school secretary took the note and read it aloud to the principal, who had just walked in. It said: "Gail has my permission to drive her own car to school and requests a permit to park in the school parking lot. Gail has my permission to leave school each day at noon when her classes are finished. Gail has my permission to request an excuse from all gym classes for the remainder of the school year."

The secretary looked at the principal and said, "This incredible note is signed with her married name. Is that legal?"

The principal snatched the note, perused it briefly, and calmly stated, "Suppose it is. Give her the permits." My senior year as a married student was off to a satisfactory start.

At home in the apartment, it was a challenge to cook; clean; launder; shop; shovel snow in the winter; keep the boots, coats, hats and mittens picked up; feed the new cat; do homework; iron SB's shirts and pants for work; pay bills; do the banking— the list was endless and there was so little time for sex. It was the most important thing we had looked forward to enjoying. June through January whizzed right by with all the work and a little loving, and soon it was the middle of winter. The days were cold and the nights colder. The little oil stove in our apartment didn't keep the apartment warm when the wind blew, and cuddling was a must. In February, there was more ice on the inside of the windows than in the freezer of our refrigerator. The floors were like a skating rink—there literally was frost on them. It cost a lot to keep warm, pay the rent, and put food on the table. School was demanding, and SB was working long hours at his job.

When bedtime came each night, SB was ready, and I couldn't wait to lie down beside him. He would caress me, and I could never wait, so I would roll on top of him. Who needed gym class for exercise when I could do this all night?

The amazing consequence of all the sex was that I could concentrate on my schoolwork. I no longer daydreamed about sex and the carnal pleasures it brought to us. I didn't have to plan, worry, or lie. Sex was always available and always pleasurable when we could find time.

When the middle of March arrived, so did the day my period was due. It didn't arrive. A week went by, and still nothing. Two weeks went by, and then three, and still no period. Finally, I went to the doctor, donated a urine sample, and the rabbit died. I was pregnant. Graduation was in three months. I had promised the principal that I wouldn't get pregnant and had agreed that if I did I would quit school. I was the first married student to ever attend my school, and I wondered if I should lie and try to hide the pregnancy until June, or if I should just tell the truth and take the consequences. Truth won out.

I told my home-economics teacher that I was pregnant and that I would have to quit school as I had agreed. She seemed upset and left the room. When class was over, I walked down the hallway, and every teacher stepped forward to congratulate me and wish me luck. When I passed the office, the principal and the secretary both came out and said congratulations. The principal said, "Don't worry. You don't need to quit. It's only a couple of months, and you'll make it just fine."

At my graduation, the principal paused before he handed me my diploma, turned to face the auditorium full of friends and families, and said, "Gail is the first student who's had to get married and still graduated." Then he tried to fix the statement and said, "Gail is the first student we've had who had to get married." Finally, amid the laughter, he said, "I am proud to award her the honor of being the student with the most improvement in her grades. She went from a C average to straight A's when she forgot about the boys." It was some night. I walked out of the school and never went back inside that building.

The pregnancy was difficult, because SB didn't want me to be pregnant. It interfered with his sex life, and he thought it would change our relationship. He was ashamed to be seen with me as my belly grew. Mom took me shopping. Sis, who was in remission from the disease that had been identified as Musculorum Deformans Dystonia,was miraculously pregnant also. We made matching maternity outfits. Friends held double baby showers for us, and my classmates had a surprise party for me.

SB drove me to the hospital when my water broke, and Mom met us. He was hungry, so while they were prepping me, he went to get something to eat and didn't come back until after our beautiful son, Andy, arrived. He more or less tolerated the baby but preferred to hold the cat. When the baby was three months old, we moved to a warmer, larger apartment in an old farmhouse. It was upstairs and had two bedrooms, a full attic and lots of closets. The living room was large, and there was an entry hall for storing our boots and jackets. The washer and dryer were in the kitchen, and a clothesline hung in the backyard. I was in heaven. The apartment was warm and pleasant, with big windows and a country view.

I settled into motherhood. Three years passed, and soon I was pregnant again. SB was furious. He didn't want any more children, but he certainly enjoyed the exercise of making them. I was delighted. I was also tired and sick. One morning, I just couldn't get up, and when SB came into the kitchen, no coffee had been made. He yelled, "You figure out how to get out of that bed and have my breakfast on the table by the time I get shaved and showered and dressed. And I mean you had better get that done."

I didn't like being ordered around, so all the next day I rearranged the kitchen to make it more efficient. The next morning, I purposely stayed in bed when he got up and went into the bathroom. He yelled at me, "You better have my breakfast ready when I come out, or there will be trouble."

I walked into the kitchen, held the teakettle under the faucet to fill it, and put coffee into the drip-o-lator coffeemaker. When the water was hot, I poured it through. While I waited, I put a bowl, spoon, cup, sugar, cereal box and milk on the table. The toast was just popping up when he arrived, and I poured the coffee and served the toast. All was accomplished in less than three minutes. I had learned time study by assimilation.

Chapter Three: Religious Control, Responsibility, Disappointment, and Divorce, 1960-1965

AROUND THE TIME WE moved from our first apartment to the old farmhouse, SB announced that he was going to attend a fundamentalist church with his father. Off he went for a Sunday evening service, while I stayed home with the baby. It was quite late when he returned, and he was animated. He couldn't stop talking about the experience and how it had changed him. He'd always been a born-again Christian; he was clean cut, conservative, and honest, with a sincere love of God. I respected that in him and felt that I exhibited the same qualities and beliefs. However, on this night, he was totally different. His usual quiet faith was aroused and excited. He paced the living room and kept throwing his hands up in the air, shouting, "Praise God. Praise the Lord."

This behavior lasted all night and through the next day and evening; then the control mode set in. He demanded that I throw away all my jeans and slacks. They were not acceptable in his new religion, and, according to him, I was going to start going to church with him. Next, it was my lipstick. "Only a

Jezebel would paint herself up like that," he said. Of course, eye makeup, face cream, and powder were not allowed, either, nor were jewelry or nail polish. He announced that there would be no work of any kind on Sundays, not even cooking. He insisted on church attendance every Sunday morning. I tried it. I found the fundamentalism embarrassing, and it frightened me. Worshipers would go to the front of the church, become overwhelmed with emotion and cry, laugh, scream, moan, or give some other visible demonstration and then fall to the floor.

I didn't mind their sincere beliefs, but I did not believe that way. The pressure to join them on the floor at the front of the church was escalating. My upbringing was unemotional and conservative. I found a middle road by volunteering to watch the nursery during church services, which seemed to satisfy everybody. The people in the church were extremely friendly, and we entertained and were entertained for dinner many times. Outside of their emotional displays, they were honest, pleasant people who didn't drink, smoke, swear, or wear makeup or jeans, and it was easier to accept them and their beliefs than to fight about it.

My parents were not impressed. Dad kept reminding me that my upbringing was much different, and we argued a lot about fundamental beliefs. He encouraged me to read the Bible for myself, and our conversations brought balance into my mind.

Meanwhile, SB spent every spare moment at the church. I stopped cooking on Sundays, and we ate cold leftovers while we read the Bible all day long. SB interpreted it for me, and I always wanted to argue the points he made.

I thought about my dad's suggestion and started to read the Bible from cover to cover so I could draw my own conclusions. It took me two years to complete the project, and I found

SB's interpretations, like the one about dancing, to be a little strange.

SB's company Christmas party and dinner/dance were going to be held at a local hotel. Mom offered to babysit for us, and she treated me to a new dress. It was light blue and quite form fitting, with sparkly sequins all over it. She also treated me to a trip to the beauty parlor, and the hairdresser put sparkles in my hair, too. After the dinner, a band started playing. SB wanted to leave, but his coworkers persuaded him to stay. One of them asked me to dance, and SB announced, "Dancing is nothing but sex standing up. No, you can't dance with my wife. She knows it's a sin and that she'll go to hell for dancing with you."

The music started, and the man held out his hand. I smiled and said, "According to my husband, I'm on my way to hell anyway. Let's go have sex standing up on the dance floor."

The next day in church, SB requested that the congregation pray for me because of my sinful behavior.

My life then dove headfirst into more hell than I could imagine.

Soon after we moved into our second apartment, our town held a parade. Mom decided to go with a friend, and they positioned their folding stools at a good vantage point. Mom was a bit heavy, and when she sat down on hers, it collapsed. She fell against the curb, bumping her side. The next day, she felt sore and touched her left side, where she discovered a good-sized lump between her shoulder and breast, kind of under her arm. She called her gynecologist and made an appointment for the following Friday. After he examined it, he told her that it was probably just a swollen milk gland and that they would watch it.

I was happy throughout the fall. I was pregnant with my second child, and Mom was waiting for her swollen milk gland to go away. Mom loved being a grandmother; Sis, in remission, was enjoying her healthy baby girl. I had Andy, just a few weeks younger, and I was due to deliver my second child in late November. We were busy with baby showers and lunches with old school friends. We all spent long afternoons on a blanket on the lawn with the babies. Time rushed by, and we didn't think much about Mom's lump. She went to the doctor each month, and the lump got a little bigger, but he assured her that it was nothing. We had no reason to doubt his judgment.

Then, in early November, the doctor wanted Mom to make an appointment with a surgeon so they could take a biopsy of the lump. The date was set for early December. Mom was a little concerned; it was pelting season for the mink, Dad was extremely busy, and it was near my due date. I told her that I would go with her. I was sure the new baby would already be born, and I planned to get someone to babysit both children.

The baby was not born on its due date. At that time, there was no such thing as induced labor, and a woman just waited as long as it took for the baby to be born.

Mom's surgery date arrived, and I took her to the local hospital early in the morning. I situated my huge body in the waiting room for what I thought would be an hour or so. Ten hours later, I was still there, and I knew something was wrong. Every time I inquired about her, I was told that the doctor would speak to me when he was through with the operation.

Finally, the doctor came into the waiting room and called my name. I struggled to my feet, my belly leading the way. I stood with my back arched, my aching abdomen sticking way out in front, and trembled as he said, "Well, your mother has breast cancer. We did a radical mastectomy. We'll send the tissue to the lab, but I'm sure it's cancer. We feel confident that we got it all. She's in recovery, and you should go home now and come back in the morning. Good evening." He was cold and unfeeling and didn't notice that I couldn't breathe or speak. I was cold and shaking violently as I struggled to pick up my purse and get out the car keys.

It was five o'clock in the afternoon. I had to get my son from the neighbor's house, tell my dad the devastating news, and then get supper for my husband.

Somehow I made it home with my little boy. My landlady said she would watch my son, and my husband had left a note saying he was going to church for a meeting. In the note, he said he was disgusted that his supper wasn't on the table.

I drove Dad's car to my parents' house, where I told my dad the awful news. He took me home and then went to the hospital to spend the night holding my mother's hand.

SB came in around ten o'clock and yelled, "Why weren't you home by five? You know I'm home at five-thirty, and you know that I expect my dinner on the table. I had a meeting, and you disappoint me when you do not do your job."

I looked at him with swollen eyes, tears streaming down my face, and started to speak, but he interrupted me. "Don't give me that tearful crap. God doesn't understand when you don't do your duty and you make me late for church. What could possibly be more important than God's work?"

"My mother has breast cancer. They cut her breast off today," I sobbed.

"Well, if she was a born-again Christian, she wouldn't have cancer, now would she?" he yelled.

"People in your church have cancer, don't they?" I asked, feeling hurt, confused, unloved, and very pregnant.

My baby was three weeks overdue that day. During the night, I had a contraction, but SB went off to work. I had contractions all the next day. Landlady Maggie kept track of me and helped with my son. She was understanding and worried about my mom as well. SB came home for supper but had to go to church to help tape a radio show for that week. The contractions got worse, and just as he came in at nine-thirty, my water broke.

He took me to the hospital; I was wheeled away to the delivery room, and I have no idea whether he stayed or not. I did not see him until after work the next day. My beautiful, healthy baby boy, Larry, was born at 11:06 p.m. I was blessed with a second son to love and enjoy.

I was in a different hospital than my mother, and I had to stay for three days. When I went home, there was no Mom to help me. My sister had a relapse, and my only aunt was taking care of Mom by visiting the hospital regularly. Dad was spending time there as well. My husband was at church endlessly, and I was sad and tired and lonely. Twenty-one: that was my age when I brought baby Larry home to meet his brother, Andy. SB was not interested in breastfeeding, declaring that he thought it was barbaric and dirty. He insisted I cover myself and go into a different room to nurse the baby. He refused to learn to change a diaper, and he thought children and babies should eat separately from adults and not bother his dinner. His church was his life, and I felt that we were just an inconvenience along the way.

Meanwhile, Mom came home from the hospital. When the new baby was three weeks old, she finally was able to visit and hold him.

She was so frail and sick and tired. I made her a cup of tea and pulled the antique cradle next to her chair so she could watch the baby and rock him a bit. We were so happy to be together and share this little boy, but we were also afraid. As we drank tea, she told me she felt bad that she couldn't help me with the workload. I felt bad that I couldn't help her with her healing process. As the weeks passed, our friendship deepened through these difficult experiences. Meanwhile, her incision didn't heal. A young nurse friend volunteered to change her dressings each day and suggested that she visit the cancer hospital. Three months later, we finally had an appointment, as well as a babysitter for the boys, and I drove her there. Tests were done, and the prognosis was grim. The cancer had spread to her ribs and maybe farther. They didn't think she would live long.

In 1961, Sis was not well, either. The doctors said her relapse was caused by lifting her little girl. Soon I found myself taking care of my niece, too. Sis was again incapacitated with the jerking spasms and involuntary noises, and a woman was hired to come in and care for her and her child. Mom was distraught over Sis's regression, even more than she was over her own failing health.

One day, my landlady, Maggie, came running up the stairs to my apartment, waving a popular women's magazine and screaming, "Gail, I just got this magazine in the mail, and here's an article about a girl who has a disease that sounds just like what your sister has." She took the baby from my arms, and I read the story. The girl's problems were identical to Sis's. I called Mom, who was able to drive again, and she came to my apartment immediately to read the magazine.

"Let me use your phone to call this doctor in New York City," she requested. Mom called St. Barnabas Hospital and convinced the staff to find Dr. Cooper. When she spoke to him in person, she explained my sister's condition and the history of her illness. Travel arrangements were made and Bernie, Mom and Sis went to New York.

After extreme risks were explained to Sis, she said, "My life is useless the way it is. I'll take a chance with the surgery." She immediately had what amounted to experimental brain surgery, avoided the eighty-five percent chance of insanity and became the oldest surviving person in the world with Dystonia when she died of breast cancer at age 75.

She lived with limited mobility; her voice was weak, and the words were garbled. She walked with a limp and had a twisted body, but she raised her daughter, loved her husband, was active in her community and travelled extensively with Bernie.

He may have destroyed my childish paper airplanes, but I will always love and respect him for his dedication and kindness to my sister.

Sis's daughter was the light of her life; she was a beautiful, healthy, bright child at three years old. She was developing faster than my boys. I often took all three of the children to a neighbor for babysitting. I helped when her caretaker had time off, in addition to helping with more of my mother's care.

Mom relapsed and was in the cancer hospital a lot. Dad had five hired men and five thousand animals to care for daily. His business grew, and he was in the planning stages of expanding it to another farming location, where there would be a new house for Mom and new farm buildings for the business.

Plans for the new house were delivered in the midst of the family crisis, and Dad considered selling the farms and going out of business. He asked me one day, "Do you think I should scrap the plans for the new house, considering your mother is so sick?"

After talking about it, we concluded that going forward with the plans would keep Mom busy and her mind occupied with positive, happy thoughts. She enjoyed picking out the materials, and we took her daily to see the progress when she was able to go. It became necessary for the contractor to build a ramp for her wheelchair so she could get inside and see her new home.

Mom and Dad moved into the house in December of 1961. Mom enjoyed the new home for two years. All the doorways had been made to accommodate her needs, and the counters were low so she could still use them from the wheelchair she called her prison.

When my parents moved into their new home, we moved from the comforting warmth of our apartment onto the mink farm. Maggie, who had become my best friend, reminded me that she wouldn't be downstairs, listening to my husband's tantrums. She said, "This might be the end, or the beginning, depending on how you look at it." She was just full of prophecy.

We had lived on the mink farm for only about six months—the boys were three and a half and six months old—when things took a turn for the worse.

One Sunday afternoon in May, I was eating a cold sandwich and looking out the kitchen window at the mink yard. It was whelping season, and new babies were arriving every day. I was thinking about checking the nest boxes for new litters when I noticed that the tar paper-covered lids were blowing off and rain was dampening the nesting, where mother mink were giving birth or had just done so.

Dad was visiting my mother in the hospital, so I put on my boots, jacket, hat, and gloves and was reaching for the kitchen door when SB came in. "Just what do you think you're doing?" he asked.

"I'm going out to the mink yard to put the lids back on the nest boxes. The wind has blown them all over the place, and the babies are getting cold and wet."

He grabbed my arm and knocked me away from the door. He got right in my face and hissed, "You are sinning. This is Sunday, and it's a day of rest, in case you forgot. You will not go out there under any circumstances, and if you do, you will go to hell. Do you want to go to hell?"

"No, I don't want to go to hell, but neither do I want the baby mink to take a chill and die. It's our livelihood, and that includes all of us who work here," I shouted right back.

"You will not go out there on Sunday. I forbid it. Take your boots off, go in the living room, and sit down. We'll listen to gospel music now," he stated.

I jerked my arm away from him, opened the door, stormed out, and slammed it behind me. I put the lids back in place and returned to the house. He calmly lowered his Bible, put on his coat, and informed me, "I can't spend another minute this afternoon with a sinner who is going to hell," and he left.

I continued to take my responsibilities to heart, care for my ailing family members, and visit my mom in the hospital, and I didn't go to hell.

One day, when I got home from visiting Mom at the Buffalo cancer hospital, Dad met me at the door. He looked concerned and pointed to his neck. There was a large lump near the base, and it throbbed with every heartbeat. I called the local doctor, and within an hour we were on our way back to Buffalo. A specialist admitted him into the hospital across the street from where my mother was being treated. The lump was probably an expansion of the main artery in his neck. Complete bed rest was ordered until a diagnosis could be completed.

I went home with a long list of assignments for the farm, three kids to retrieve from the neighbor, a sister to help, two farms to manage, three dogs to feed, and five hired men to supervise. I gave no thought to dinner for my unfeeling, uncaring, unhelpful young husband. Boy, was that a mistake. He was waiting at the door when I trudged in with two sons and a niece to feed and bathe and put to bed.

"Where's my dinner? Don't you know that it's five-thirty and I have church in an hour? What's wrong with you that you can't seem to keep a schedule?" he yelled.

Just above a whisper, I recounted the day's events. I was exhausted, frightened, and preoccupied with the new load of responsibilities I had just acquired. He threw his coffee cup into the sink, pushed me aside, and stormed out the door. "I'll eat out," he snarled on his way.

Time passed in a blizzard of events. Mom was discharged while I was visiting her, and Dad was not discharged. I didn't know how I could take on anymore work. How could I care for Mom at home with SB acting so nasty, all the kids to care for, and all the farm work? But there was no choice. I considered it for only a few minutes and then said, "Let's get her packed up, and I'll take her home." While the nurses got her ready to go home, I called Sis's husband, Bernie, who also worked on the mink farm, and asked him to take my bedroom furniture upstairs and get a hospital bed from somewhere to put in the downstairs bedroom of my home. He enlisted the help of the other hired men. In the two hours it took me to get home, he got it all ready. SB had a meeting right after work and then a church service, so I got home with Mom first. She was already settled in the hospital bed in our bedroom when he got home at ten that night. He was livid. He screamed accusations loud enough for the whole state to hear. "You are a stupid idiot. Where am I supposed to sleep, upstairs? You expect me to sleep up there and use the bathroom downstairs and keep my clothing in the closet where your mom is moaning and groaning and dying? You are an inconsiderate, useless piece of crap." Fortunately, Mom had taken her sleeping medication and was sound asleep.

Dad was discharged with instructions for absolutely no lifting over five pounds for the rest of his life. That lasted about three months. Then, one day, he announced, "If continuing with my normal, daily work-related activities is gonna make me die, so be it. I will not live like this anymore."

Mom struggled against the cancer for another year and a half, and I watched it consume her body mass and then her mind. It was relentless and cruel, as all cancers are. Finally, although I thought it was the last thing I would ever do, I prayed for her life to end. She died at the age of fifty-seven in the Buffalo hospital. Her funeral was on my parents' thirty-fifth wedding anniversary. The next day, SB demanded that I pack up and go on a week's vacation with him. I did it out of guilt and the knowledge that he thought I had neglected him. We took the boys to the Adirondacks, but I couldn't make myself participate or smile; I took care of the boys out of habit. We stayed at a Lake George resort. The second night, I discovered a lump in my left breast. I was terrified and begged to be taken home so that I could see my doctor. In answer to my request, SB criticized me for not depending solely upon God to heal my breast.

We got home on a Saturday, one week after my mother's funeral. I called the cancer hospital where she'd been treated for three years and where she died. A nurse I knew by name answered the phone. I explained my panic, and she immediately put me through to Mom's doctor. He insisted that I be at Roswell Park Memorial Hospital in Buffalo by ten the next morning.

I was examined as soon as I got to the clinic. This was unusual, since it was Sunday morning; but because Mom had been a patient there for so long and I had bonded with the staff, I received really special treatment. The doctor ordered me to be admitted. The nurse who processed my paperwork looked distressed and came around to the front of the desk at the nurse's station. She put her arm around me and said, "Gail, I can't believe this is happening. The only bed we have available is the same one your mother used. The doctor wants to biopsy your breast tomorrow morning at six. I don't have a choice here. I'm sorry."

SB wanted me to just go home and do it some other time. I said, "No way. Mom would want me to get it taken care of immediately. I'm deciding to feel even closer to her if I'm going to be in that room, in the bed where she died. Let's go."

As soon as I was settled in the bed, they began to draw blood for testing. SB announced that he had wasted the whole day and needed to go home; he didn't want to be late for Sunday-evening services. He left me there, alone, in the same bed where my mother had died just seven days before.

SB did not come back the next morning, nor did he call. I had some complications from the anesthetic, but the lump was benign, thank God. I needed a drain for the deep incision, so the doctor wouldn't release me for three days. Then I had to put my clothes on and declare that I was going home. A friend of my mother's heard I was having problems and came to see me when she brought a patient in for treatment. I begged for a ride to my home, which was sixty miles away. The whole way home, the patient was vomiting from chemo. My mother's friend asked me to walk the last mile from the main highway so she could get the woman home faster. The detour to take me to pick up the kids and drive on to my house was out of the question. I made it to the babysitter's house, got my children and niece, borrowed a wagon, and pulled them the last half mile home.

SB came in from work just as I sank into a chair in the living room, exhausted. The kids were playing in their rooms. He said, "What are you doing home? Why isn't my supper ready? I have a church board meeting at six-thirty, and I need to have my supper."

He didn't ask if I was all right, what had happened, or how I'd gotten home. I fixed him a hamburger. I was relieved to have him go out for the evening.

A week or so later, I felt much better, thankful that the lump was benign. One night when we went to bed, I was feeling quite frisky. I rolled over next to SB and put my arm around him. Then I ran my fingers slowly down his tummy. Just as I touched his penis, he shot up and screamed at me, "Don't touch me. There's something wrong with you. All you think of is sex. There will be no more sex in this marriage. The Bible says sex is for procreation only. We have two kids, and that's all we're ever going to have. Get your filthy hands off me."

I was only twenty-four, too young to hear a death sentence for my sex life. He undressed in the closet from then on. It was the last time we even discussed sex. He spent more time at work and his church after this.

A few weeks later, a high-school girlfriend of mine called and asked me out for lunch. I left the boys with my aunt. When we arrived at the restaurant she had chosen, she said, "Now if you don't like what you see in here, just tell me. Don't yell or say anything; just tell me you want to leave."

I thought that was strange, but I followed her into the dimly lit bar and restaurant. She made me sit facing the back corner, which was so dark I could hardly make out the faces of the people seated there.

She said, "Look over my right shoulder at the booth in the back corner. Don't scream, just look."

When I looked, I thought I was going to throw up. There was SB, my overly religious husband, with his arm around a woman who had her head on his shoulder. "Let's get out of here," I whispered.

When we were out in the bright, clean sunshine, she said, "Gail, I didn't want to tell you about your husband. I thought it best if you saw for yourself, with your own eyes. I work in the same office complex as him, and I eat at that bar every day. I thought you needed to know," she said, holding me while I sobbed.

I went to get the kids, and my aunt advised me to go to the bank and withdraw all the money in our savings account. She reasoned that if he was having an affair, he would not give it to me, and I would ultimately have to support the boys.

SB and I had bought a building lot, drilled a water well, and opened a special savings account to plan for the down payment on a prebuilt home we loved. It was secondary to all the trouble in my life, but it was a positive, happy thing to look forward to during dark times. There was a balance of $996.92 recorded in the savings-account passbook.

I agreed with my aunt, left the boys a bit longer, went home to retrieve the passbook, and took it to the bank. I stepped up to the teller and handed her the book.

She looked me straight in the eye and said, "That account is closed. There's nothing in that account." She never even opened the book or checked the names or account numbers.

I stood in disbelief, wondering how she could know that information without knowing me; and then I realized she resembled the woman I had seen in the booth with SB.

Later, I learned that she was also an organist and substituted at local churches occasionally. At the time, I believed that she met my husband one of those times.

I found my dad in the mink yard that afternoon and told him I was going to confront SB. He warned me that I should remove all the ammunition from the house first. He said that if things got rough, I should turn on the front-porch light; he'd watch from my sister's house to be sure I was safe. I told him, "That's ludicrous; SB is a born-again Christian, and he won't harm the boys or me." I finally gave in, handing over all the ammunition and some of our handguns.

Andy was seven years old by then and could understand and carry out directions. I instructed him to turn on the porch light if I told him to, and he agreed.

SB did not take the accusation lightly. "You're a liar and need to see a psychiatrist. You need to get right with the Lord and maybe admit yourself to a mental hospital. You make up stories and tell them so often you actually believe them," he had the audacity to yell at me.

I presented the bank book and told him about lunch. He ran to the closet, grabbed his shotgun, and looked for some shells. When he couldn't find them, he grabbed me just as I told Andy to turn the light on. He slammed me into a closet and choked me until my neck was black and blue. Then he jumped into the car and nearly crashed into Dad and Bernie as they turned into the driveway on their way to rescue me.

SB got away. Dad and Bernie helped me gather some clothes and bedding and some of the boys' toys. Dad had been alone since my mother died, so we moved to the house he'd built for her.

We each filed for divorce.

Chapter Four: Learning to Be Single, 1965-1968

THE ATTORNEYS ENTERED THE arena like two fighting cocks at a gambling ring. Paperwork containing threats and accusations filled the mailbox daily, and my little boys missed their home on the mink farm. They had left their friends behind, and Andy was forced to start a new school. Larry was only four years old, but he felt the loss of his closest playmate. Instead of having their own rooms, they now had to share space in Grandpa's house. I inhabited the laundry room and office area.

A year passed slowly, punctuated by regular panic attacks. I was fearful of going out in public, sure that everyone would know I had left my husband and was getting a divorce. Local EMTs made several visits to administer oxygen to me when I couldn't breathe. The folks who sang the "I told you so" song were always in the shadows of my thinking and my self-esteem was nowhere to be found.

Dad and his lady friend, Freddie, who had been his high-school sweetheart, called a meeting at the dining-room table. They brought lists of ideas, contacts, and offers to look after the boys if I would get on with my life.

"Gail, you need a part-time job off the farm, preferably one where you could meet people," Freddie said, kicking off the conversation in her take-charge manner.

"I don't want another job. I cook, clean, mow the lawn, work in the mink yard, take care of the boys, do laundry, and shovel snow in the winter. What more do you people want from me?" I cried.

"We love you, Gail, and we're worried about you. You're becoming a recluse. You work, eat almost nothing, and sleep. What kind of life is that for any young woman?" Dad asked.

Tears streamed onto my cheeks.

"We have a plan," Freddie continued. She then gave a speech as detailed and perfectly executed as her hair, clothes, and makeup. "I made an appointment for you to apply for a waitressing job at the ski-lodge hotel, just over the hill. You need to go for an interview with the owner at ten tomorrow morning. That will allow the boys to get off to school. With Larry in kindergarten, you'll have time in the morning before he gets home. Your dad says he'll take care of some of the chores in order to get you there on time."

"It sounds like I don't have a choice. Who do you folks think you are to plan my life for me?"

Dad slammed his fist on the table and sternly said, "Enough whining. This plan isn't the only one, and it isn't just about you. The boys deserve at least one normal parent, and the other one is a crazy religious fanatic. I want you to yank yourself up by the bootstraps and get on with living. On Saturday night, you'll go to the YMCA and attend the Parents without Partners meeting. We feel that you need to reestablish your life with a different crowd, one in similar circumstances to your own. The meeting is at seven o'clock, and we'll stay with the boys for that, too."

Freddie chose clothing from my closet that was appropriate for the planned appointments, and the issue was settled in spite of my objections. I was amazed that I got the waitressing job with just one interview and no experience; I learned the meaning of the old saying, "It isn't what you know, it's who you know"—or, in this case, who Freddie knew.

Soon I implemented the next part of their plan. When I arrived at the Parents without Partners meeting, I found a room full of middle-aged men and women who were old enough to be my parents. Coffee and donuts were provided. Everyone took their seats, balancing their refreshments on their laps. Coffee and donuts weren't my thing. I slunk back into a corner seat and tried to look small so I wouldn't be noticed by any old codgers on the prowl. But soon enough, one of the fatherly types sauntered over with his paunchy pouch of a belly and asked, "How would you like to play golf tomorrow morning, babe?"

I willed away a whole-body shudder, silently cursing my dad and Freddie. Barely above a whisper, I answered, "No, thank you."

The meeting was called to order, and plans for picnics, movies, and woodland hikes were discussed. The activities were meant to provide children with single parents an opportunity to enjoy a mixed-gender outing.

Suddenly, the meeting-room door flew open; a six-foot-tall blond man in his thirties commanded the doorway. He surveyed the room one person at a time until his eyes met mine. He stepped just inside the room and bellowed, "Is this the Parents without Partners meeting?"

The meeting leader answered, "It is. Please have a seat and join us."

"Wow," the stranger replied. "I'm from Paterson, New Jersey, and back there the PWP meetings have six hundred swinging young cats attending. What in hell happened here?"

I sat up in my chair. His observation was exactly right. These were middle-aged, out-of-shape losers, in my opinion. He made his way to the empty chair next to mine. When the meeting resumed, he whispered, "I was relieved to see at least one normal-looking person my own age. What do you say we get out of here when they take a potty break?"

He was incredibly handsome and personable, and it had been a long time since I had noticed a man. I said, "Okay."

A few minutes later, walking out into the fresh evening air and setting summer sun, he asked for directions to the nearest bar.

"I don't drink," I said. "I've never been in a bar except where I'm going to start a waitressing job next week. They gave me a tour, but I don't know one drink from another. I buy clothing over on Main Street, and I think there's a restaurant that serves drinks next door to that store."

We headed that way for a couple of blocks, and he said, "I'll order for you. I know a perfect orange-juice blend I bet you'll love."

The drink, a screwdriver, tasted like plain orange juice, so I swilled it down. He ordered another one and commented on the temperature and what a warm summer we were having. I drank the second one, too; I was really thirsty. Then I tried to get up to use the restroom and nearly fell. He leaned close to my ear and said, "Don't worry, babe. I won't let anything happen to you. And just so you know, I have my final divorce. I also have nine kids and a vasectomy, so you don't have anything to worry about when we get friendly later. Let me help you to the ladies' room."

"I don't have to go anymore. I'm leaving now and going home. Thank you for the orange juice, and I'll see you around," I said as I raced for the street.

He was behind me in a flash. I was nearly to my car, a brand-new Mustang Fastback that required huge car payments.

"Where do you live? What's your phone number? Would you go out to dinner next Friday night?" he huffed as he tried to keep up with me.

"No, no, and no," I spat as I jumped into my car. I locked the doors and peeled out amidst squealing tires. I kept checking my mirrors as I quickly made my way out of town toward home, which was about twenty miles away.

Sure enough, he caught up with me at the edge of the city. I used the Mustang's full capacity and left him and his brand-new gold Cadillac convertible somewhere on the horizon about five miles out of town.

Dad and Freddie were anxiously waiting for me. "How was it? Did you meet people your own age, and did you make any new friends?" they asked in unison.

"Ha. The only one I saw who wasn't old enough to be my great-grandfather was a guy from New Jersey who told me he'd had an operation and I had nothing to worry about if we got intimate. Thanks a lot, folks, but I won't be going back there. I'm not interested in paunch-bellied old farts who play golf, or some guy trying to score," I said over my shoulder as I went to check on my boys. They were fast asleep.

I worked the waitressing job during the winter ski season and befriended the ancient cook, who constantly compared me to his daughter and sent me to wine-serving school. He quit, took a job at a roadhouse a few miles down the highway, and asked me to work there. I did, for about three months, until the owner met me at the door one fish-fry afternoon and said, "Don't put your apron on. You don't work here anymore."

I felt like I'd taken a fist in my gut. I thought I'd been doing a great job serving the fish fries and beer. "What did I do wrong?" I gasped.

"Nothing at all, darling. You're now the new cocktail waitress at the Elks Lodge in town." He smiled.

"I can't do that," I insisted. "I don't know one mixed drink from another."

"Not to worry, sweetheart. The two bartenders will teach you everything you need to know. Here's the address. They're waiting for you," he said, handing me a slip of paper.

I went to the posh private club with trepidation and found two older men named Fritz and Skip in charge. They had me hang my coat at the end of the bar, and my instruction began immediately.

Carrying the round, cork-covered tray, I made my way to a table full of men and wrote down their order for six bottles of beer. The bartenders filled the order, inverted six weighted beer glasses on the bottles, and helped me figure out the bill. Then I lifted the tray to go to serve my customers. Because I was short, I couldn't clear the thick leather padding on my side of the bar at the waitress stand. The edge of the tray caught, and the weighted glasses toppled the beers, causing the whole thing to hit the back edge of the bar. The broken bottles cut and splattered the bartenders. Beer, broken glass, and blood flowed freely across the bar.

I looked at the mess with horror.

"Oh, my God, Fritz, you're bleeding," Skip yelled.

"So are you," Fritz replied.

"I'm leaving," I said, reaching for my coat. Out of the corner of my eye, I noticed that the barstools were filled and people were waiting for tables.

Just as my hand closed over my jacket, Skip thundered, "Don't touch that coat. Grab another tray and get to work while we clean up this mess and put on Band-Aids."

I did as I was told. I took my order tablet and marched straight to the next table. There were six men and women, and everyone except the last one ordered a different mixed drink. The only drink I recognized was the infamous screwdriver, and the last one was the most strange of all: the guy wanted Anacin. I turned in the order, picked up the six replacement beers on a clean tray, and served them.

The new order was ready when I stepped up on the stool that now graced the waitress stand. The new height helped me see the bar a lot better. I took the order to the table, served it all around, and gave the last guy his Anacin on a napkin, plus a glass of water. He looked surprised. His deep voice caught everyone's attention when he asked, "What's this, doll?"

I answered timidly, "It's the Anacin you ordered. I brought you a glass of water so you could swallow it easier."

The whole bar and all the tables roared with laughter when he informed me, "I said anisette, as in liquor."

The instruction continued for two years. I learned to grab myself by the bootstraps, get a thicker skin, and roll with the punches like my dad told me to. A few years later, that thick skin also provided me with some laughs as I remembered the bank teller/organist who had alienated my husband's affections. I was able to replace hurt and anger with humor when I realized she knew how to play the organ better than I did.

My boys never minded when I went to work as a cocktail waitress. In the middle of the night, I would put an apron full of tips on the foot of my bed. In the morning, they would run into my room, dump the change on top of the covers, and count it. We had a special bank where we saved all those silver coins for a home of our own someday.

One season changed to another on the mink farm, and soon it was time to breed the mink for next year's crop. That happened in February and March, in the dead of winter, in the middle of New York State's snowbelt. One particularly windy morning, when snowdrifts reached to the peaks of the dozen twelve-foot-high, two-hundred-foot-long aluminum mink sheds, we ventured through the snow tunnels we had dug between the sheds. Dad and I needed to take a break from our daylight-to-dark pedigree matching and mating-season work. We were shaking with cold as we plodded through the drifting snow to warm our hands and souls with a cup of hot tea in the heated barn.

As we walked, heads down against the swirling whiteout of snow, I caught sight of something in the driveway, just outside the security fence. Dad saw it, too, just as a man emerged from the blizzard. "Ah-ha! I've found you, Gail Love," the man shouted above the howling wind. I couldn't believe he called me by my maiden name. I couldn't believe he found me at all. It was the handsome jerk in the gold Cadillac whom I'd met at the Parents without Partners meeting the summer before.

"How the hell did you find me?" I shouted back over the wind.

"Aren't you going to introduce me to this man?" Dad asked.

"Dad, meet Sam. Sam, meet my dad," I said.

Dad stuck his hand out, recognized the guy from my past description, and said, "Come on in out of this blizzard and join us for tea and for lunch, too." God, I was upset.

Dad walked right past the barn and led us through the accumulating drifts to the house. I thought he must be desperate to marry me off and get rid of me.

I learned that Sam had gone back to the PWP meeting and looked at the sign-in sheet, where I'd written my maiden name. He visited every post office in the direction I'd travelled the night he tried to follow me until he found someone who recognized the name and was willing to give him directions. He turned up every few weeks or months to ask me out. I always refused. Finally, I introduced him to a friend, and they hit it off. As a return favor, they arranged for me to join them on a blind date.

Chapter Five: Predestined to Find the Farm and Marry Again, 1968-1970

TWO YEARS AFTER MY Mexican divorce and several attempts at dating, that blind date led me to the chief of police in a nearby town. He was five feet eight inches tall and impeccably dressed, with a full head of thick black hair, a misshapen face, and ears that stuck out. He was happy to show my family newspaper clippings about his police work. My young sons were fascinated with his uniform and gun belt, and the chief enjoyed showing them some self-defense moves. A few days later, on my birthday, he surprised me with flowers and an Eddy Arnold record, telling me that we shared the same birthday and that he was three years older than me. Although he wasn't the most handsome man I'd ever dated, he loved to dance and was fun and smart. It wasn't long until he took me to meet his mother and stepfather.

Saturday nights, he would pick me up in his police car, which was covered with antennas, and we would dine and dance at the finest restaurants in western New York. We saw the latest movies, took the boys to museums and on historic train rides, and had picnics in local parks. He even attended PTA with me. He impressed me with his interest in my boys.

A pretty diamond ring graced my finger on the evening of the second birthday we celebrated together, and the courtship was fun; I was happy again. My boys didn't complain when I left for an evening—they could watch TV, and Dad would make popcorn. Dad asked, "So, when's the big day?"

The chief said, "As soon as we find a house and make sure the boys are prepared to change schools. It'll take a while."

His police contract stipulated that he had to live within the Village of Westfield, where he worked, so we began to search for a house within the incorporated limits right away. I drove around looking for one that would suit our needs, but because I had two young boys, an Airedale dog, two cats, seven rabbits, twelve mallard ducks, and a pet raccoon, the task was daunting.

After looking for two months, I finally introduced myself to the mayor and told him my problem. "Well, I'm an old farmer myself," he said. "We'll just change the law to include a five-mile radius for employee residents."

I was surprised that the problem could be solved so simply, but I thought it was because the chief was valuable in his job and the mayor wanted to accommodate him. I spent another month driving the back roads and hidden lanes outside the village limits trying to find a home that would accommodate our menagerie. It seemed impossible; each possibility had a major flaw. The chief instructed me, "Whatever you do, don't look at big, drafty old places."

While I was feeding the mink, which had been a daily five-hour task for years, I had what I would now describe as a vision. People immediately raise their eyebrows when I say that, and I am tempted to call it something else. Whatever you want to call it, it was a mental picture of an old house at the end of a long driveway, and it overlooked Lake Erie. The mental picture wouldn't go away. I tried hard to ignore it while I kept on working. I even sang to distract myself, but nothing seemed to obliterate the scene in my head. I felt an intense directive, message, or command, no, all of those things, insisting that I should leave right then and go to Westfield, where I would find the house that was right for me. After several unsuccessful attempts to get rid of this ridiculous mental state I gave up, took off my feed apron, went to my dad, and announced that I was leaving to follow the persistent daydream.

Dad was a practical, self-made, self-disciplined man who did not believe in such "hogwash." He blew up. "What the hell do you mean? You can't just walk out on feeding six thousand animals. Have you lost your mind?"

I answered, "I think so, but I have to go right now." I walked away, which I had never done in the twenty-six years that I had helped him feed the mink—something I'd done since I was four years old, when I was issued my first tin cup for measuring each portion.

On my way out of the mink yard, I gathered up Larry, who was at that point nine years old. I left Andy, then twelve, to help his grandfather. Then I called my future mother-in-law, Nellie, and asked her to go for a ride with me. Soon we were on our way. The mental picture, vision or whatever it was, remained firmly imprinted in my mind.

As we drove the twenty miles to the grape-growing microclimate along the south shoreline of Lake Erie, I told Nellie about the overpowering, unending, invasive, surreal picture in my mind.

She said flat-out, "You're crazy. You've lost your mind. You just want to find a house so badly that you're imagining this."

I drove on. I believed that I could drive right to the house I saw in my mind, so I went where I thought it was located: on the escarpment overlooking the endless expanse of water in Lake Erie. I drove the length of the escarpment in the Township of Westfield, all of which was within five miles of the village limits. I found nothing. Nellie insisted we turn around and go home. She reminded me that I was crazy, but I drove on and on. I still couldn't get rid of the image on what I imagined was a TV screen on the inside of my forehead.

Finally, in desperation, I turned into a service station. I asked the woman in charge, "Do you know of any old house that sits at the end of a long driveway, high on the hill that overlooks Lake Erie, and is for sale?"

She thought for a minute and said, "No. I don't know of anything like that."

Out of my mouth came the words, "Well, you should, because you deliver fuel oil there." I was shocked by my own voice; I had no idea where the words had come from. I certainly had not known that the gas station also had a home-heating–fuel business or where they delivered fuel.

She said, "Wait a minute. An attorney here in town just got his real-estate license. He was in here this morning and said he'd just listed a house that's something like that. But it isn't up on the hill, it's down by the lake."

"Can you call him?" I asked.

"No, I can't. He and his wife left for a two-week vacation. He was in here gassing up his car, and then he was going home to get his wife and leave town."

"Call him please," I pleaded. "Just go to the phone and call him now."

She sighed impatiently while she dialed, muttering that he was already gone. To her surprise, he answered the phone. "A woman is here, asking about that house you just listed," she said. "She insisted that I call you. She wants to see it." She listened for a moment and then hung up.

"He said for you to meet him at the New York State Thruway entrance on Route 394. He'll just give you a key, because he's headed that way to leave on vacation. He said you can look for yourself."

In 1969, as now, that was unheard of. No one just gave a stranger a key and left for two weeks. I hurried to the thruway entrance, while Nellie protested that I truly had lost my mind. When we got there, Mr. Tennant, the real-estate agent, got out of his car and said, "I've changed my mind. I'll go with you for a few minutes. I don't think you can get the door open by yourself. Just follow me. It's only a mile or so."

I shivered with anticipation as we followed him down the long driveway in a cloud of dust. When the ancient farmhouse finally peeked out of the overgrown brush surrounding it, I saw that it had a green shingled roof, clapboard siding with no visible paint, and a broken cement slab for a front porch.

Nellie said, "It's so isolated back here in the woods. You can't see another soul; it's so far off the highway. I'd be scared to live here."

"Not me," I boasted. "I'm marrying the chief of police. How much safer could I get?"

As we got out of the car, I told Nellie and Larry, "I'll know if this is the right house when I get inside. There will be five dark beams across the ceiling."

Nellie stated, "You're nuts."

While Mr. Tennant struggled with the lock, we looked at the dilapidated, unpainted, ramshackle house, covered with brush and vines. I kept saying, "This is it. This is it."

Little Larry followed me to the front door. Mr. Tennant opened it and there, before our eyes, was a living room with five large, dark beams across the ceiling. Then the smell hit us full-force. Boy, did it stink. Nellie gagged, and Larry ran out. I said to Mr. Tennant, "I'll take it."

Mr. Tennant replied, without a pause, "Okay, here's the key. You haven't even seen the property or the rest of the house yet, though."

"It doesn't matter. I'll take it. I'm supposed to be here." He handed me the keys and insisted that we walk through the rest of the house. The pungent smell gagged me. I noticed that the kitchen floor had rotted through in one place. But I was so excited to actually find the physical object of my vision that I hardly noticed the rest of the inside on the tour.

Mr. Tennant insisted on giving us a guided walk down a path toward the lake. When we got to the end of it, we saw that we were at the edge of a twenty-foot cliff. The view was breathtaking. We could see more than a mile to the west, past a boat harbor, and we could see a city twelve miles to the east. The diamonds of reflected sunlight dancing and sparkling on the water stretched north, beyond the horizon, toward Canada. The cliff dropped straight down without any access to the water and no fence at all.

The stench of the lake on that hot summer day was disgusting. Dead fish had washed up on a little beach in a cove, and decaying seaweed sloshed against the shale at the base of the cliff. In spite of that, all I could see was the vision in my head and all I could feel was the overpowering sense that I was home. This place was meant for me. It was beautiful, and it was ok, rotting floor, sticking front door, lake-water stench, and all.

Mr. Tennant said, "You haven't even asked me how much it is."

"It doesn't matter. It will all work out. I'll take it," I said. He handed me the keys, and I asked if I could clean and paint.

He said, "Do whatever you want to do. I'll be back in two weeks to complete the paperwork."

As he walked away, he continued, "Your timing was lucky. We got to the thruway entrance, and my wife couldn't remember if she'd unplugged the iron, so I turned around. As I was taking care of that, the phone rang. I'll see you in two weeks. What's your name, and where are you from?"

I said, "I'm the new police chief's fiancée. You can contact me through the police department."

"Nice to meet you," he said as he left. I had bought a house.

We walked around in the house a little more, where I discovered that a lot of the smell was garbage that had been left in a cabinet under the kitchen sink. Then we left to finish work at the mink farm. It was seven o'clock by the time all the little critters had had their supper. I couldn't wait to show the place to the chief, Andy, and my dad. We left for Westfield and met the chief there around seven-thirty. One look at the grim expression on the chief's face told me he didn't like it at all. Dad just shook his head in disbelief. I unlocked the door, and the smell overwhelmed all of us. As we made our way upstairs, we all held our noses, overcome by the smell of something dead. It was bat manure in the attic. In the downstairs back bedroom, an eye-watering odor overwhelmed our senses. The chief stepped into a closet in the darkness and fell off a ten-inch drop. He was not impressed.

They wanted to know what I had agreed to in terms of money. I said I didn't know. They asked if I'd shaken hands on the deal. I said, "I shook hands and agreed to buy it. You might as well accept that this is where I'm supposed to live. I'm positive about that." They were both in complete despair and angry.

The boys returned from exploring the lake and declared, "Lake Erie is full of dead fish, and it stinks."

I assured them that after I cleaned up the house, cut some brush, and picked up all the trash, it would look different and smell 100 percent better. The chief returned to the village and his neat, clean, well-kept apartment. The rest of us rode back to the mink farm in silence.

I thanked God and asked him for at least twenty years in that house. I slept well that night because I knew in my heart that I was predestined to live there. The mental picture was gone, the overpowering message was quiet, and in their place was a serene knowledge that this was exactly where I was supposed to be. I had always believed in divine direction.

Mr. Tennant returned from his vacation and was surprised and pleased to find changes to the old house's appearance. We had chopped the brush away from the windows and doors and swept the whole place. Trash had been hauled away, and the boys had opened up a wide path to the lake. Mr. Tennant informed me that the mortgage was transferable but that I needed a $3,000 down payment. The remaining balance would be $6,000, and the monthly payments would be $150.00. The chief had no money and I had no savings, but I knew that my portion of the net profit from the mink harvest would cover that down payment. Dad agreed to let me have it early, so we signed the papers and continued making the house livable, one room at a time.

My plan was to do all the things that didn't cost money first. I filled a bucket with Clorox and hot, sudsy water, grabbed a mop, and said, "Once begun, half done." In the back bedroom downstairs, the finish of the linoleum floor looked like it had been stripped. I thought I could at least clean it so the smell would no longer sting my nose. I threw the Clorox and soapy water on the dark, sticky mess, and it was immediately clear that it was covered with years of cat manure. It had been walked upon until it resembled tar and the only way to get rid of the scummy mess was to scrape it up with a putty knife after softening it with the hot water.

The room was sixteen feet by sixteen feet. Underneath the mess was a new-looking linoleum floor. After three days of gagging and vomiting from the odor, I had a new floor at no cost. A week of leaving the windows open and some new paint resolved the problem.

The chief approved of my laborious improvements and agreed to join me in a massive cleanup of the grounds surrounding the old house. I borrowed an old wheelbarrow and we began to gather up the years of accumulated debris.

The chief had an aversion to getting his hands dirty, so he donned some rubber gloves and picked things up while I pushed the wheelbarrow along. He stepped carefully through the debris, onto a decaying pile of brush. *Whomp!* He fell through the pile like it was a bear trap. He managed to stick his elbows out just in time to escape total submersion in the septic tank. I laughed, but of course he didn't see any humor in the incident. It was the beginning of a pattern.

My kids took up the slack when the chief quit the cleanup effort. We were moving right along when we encountered a heap of trash. Twelve-year-old Andy slammed his shovel under it and used condoms hung from the dirt he slung into the wheelbarrow. "Look, Mom," he exclaimed with a sly, knowing smile, cocking his head toward his little brother, "ghost balloons."

We found an abandoned baseball diamond and backstop in the overgrowth. We found nearly perfectly round stone balls and put them all down woodchuck holes, only to learn years later that these stones were probably used by the Erie Indians to grind corn. We found marbles and silver spoons and pieces of pottery. Larry stumbled over something and discovered it was an Erie Indian skinning stone. When we took it to the Buffalo Science Museum, we learned it was four hundred to six hundred years old. Because of it and the stone balls, the expert thought there might have been an Indian farming community on the property.

We moved inside. Larry was in charge of removing trash from the upstairs. He was busy putting bits of paper in a trash bag when he yelled, "Mom, I found a lot more ghost balloons under the baseboards in the bedrooms. Bring a flashlight up here. There's writing on the walls in the closet. It says, 'Frank has a big something.' I need the light so I can read it."

The boys and I cleaned, removed cobwebs, scraped and painted, nailed boards back onto the outside steps, and repaired an old picnic table. Finally the house was in move-in condition. We celebrated with a picnic at the refurbished table. When the chief came to inspect our progress, he said, "You guys have done a great job. I can't imagine how nice this house will be after we're married and you quit the mink farm. You'll be a full-time housewife, with time to make all kinds of improvements."

"I don't intend to quit the mink farm. Dad and I are partners, and I have years invested in the business. I can do both, believe me," I asserted.

The chief picked up one of the square, blue, china plates I had brought for the celebration, smashed it on the edge of the old table, and said, "We'll see. You don't need to be a dumb farmer when you're my wife."

The incident upset all of us. He stomped off to his patrol car and drove away, but just before dark, he returned with a bouquet of flowers for me, candy for the boys, and an apology. We forgot about it.

I had hung the old family heirloom I called Mirror in the front hall to cover a tear in the wallpaper. One day, I was walking out the front door when I thought I heard Mirror caution, "The chief might be good to the boys now, but you always pet the calf to catch the cow." I scoffed at Mirror and went ahead with the house cleaning and wedding planning.

Ten weeks of cleaning, repairing, painting, and preparing for a wedding, along with my regular schedule of farm work, exhausted me. I was confident that I had bought the right house and found the right man to be my second husband and that life was going to be great.

The broken-plate incident and the comment about giving up my partnership in the mink farm lingered like a shadow in my mind, but I was convinced that things would work out when Dad reminded me of the flowers, gifts, and time the chief showered upon us. A broken plate and the chief's desire for my undivided attention didn't outweigh all that. I desperately wanted a home of my own, and Dad's lady friend, Freddie, had made it clear she wished I would move out. Still, the broken plate and the yelling, red-faced man at the picnic table stayed shaded in my mind.

My wedding day finally arrived. I remember riding in my dad's car with my two boys when it was time to go to the church. We were almost there when a tiny shaft of sunlight tried to pierce those shadows of doubt in my mind. I said, "Dad, stop the car. This is a mistake. Take me back home; I don't want to get married today."

"Gail, you just have the wedding jitters. As soon as the ceremony is over, you'll be fine," Dad said. He kept driving toward the church and the end of his commitment, care, and responsibility for me and my children.

The reception was at Vinewood Acres, the name the boys chose for our new house by Lake Erie because it had grapevines and acres of thick, dense woods.

A hundred people came. The cake was in place, finger foods were on the table, and my aunts and friends were in charge. It was a lovely celebration. The boys went home with their grandfather when it was over, and the chief and I left for a honeymoon.

Trouble started on the first morning in our home as a new family. The boys left on the school bus, and I was about to leave for the mink farm when the chief grabbed my arm hard enough to hurt. He spun me around, looked me in the eye, shook his finger in my face, and said, "Don't drive your car into the Village of Westfield. Do you understand? Don't come anywhere near the village, or I'll arrest you for bald tires."

"You know I don't have money for new tires," I said, shocked. "Would you really give me a ticket, knowing that?"

"Trust me, I will if you come into the village. You're the police chief's wife now, and you have to behave to the letter of the law. You better listen up. I'll give you a ticket for bald tires, rolling through a stop sign, or anything else you do wrong," he snarled. He pushed my arm away in disgust and stomped out the door. "Don't think you or your kids can get away with anything. You're all on probation, as far as I'm concerned."

When the chief came home that evening, he held up his hand like he was stopping traffic at a busy intersection and said, "You might as well get adjusted right now. When I come home, I want you to ask how my day was and then leave me alone for thirty minutes while I change out of my uniform and have a drink. Then I expect my dinner to be on the table. After that, you can talk to me." On his way through the kitchen, he added, "Oh, yeah, I don't want any trivial chitchat at the dinner table, either. Tell the boys that. They should be seen and not heard."

It was just the beginning of difficult times. I had settled the divorce from the boys' father, agreeing to only minimal support payments and an agreement for a few dollars a month to be invested in a college fund for them. The boys were beginning to ask questions about money from their dad, and they were wondering why they hadn't heard from him since I had announced my engagement and bought the house. It was the end of their relationship with their fanatical father. He made no phone contact, arranged no visits, and sent no Christmas or birthday cards. He made the support payments only because he had to. He never contacted the boys as they matured.

Life in the grape-growing region along Lake Erie was foreign to us, which added to the stress. Loud noises and flashing lights woke us on the second night we slept in our new home. Lights flashed everywhere and rumbling noises filled the darkness. We heard yelling, metal clanking, and engines roaring as spotlights illuminated the windows. We all woke up to hear the dog barking and howling, adding to the din.

I was terrified. I peeked out the window, expecting to see a flying saucer, but instead my yard was filled with tractors, wagons, and people, and trucks were in my driveway. The first grape harvest was in full swing. Men with log chains were swearing and yelling as they tried to get the harvester unstuck with a bulldozer. I was relieved; it wasn't a UFO.

The harvesting season was festive. There was no more sleep that night as we watched from the house. The aroma from the Concord grapes intensified with the harvest, and on that warm October night, we just wanted to drink the air.

The next morning, the chief's coffee was too hot. He burned his tongue and then threw the mug of scalding coffee at me. It burned my hand and dented the refrigerator behind me, but he just glared at me as he walked out the front door. I excused the behavior, because we were all tired from watching the grape harvest, and we were still getting used to living as a family.

As we struggled through the first year of living in the old house, I reached into the reservoir of experience and knowledge I'd acquired while maintaining Dad's rentals. I knew how to deal with a leaking roof, broken plumbing, cold drafts that blew through the windows and doors making it impossible to keep warm, and much more. As soon as I earned a dollar, I spent it on roofers and plumbers and a variety of used storm windows that I adapted to fit the mismatched windows of the old house.

One afternoon, I came home tired and dirty from the mink ranch. I had budgeted just enough time to get dinner for my boys. I planned to wash my hair for an official dinner in the village. The chief was going to be the speaker, and I had a new dress to wear. We had adjusted to one another and fallen into a routine. I put a leftover casserole in the oven for the boys and ran to the bathroom. I wet my hair and massaged some shampoo into it, but then the water stopped running. I turned it off and on several times, but nothing came out of the faucet.

I ran with dread to the door leading to the hole under the house, which we called a cellar. The single dim light bulb down there was draped with cobwebs, which were, in turn, draped with dust. Something smelled like burning electrical wiring so I made my way across the cellar in the semidarkness and pulled the fuse for the water pump. The humming stopped, and the smell disappeared.

I ran back upstairs for a flashlight, screwdriver, and pliers. I was sure they were in a drawer in the kitchen. They weren't. I jerked the drawer completely out, but the only thing I found was a folded, yellowed piece of paper that said, "To whoever buys the house: instructions for when the water quits." I couldn't believe it. I had budgeted just thirty minutes to transform myself from the farmer my new husband despised into a wife he could present to the community.

The yellowed paper said to prime the pump with the gallon jugs of water that were on the dirt floor of the crawl space. When we moved in, I had wondered why anyone would keep twelve gallon jugs of water, and when I couldn't figure it out, I had dumped them.

There I stood, shivering in the damp, dank, musty cellar with lather in my hair and not much more than a smile on my body, when the chief arrived on the scene.

I explained my predicament, and he said, "I should have known you couldn't be anything but a dumb farmer. I'll just go to the dinner alone." He left in a huff.

I eventually primed the pump with water I found in the teakettle, but there was not enough water in the well to take a bath. I finished rinsing my hair and filled a couple of gallon jugs for future priming, and that was that. I ate supper with the kids. The chief and I didn't speak for a couple of days, but the difficulty eventually faded into the past.

Colder weather caused frozen pipes under the house. I was the only one small enough to make my way through the crawl space to thaw them. I took a candle and matches and made my way halfway down the cellar stairs. It was tricky to boost my body into the sixteen-inch space under the rotting kitchen floor. I had to lie on my belly on the crawl space's dirt-and-clay floor and then wiggle like a snake through cobweb curtains for thirteen feet to the stone foundation wall on the outside of the house. There were many open spaces between the stones, letting the wind and snow howl and whistle through, which had frozen the water pipes feeding the kitchen sink. Finally I covered the distance, worked my arms into position, lit the candle, and held it under the old iron pipes. The pipes sizzled as they started to thaw, and droplets of water formed. I stuffed an old rag into one of the holes in the stone wall, only to have it blow out again when the wind howled. When I slithered back out, my head was covered in cobwebs and my clothes were dirty, but I could hear water running in the kitchen sink. It's a wonder I didn't burn the house down with the candles I used.

The furnace burned up the first winter I lived in the house. The boys, who were not yet teenagers, were in bed upstairs, and the chief and I snuggled in our bed; we'd been married only three months. My big Airedale, Buster, was asleep on the floor on my side of the bed. Around one in the morning, I awoke to a trembling sensation. The dog suddenly began to growl and then the trembling became violent shaking. It was the bedroom shaking; our newlywed lovemaking was not the cause. I jumped out of bed, ran down the hall to the cellar door, and smelled smoke. The dog already had the boys up and in the kitchen, and we all ran out the door.

A freight-train wind howled off Lake Erie which shivered and shook our pajama-clad bodies in the harsh fifteen-degree night. The chief ordered the boys and the dog into his police car and told me to call the fire department. Then he raced off to pry open the old door to the dug-out hole under the house so he could get to the fuse box. I pulled my pajama top over my nose and ran just inside the front door to the phone. The rumbling and shaking intensified.

In a matter of minutes, a local police car screamed down the long driveway, followed closely by the fire chief and fire trucks, all leaving a wake of snow behind them. Then the sheriff's department arrived, and they began take furniture out of the house while we huddled with the dog in the police car, which was now stuck in a snow bank because I'd moved it too fast when I tried to get it out of the way. At least the car's heater worked. Before long, everything was under control. The fire chief said that the furnace was actually a combination of five different furnaces that someone had hand-assembled.

An accident a mile down the road had severed a utility pole, and the electric company had turned the power off while they replaced it. When they turned the juice back on, a power surge fused the old wires in the makeshift furnace together, causing the oil to get hot and smolder but not ignite. Another few minutes and the furnace would have exploded and the house would have burned down. We were thankful to have our home unharmed. One of the firemen owned a heating business and soon we had a new furnace to keep us warm against the winter winds.

Chapter Six: Hard Times, Hard Work, Angels, and Abuse, Spring of 1970

THE STORMS OF WINTER finally passed and spring bloomed. It seemed to be the perfect time for entertaining. We decided to have an extended-family picnic, so I invited my sister and her family; my dad and his lady friend; the chief's mother and her husband; Gramps, the chief's step grandfather; and a local judge and his wife. I thought it would be a lovely celebration. We had weathered some bumps in the road, and we still had problems, but we had survived the winter, and it was time to celebrate.

Gramps arrived first, along with his dog, Shaggy. Shaggy charged into my kitchen and left muddy tracks all over it. More guests were expected momentarily, so I grabbed the dog, yelled at her, booted her out the door, grabbed the mop and began to clean up the mess. My husband of eight months suddenly grabbed me by the neck, dragged me into the living room, punched me just below the ribs, and said, "My grandfather's dog can do anything she wants, and you will never yell at her again. Do you understand?" He yanked my hair and pushed me into the stairway as he growled, "If you hadn't yelled at Shaggy, I wouldn't have to hit you, you miserable bitch." Then he went to the door and greeted our next picnic guest as though nothing had happened. He did that right in front of Mirror.

I clearly heard Mirror hiss at him, "You're the son of a bitch. She didn't deserve that," as the chief escorted another guest into our home.

I covered my face in shame and hid in the upstairs bathroom to cry. I put cold water on my face to hide the tearstains, waited until the shaking stopped, and returned to the party, which was now in full swing. I didn't think anyone guessed what had just happened to me; I was so ashamed. I thought I must be the most awful wife in the world. The words "I'm a bitch" ran through my mind over and over again.

The next day, the florist arrived with a big bouquet of roses from the chief. He came home for lunch, apologized, and said it would never happen again. He said he'd been stressed because it was our first attempt at hosting a family picnic and entertaining made him uptight. I forgave him.

———————————

We planted our first garden that year and made improvements to the lawn and driveway. Other picnics were fun and uneventful. Dad bought the boys an inflatable raft to use in the lake. He attached a long nylon rope to it and tied it to a tree at the top of the cliff. We played hide-and-seek, cleaned up the trails in the woods, and built steps down the cliff so we could go swimming on the days the wind blew the seaweed away. We worked as a family. The chief was good to the boys, as he had always been. He liked the improvements and enjoyed showing them off to his friends.

However, Mirror reminded me, "Don't let your guard down; you know better."

When our first anniversary rolled around, I arranged for the boys to spend the weekend with their grandpa. I made a special trip to the grocery store and bought thick T-bone steaks and all the extras. I stopped at a specialty store to buy some scented candles and picked up a pretty cake at a local bakery. I was so excited, imagining how romantic it would be for the chief and me to have a candlelit dinner in our own dining room. I envisioned soft music and a romantic moonlight walk to the edge of the lake.

I was singing and smiling when I grabbed the bags and got out of the car. "Hi, sweetheart," I called to the chief, who was on a ladder at the front of the house, painting the gutters with white Rust-Oleum. "I have a surprise. I'm going to fix us a gorgeous steak dinner with candles and music and all the trimmings—just you and me. Happy anniversary! The boys are spending the weekend at my dad's house."

The chief turned so he could see me standing there below him, my arms loaded with groceries and goodies, and he yelled, "Where the hell have you been? It's five-thirty, there's no supper cooking, and I don't give a good goddamn about your stupid surprise." He raised the paintbrush filled with white paint and snapped his wrist as hard as he could, whipping paint all over my hair, face, and clothes. Then he barreled down the ladder with murder in his eyes.

I ran back to my car, hurled the groceries on top of the cake, slammed and locked the door, and got my keys out of my pocket. I was shaking so badly I couldn't get the key into the ignition. I poked and poked at it while he covered my car with the white paint, dipping the brush repeatedly in the paint bucket and flicking it at the car. I put the vehicle in reverse and left in a cloud of dust that stuck on the paint. I could barely see out of the windshield.

When I drove to the mink ranch and found my dad and boys, I was shaking so badly I couldn't talk. They looked incredulous when they saw the car. The maroon Mustang Fastback was splotched with white paint and road dust. It took us four hours, working as fast and carefully as possible, to clean off the mess, while I explained how it had gotten on there in the first place.

Finally we brought my groceries inside. Dad cut up the lettuce, the boys scrubbed four potatoes and set the table, and I cooked the steaks and cried.

"You must have ticked him off because you were late or something," Dad mumbled, his mouth full of anniversary cake.

"I swear to you, I didn't say or do anything except get out of the car with the bag of groceries and the pretty cake we're eating right now. Dad, you helped clean the paint off the car, and I still have paint in my hair. How the hell could you even think it was my fault? Only a maniac would throw paint on someone."

"Something must have happened, Gail. He didn't just fly into a rage because you came home with steaks and a cake," Dad insisted. The boys stopped eating and stared at me, waiting for an explanation, but there wasn't one.

"I can't go back. It's our anniversary, and he did this to me. I can't go back—ever."

"You have to. You have a life there now. The boys have school and friends, and their life is in Westfield. You raised a garden and canned and put all that food away in the new freezer you struggled to buy. Why don't you just wait and see if he shows up with an explanation?" my old-school father suggested.

We worked in the mink yard all the next day, which was Sunday, and in the middle of the afternoon, the chief showed up. True to form, he got out of his car with flowers, an apology, and a string of excuses about how the endless work on the old dump of a house I had insisted on buying and the stress and responsibility of his job had made him overtired.

I physically trembled throughout the cold, self-serving presentation. I looked at my feet and glanced at my dad to see if he would come to my defense, but he said, "There, Gail, you see? He had a reason, and I guess it wasn't your fault after all. You can get your stuff and the boys and go home again. I'll finish the chores. Everything will be okay. Just forget about it."

I packed up our things and went back, cold, shaking, disillusioned, and waiting for the next time. I reminded myself that Mirror thought I was a good daughter, a good mother, and a good wife. I convinced myself that upsetting the apple cart and disrupting everybody's life would be selfish, just like my dad had indicated.

I began to believe that my work on the mink farm was making the chief disagreeable. I decided that maybe I should work fewer hours and find something else to do.

———

A year and a half passed without incident. In the fall, my neighbor, who aspired to having her own restaurant, knocked on my door and said she'd discovered that I had a first-refusal option on the vineyards surrounding my farmhouse. She asked if I would consider signing off so she could build a truck stop restaurant. She informed me that she already had a franchise deal with a national chain.

I was devastated. I loved the acres of grapes, which provided a buffer of privacy around my house, and I didn't want to live behind a truck stop. I heard myself say, "Nope. I'm going to buy them and become a grape farmer."

I wasn't surprised when Mirror said, "Now you're thinking. Grapes don't bite and stink and you won't have to commute to work on them; they're right in your front yard."

I went to the bank the next day and asked for another loan. I had assumed the mortgage on the old house and surrounding acres. They informed me that they would be happy to do that with one-third down payment and my husband's signature on the loan.

The chief flatly refused, yelling in my face, "I hate the house and the place; the well has gone dry, the roof leaks, the pipes freeze up every night, the furnace burned up, there aren't enough storm windows or doors, and the wind blows through all the cracks, making the heating bills outrageous." As he stepped over the rotted hole in the kitchen floor, he snarled, "The septic tank has no cover on it—only a piece of plywood. There's no money to buy bread and milk. What the hell are you thinking? I'll never become a goddamned grape farmer, and I'll never cosign on a loan to buy grapes."

I went to my dad next. He and I were business partners in the mink farming business, and I worked for minimum wage plus half the net profit each December 31. I had already borrowed the money to cover the down payment for the assumed mortgage. He said no.

I went back to the bank and asked again. The loan officer asked me to sit down and quietly said, "From my perspective, you're out of your mind. You have no knowledge of the grape business, no money, and no equipment, and you're so tiny—you lack the physical strength to succeed. In my humble opinion, I see a resounding failure." He also informed me that he had seen my husband and knew that he wanted no part of a grape farm and would oppose my efforts.

I kept hammering away at the chief. The more the wind howled and the lake-effect snow blew outside, the more I insisted that I was going to buy the damned grapes. While I dreamed of working at home, my work on the mink farm continued to cause stress in my marriage.

It was harvest time on the mink farm. Mink have scent glands just like skunks. When they are skinned for their hides, which are ultimately used for coats, they stink. They don't just smell bad; they really *stink*. I was the primary skinner and was working my way through about six thousand hides over a six-week period. The scent permeated my clothes, skin, and hair.

The lanolin in the fat on the carcasses made my hands soft, but they smelled rank. The chief hated the smell, the mink, the grapes, and all farming. Each night when I came home, he would greet me with a pail of water and bleach. Before I could enter the house, I had to strip, wash, and leave my stinking clothes outside, regardless of the cold, before I could enter our house and make my naked way to a perfumed bath. Even that daily ritual didn't stop stray dogs from howling and following me because of the scent embedded in my skin and hair.

As I harvested the mink hides, I envisioned working at the vineyard, where I knew I would not smell bad. Grapes grew in front of my house, not twenty-five miles away like the mink farm. I put forth that argument one evening. I guess the chief thought I would quit the mink-farming business, silly man. I fully intended to do both, in addition to my new part-time responsibilities as secretary for the police department and police matron on call.

My next stop was the bank again. I went by the loan officer's cubicle on my way home from skinning mink, before my Clorox treatment. Heads turned, bank customers stared, and tellers gagged, but I marched right into the loan department and said, "Are you ready to give me the loan to buy the grapes?"

He said no.

I repeated the drill every afternoon on my way home, throughout mink-skinning season. Each day, my "outfit" got more disgusting. It was useless to wash my skinning clothes until the six-week season ended. Besides, I just left them on the front porch to air out every night. After a while, I couldn't even smell them myself.

During one daily visit, the bank president yelled at me, "You don't know how to prune grapes or how to take care of them. You don't have any equipment—no tractor or tools. You're a woman, for God's sake." The loan officer crossed his arms on his chest and scowled.

That made me furious. I stood there in my stinking, bloody, greasy, filthy, stand-alone Carhartt coveralls and farm boots and yelled, "I'm a mink farmer. I raise eight thousand animals a year, which requires me to be a nutritionist, a veterinarian, an expert in genetics, a mechanic, a truck driver, and a businesswoman. How much more damned experience do you want? And, yes, I am a 'woman,' and I think that's the real problem."

Everyone in the bank stopped what they were doing and waited in total silence for his answer. The president said, "Gail, if you promise to never come in here again looking and smelling like that, we'll give you the loan."

"Thank you. I promise. Furthermore, one day I'll come in here and you'll beg me to put my money into your bank. I won't need to beg you for a loan," I answered.

"Just how will you learn the grape business?" he asked.

"I'll find somebody to teach me."

"There isn't a man in this county who will teach you."

"I know a farmer's wife, and she'll teach me."

"Good luck. The bank will own the grapes before it's all done," he said.

I won.

Back home, Mirror said, "Congratulations. You done good. I knew you could. As tough as you are, I even think you'll succeed."

I got the loan, and I got acquainted with my first female angel and mentor. I called the woman I had in mind, introduced myself, and stated my need for her instruction. She agreed. When the mink had all been skinned, I disinfected my "uniform" and followed her and her husband through their vineyard, learning to prune and listening to their dissertation on the grape-farming business. Eventually, the fresh air eradicated the mink scent from my clothes. The farm where I was learning my lessons was on my way to the mink farm, where I still had to care for the breeding stock every day.

I bought new pruning shears, loppers, and a new pruning saw. I invested in heavy sheepskin-lined gloves, and my face became tan from the winter sun and wind. One day, I was obsessing about which vines to cut off in the tangled grapevine growth. Mary said, "Gail. I cannot hold your hand. Just cut the damned thing off. You know the basic selection process. You can't kill a grapevine. Just cut them."

I knew I had worn out my welcome; they needed to go on with their work without my interruptions.

I went home and began to prune my mortgaged vineyard. It took three and a half hours to prune one row, and there were seventy-two rows. I estimated the time needed to finish before I had to make a little maple syrup in March and carry out the breeding season with our remaining 1600 female and 400 male mink. It meant that I would have to work in the grapes every daylight hour available.

I've always been a get'er-done kind of person and I finished the pruning in time to spend the lengthening daylight hours breeding the mink. Each animal had a pedigree tag attached to its nest box. The genetics, records of size, quality of fur, and other pertinent information were important to maintaining and improving the fur bearing herd. Matching up pedigrees for optimum herd improvement was an exciting part of my mink-ranching career.

The male mink knew me on sight. They would see me entering the sheds, peek over the top of their nest boxes, and make a chuckling, purring sound deep in their throats to let me know they were ready for some female company.

I would match up the genetic records and turn each selected male loose in a pen with an appropriate female. Four hundred males had to go visiting each day, and the wooden nest boxes I carried them in weighed forty-five pounds. The month of March was a blur of mink, maple syrup and grape vines.

March turned to April, and while I waited for the mink to whelp, which took about five to six weeks, I had to install 1600 specialized nesting materials into the females' nest boxes, as well as 1600 fine-wire-mesh false bottoms in their large litter pens, so the tiny, furless, new babies, the size of my little finger, would not fall on the ground.

My extra job as police matron and secretary carried responsibilities that included attending many functions. One day, an invitation arrived for the dedication of a new youth-detention center at the county office building.

I arrived at the mink farm just before daylight, had a cup of tea with Dad, and finished my chores there by midmorning. I jumped into my reliable old Mustang and headed home. As I drove, I planned what dress I'd wear to the dedication.

Cresting a hilltop, an oncoming driver made a left turn in front of me. I remember seeing him on my side of the road, trying to avoid the impact, and deciding to pull to the right shoulder in case somebody else was behind him so that I would avoid a head-on collision. I remember screaming, "You dumb bastard," and then I remember nothing.

Waking up in our tiny rural hospital was a shock. I couldn't move my head. I couldn't move my body, and my legs were terribly heavy. I rolled my eyes around, and there stood the doctor, my dad, my two young sons, and the chief. My speech was slurred, slow, and heavy from sedation as I said, "Wh's go'n on?"

The doctor said, "You've been in a terrible accident. You have three broken ribs, a broken pelvic bone, and a broken left hip, and your collarbone is dislocated from your breastbone. You have whiplash, and you're lucky to be alive."

Tears rolled in rivers down my cheeks. All I could think about was the unfinished spring grape work and the baby mink due to be born, counted, and nurtured. I tried to move. The doctor said I should lie quietly and that the sandbags and traction would prevent any motion. The chief stood at the foot of my bed, unsympathetic and stone-faced, his arms folded across his chest. "Your Mustang is a pile of junk. It was destroyed. The bank was right. They'll own the grapes now," he said.

I kept thinking I had to get up and go to work. I owed that damned bank a lot of money, and I had no funds or cash flow to hire any labor. God, what a mess I was in. "The bank will end up owning the grapes" kept echoing in my foggy, pain-medicated mind.

I lay there, sedated, for a few days. Every time I woke up, I found a police patrolman, my husband, my sons, or my dad standing guard.

One day, when just my dad was there, I managed to reach up and grab the triangle thingy and sit up out of the sandbags. Oh, it hurt. Dad was dozing in the chair. I knew that the longer I lay there, the weaker I would become. I reached down and found a way to unhook the weights on my left leg, and they crashed onto the floor. All hell broke loose.

I was a terrible patient. I refused the pain meds, refused the weights and traction, stole the wheelchair from my roommate, and found the service elevator. I offered my help to the cafeteria ladies and dried dishes, while tears of pain flowed like the rinse water in the sink. The nurses finally caught me, and the doctor reprimanded me.

I begged for a day off, out of the hospital, and finally the doctor agreed to let the chief take me out for a day. I bought a new pickup truck with the promise of payment from the insurance money. I was never going to own a little sports car again. The truck had an automatic transmission, so I wouldn't have to shift with my injured left leg. I could put my walker in the back and pull myself into the driver's seat with my right arm.

A few days later, I prevailed upon the doctor to release me. I went home with a wheelchair, a walker, and a traction device for my neck. The chief dropped me off. When he was out of sight, I hobbled over to the closet, got my grape-tying apron and my hooded sweatshirt, and headed slowly and painfully across the lawn to the grapes. They had to be tied to the trellis wire before the buds emerged. It hurt to walk, but the work had to be done because of my debt at the bank. I thanked God the heavy, post and wire trellis work was all done.

As I painfully made my way to the end post and turned into the first row of grapes with my tools and supplies tied to my walker, two women I had never seen before came running down the row. They were waving their arms, yelling, and shooing me out of my own grapes. When they came closer, I saw that they were wearing tying aprons with bundles of tie twine at their waists. They looked like they were wearing hula skirts. They yelled above the wind, "What are you doing out here?"

I yelled back, "What are you doing in my vineyard?"

"We're tying your grapes."

I stood still. My mouth hung open in disbelief, "I don't know you," I said finally. "How did you get here? Who hired you? I don't have any money to pay you."

One of the women said, "Our names are Mrs. Foti and Mrs. June, and you don't have to pay us anything. We saw how hard you worked every day this winter, even though it was below zero. We watched you work your way across this vineyard, pruning these vines. We heard how you got the loan. Then we read about your accident in the newspaper, and we decided that you just couldn't possibly tie these grapes yourself. This is our gift to you—woman to woman. We both love to tie grapes, and we don't have any since our husbands sold our vineyards. Now you go on back into the house and rest. Take that apron off, and take care of yourself. There will be a lot more to do, but the tying is almost done. There are only six more rows to go. We'll come in and have a cup of coffee when we finish them."

My chin dropped to my chest. My neck couldn't hold my head up another instant. Tears of gratitude ran down my cheeks as I limped back to the house. When I made my way through the front door, Mirror said, "Ya had a tough break, but somebody's looking out for ya."

A few minutes after I sank into my wheelchair and rolled to the kitchen to make coffee, someone knocked on my back door. I rolled around the rotten spot in the kitchen floor and there stood the neighbor who had wanted to build a truck stop. She had a huge smile on her face and a hot casserole in her hands. "Tough break you had," she said, "I'll be here every day, same place, same time, different supper. Here you go." And she set the dish in my oven. I had never known women would take care of each other like that. True to her word, she arrived each afternoon with supper in her hands. She brought a smile, her little girl and many other surprises. She turned out to be a treasure, another angel in my growing portfolio of angels. Still, the challenges seemed overwhelming, and I couldn't find a way to escape them.

Meanwhile, the baby mink were being born at the fur farm. I was the one who counted them and monitored and recorded their health, growth, and ancestry for future reference when selecting healthy breeding stock.

Every day I hobbled to my truck with my walker, threw it in the back, and pulled myself into the driver's seat. At the mink ranch, I withdrew the walker and then made my way up and down the 225-foot-long metal sheds full of cages, listening for the faint squeaks of newborn mink. The babies were less than two inches long, hairless, and pink. They were supposed to be kept warm. Occasionally, one would fall through the fine mesh wire that was supposed to keep them contained, and I would find it stiff and cold on the ground, dead. I had to move slowly with the walker, and it was painful to bend over and pick up the tiny babies that had fallen through. I was so focused on my pain and balance that I forgot to get a container for the lifeless little babies I picked up. There was no way I was going to walk somewhere to get a bag or can, so I just slipped the ice-cold little things in my bra, between my breasts. As I hobbled along, listening, opening nest boxes, and counting the little ones, I was startled by movement in my bra. The little dead babies weren't dead at all. They had hypothermia and my body heat was the perfect way to revive them. Eventually Dad said, "You have saved a hundred times more mink than it takes to make a coat. This fall, I think you should have a coat made to repay you for your work with your three-sided heater." And I did. It was a bright moment in my bleak, hard working life, when money was so scarce it was difficult to buy groceries. With my injuries, I couldn't work as a police matron, and my chores at the mink ranch decreased. I spent less time there, so my weekly paycheck was less.

At home, the vineyard had sucked up a lot of my savings; I had to pay for work I couldn't do because of the accident. I had to hire people to finish cutting the suckers off the bottoms of the vines after I fell and stuck the pruning shears into my hand. I had to pay for chemicals and fertilizer, and I was worried about the first year's crop.

A terrible frost hit the Lake Erie grape belt that year, and almost all the grape buds froze, turned brown, and fell off. Some secondary and tertiary buds survived, but basically there was not a sustainable crop. People were worried about the money that had already been invested for pruning, tying, fertilizer, and early fungicide applications. When I was able to assess the damage, I was relieved and thankful because I was spared. Not a hint of damage was evident in any part of my vineyard. My vines grew leaves and then tiny buds that developed into full clusters with higher-than-average berry count and size. Other farmers came to see my grapes, marveling at the sight because they had none.

A record crop of ten tons to the acre came off my farm that first harvest season. The grapes brought over $300 a ton. I had seventy tons of grapes and would easily net the $9,000 I'd paid for the grapes. I couldn't wait to take the money to the bank president and remind him that I was a woman with no experience in the grape industry.

Mirror was quick to remind me, "So, now you think you control the weather? How about being thankful to a higher power and predestination or did you forget?" Mirror caused me to remember my dad's belief that pride goes before a fall. I thought about my success and was thankful for all the help I'd received.

For months I used crutches and a walker and experienced pain, but I was able to work the vineyard and the mink ranch in a limited fashion as long as I rested when I was tired.

I had been lying down with a headache and neck pain one summer day when I heard someone at the door. I struggled to get up. When I opened it, I found a huge man with his hands fisted and his face red.

"You Gail Black?" he growled.

"Yes, I am."

"I'm here to give you an insurance-settlement check for the car accident you were in," he said. He thrust his hand into his inner coat pocket and tried to hand me an envelope.

"I'm sorry, but I don't know anything about this, and I'm not going to take anything from you," I responded.

"You better take it, because it's all you're gonna get," he asserted.

I shut the door in his face, more because of my headache than anything else, but it was a good thing I didn't take the check.

The goon, as I called him, returned monthly with his threatening demeanor and actions. He always brought a check, and each time it was worth a bit more. I never knew where or when he would show up, and he was more distasteful with each visit.

My injuries slowly improved. I had a contraption to stretch my neck and Valium for the seized-up muscles. I flushed the Valium because it impaired my thinking, but finally the headaches abated. My broken hip healed. So did the ribs and pelvic bone. My shoulder took longer, but eventually I could lift things and rotate the shoulder normally.

The goon was on the front porch one morning when I opened the door. "This is the last time I'm going to make an offer for the insurance company," he said through gritted teeth. "I've wasted a lot of trips here, and you better take this check if you ever want to settle this peacefully and keep out of court." He thrust the envelope at me. I took it, pulled the check out, and realized that it was the exact amount left on our mortgage.

"Thank you. I'll take this. You must have done your homework to know this exact figure," I said.

"It's enough to pay off your mortgage. You're a fool if you refuse it," he snarled as he started to leave.

"I'll miss your rotten attitude." Then I slammed the door and changed my plans for the day.

My first stop was the bank. It was such a pleasure to walk up to the bank president and hand him that check. "Here you go, sir. I don't owe you anything more on the house. I want a mortgage release, and I want you to know that as this year's grape checks come in, I'll pay off the vineyard loan, too." When he looked sour and perplexed, I added, "I'm supposed to be there—predestination, you know."

When the chief came home for supper, I informed him that I had accepted the insurance payment. His face lit up and he said, "Great! How much did we get? I know what we can do with it. I saw a new Harley-Davidson motorcycle. Is there enough to get it, and do you feel like going shopping tonight? Did you cash the check yet?"

I handed him the mortgage-payment book stamped "paid in full." He slapped me across the face and said, "You stupid, dumb farmer. You could have held out longer and got more."

Mirror asked me, "What's this 'how much did we get' crap? I don't recall that bastard with any broken bones. The money was yours, and you did right."

I considered telling the chief to shut the hell up, but it wasn't worth the risk of being punched, slapped, pushed, or degraded further. I silently vowed to never have a mortgage on my home again. I reminded myself that I was predestined to be a grape farmer; now the place was really mine and mortgage-free. I kept quiet. Only my marriage was a rotten failure.

Mirror confirmed my thoughts. "You're not a dumb farmer," it said. "You did the right thing with the insurance money. You're a smart woman who is supposed to be on this farm. Some would just call it luck, but you and I know better. You will succeed with this farm, because it is meant to be."

Chapter Seven: Escape into Sweet Work with More Angels, 1973

THE MINK HARVEST WAS completed in December, I was well enough to prune the vineyard for the second time, and winter worried along with more frozen water pipes and wind-driven drifts across the long driveway. One winter day, tired from shoveling snow on top of my already excessive workload, I sank into a kitchen chair with a cup of hot coffee and unfolded the local newspaper. As I read an article describing how a Native American squaw discovered maple syrup while cooking over an open fire under a sugar-maple tree with a broken branch, I lowered the newspaper and thought about all the sugar-maple trees around the edge of my vineyards. It went on to tell how Native Americans used elderberry branches for spiels by removing the pith from the inside of the branch, making it into a hollow tube. The tube was then put into a hole made in the side of a sugar-maple tree, and the sap dripped out into a container on the ground.

Elderberry bushes and maple trees were growing in my backyard. I couldn't afford to buy maple syrup, and, immediately, I saw an opportunity to make my own pure, sweet, golden topping. First I went around to the corner of the old farm house where the elderberry bush still grows today. I had an old pair of pruning shears so I cut off a long branch. I wondered how I was supposed to get the stuff, the pith, out of the middle of the branch so sap could flow through. I found an old piece of rusty grape trellis wire and poked at the stick until the pith disappeared. Then I borrowed my dad's brace and bit, drilled a hole that looked about the right size and pounded a six-inch section of the elderberry branch into the sugar maple tree. I didn't even finish before the clear, sparkling sap water began to drip out.

I found an old galvanized tub, a rusty iron bed frame in the brush at the edge of the woods, and enough cement blocks and bricks to construct a makeshift fireplace at the end of a crumbling cement patio on the house. I could hardly wait to gather enough sticks and limbs from the woods to start a fire. I drilled holes and put elderberry stems in trees all the way to the road. It was cold work and my fingers ached from the cold. I noticed that the sap didn't drip when I drilled anymore, and I thought it was because the temperature had dropped to freezing. My arms ached. I gathered up my tools, but when I started back to the house, I couldn't believe my eyes. I had tapped every ash tree and not one single sugar maple. It was no wonder the sap wasn't dripping! Only sugar maples produce dripping sap.

All that work was for nothing and had to be repeated. It was a couple of days before I could even raise my arms to comb my hair. Finally, the gathering began, and my arms ached even more. Every vessel was full. I carried and carried. I filled the makeshift boiling tub, scrubbed the garbage can I used for sap storage, and filled it with sap, and started the fire. I was so excited. But a strong south wind was blowing that day, and the first sparks set the house's old wooden siding on fire. I threw all my sap onto the flames and didn't have to boil it down after all. It got cold and snowed some more, and the sap flow halted.

A week later, the sun came out, and the sap flow resumed as the spring warmth of the sun thawed out the tree trunks, and the frozen sap in the elderberry spiels thawed, and the vessels began to fill. I carried and carried again and again. When I finally lit the fire this time, it was a sunny winter day. Steam began to rise from the old tub, and the sap began to boil. It wasn't long until I could smell the sweet aroma of boiling maple sap. I boiled and boiled and boiled and boiled. I put all the extra sap from the garbage can into the boiling tub and boiled some more. I boiled for two days. When I wasn't picking up every burnable piece of wood I could find, I was carrying fresh sap to the tub. Finally, I let the fire go out and transferred the reduced sap/syrup to my kitchen stove. I had about two gallons of the brownest, dirtiest liquid you could imagine. I strained out what ashes and bark I could and turned the burner on. It smelled heavenly. I got out pancake and waffle recipes, the griddle, and the waffle iron. I put sausages on to cook slowly.

The brown liquid didn't reduce very quickly, and while I waited, I remembered hearing that old-timers used to throw eggs in it to cook and eat. I cracked a couple into the kettle. Immediately the top of the liquid turned to a foaming, gritty brown scum that rose to the top of the liquid. The old-timers didn't put eggs in there to eat—they put them in to clear the syrup. Then they skimmed off the mess and threw it away. That was a new lesson learned.

Mealtime came and went over the next few days, and the brown liquid was finally thick and sweet. I poured it into a jar— my first maple syrup—a project completed successfully. It was exhilarating and an extremely interesting learning experience. I had learned to identify sugar-maple trees, put out fires, and boil eggs in hot sap. I was bursting with pride.

I carefully drained the last of the boiling golden liquid into a glass canning jar and I had a whole half pint. Then there was a sharp cracking sound and the damned jar broke. The syrup just drained away down between the washing machine and the end of the kitchen counter right into the dirt space under the house where I crawled to thaw the frozen pipes. I sat down on the kitchen floor and cried.

Just like every year in the history of maple syrup, the sap was still filling the vessels in the woods. Once sap starts flowing, it doesn't stop until the frogs begin their chorus of croaking in the spring. I was so tired, and my arms hurt so much, but I'd been brought up to waste not, want not. With memories of my grandma in mind, I went out to begin the process all over again. I finally made two quarts of pure, delicious maple syrup that year.

Around that time, a new friend appeared in my life. She was the mother of one of my oldest son's classmates. Peggy, the second oldest of sixteen children, had grown up on a potato-and-dairy farm at the northernmost border of New York State, and her family had produced maple syrup throughout her childhood. When she learned about my amateur sugaring operation, she told me she also enjoyed the challenge, exercise, and fresh air of sugar-bush season.

We took turns gathering sap and wood, and we each made about a gallon for our families. While we tended the fire, added the sap, and gathered the wood, I learned that she taught in our local school, was crowned Miss Chautauqua County, and married a local young man. Making maple syrup was an added bonus for her.

Peggy taught me many things during the long hours we boiled sap. She was beautiful on both the inside and the outside. She volunteered at our local hospital, school, library, and YWCA, and she was adept at organizing and directing charity events. We became lifelong friends. I helped her cut saplings from my woods to use as decorations for a charity ball. We collected food for charity baskets and clothing for distribution to the poor.

As word spread about my little maple syrup distilling operation, more friends and neighbors wandered in to help. One of them built us a little fireplace inside a pole-barn–type shed my son, Andy, had constructed to house the lawnmower.

With the new setup, Peggy and I no longer had to cover the boiling tub with scrap plywood or aluminum siding scraps. We retired our rain suits except for stick or sap gathering, rested in lawn chairs by the warmth of the fire, enjoyed the delicious odor of boiling syrup, and found that we couldn't stay awake. Oh, my, it was so cozy in there. When the chief finally took an interest in the process, he found that it was a perfect place to drink his beer while he complained about his late suppers.

Every time I began to feel complacent, Mirror would say, "Look out—it's the calm before the storm."

One day, the village mayor stopped by to check out our syrup operation. He thought it was so novel and delightful that he asked to bring his family so they could experience the hard work and pride of making maple syrup. He arrived early Saturday morning with his wife and three kids. I explained the operation, pointed out the dangers of getting too close to the fire with loose clothing and of getting too close to the high cliff edge of Lake Erie, and reminded them that they were there at their own risk. Then I went into the house. They boiled and boiled. They gathered and gathered. They finally let the fire go out around five o'clock, but they were back on Sunday morning and did it all over again all day. Around four o'clock, Mrs. Mayor went home to get split-pea-and-ham soup for all of us for supper.

She had just gone up the driveway when Mr. Mayor knocked on the front door. My younger son, Larry, let him in on his way to buy some milk and bread to go with the soup. Mr. Mayor calmly said, "Uh, we have a little problem."

I said, "What?"

"Look out your window at the lake," he replied.

"Oh, my God, I'll call the fire company," I screamed when I saw the bright orange glow of the small but raging fire in my woods. I was anything but calm! The March wind was whipping the leaves and sticks into a wildfire. A spark from the chimney at the maple shed had stuck in the limb of a dead tree. When the limb burned off and dropped to the ground, the fire spread quickly.

"No, no, you can't call them. They'll never let me live it down. Just get me a garden hose, and I'll put it out," he said naively.

"You can't put that out. The hose won't even begin to reach," I screamed. The flames leaped higher and higher in an old, dead, snag tree. As pieces fell off, dry winter leaves ignited and then blew around, spreading the fire rapidly.

I called the fire department. The last I saw of the mayor was his back as he ran across the lawn to the old tin shed, where sparks were spiraling out of the smokestack, whipped by a howling March wind.

Suddenly, sirens and lights were everywhere. Ambulances, fire trucks, pumpers, and the fire chief's pickup lined the driveway. Firemen arrived in their own vehicles with blue lights flashing. They dashed into the woods with hoses and backpack firefighting equipment and extinguished the flames in minutes.

While they monitored the situation to make sure the fire didn't restart, I overheard the fire chief and some of the firemen speculating on how it had started. "There aren't any electric lines down there, so it couldn't have started from that," the fire chief said.

"There's no road close by, so nobody threw out a cigarette butt," one of the firemen observed.

"What in the world do you suppose could have started it?" another questioned.

All of a sudden, I realized I didn't see any sparks swirling out of the shed's smokestack. There wasn't even a bit of smoke. I wondered how that could be, but I said nothing; the mayor didn't want them to know he was to blame.

Finally everyone except the fire chief left. He was in his pickup truck, filling out some paperwork, when up from the shed came the mayor, a bucket of pure, golden maple syrup in each hand. He hadn't seen the fire chief's truck. The fire chief was out of his truck instantly. "Why, hello, Mr. Mayor," he said. "And what brings you out on this windy March evening? What have you there?"

"Uh, oh, I was just making a little maple syrup in Gail's shed. The wife and kids helped me for the last couple of days. It's a lot of work for what you get," Mr. Mayor replied.

"I see. Where were you a few minutes ago, when we had the big fire? I didn't see you."

"I must have been in the shed, draining off the syrup."

"Well, perhaps we know now how the fire started. How did you extinguish your fire so fast, Mr. Mayor?" the fire chief asked.

With a sheepish grin, Mr. Mayor replied, "Why, I used the rest of the raw sap to put it out."

After the fire, we washed and stored the sap buckets and put the tin shed to rest in anticipation of the next maple-sugar season. I felt relaxed, content, happy, and—just like Mirror had said—complacent.

Spring arrived with warm sunshine and soft breezes. Flowers bloomed in a quilt of pink, yellow, and green as far as the eye could see through the woods, right to the edge of the cliff and the blue water of Lake Erie. Birds sang, and breezes caressed the new buds. It was nearly Mother's Day and my birthday.

Adjustments had been made to both the old house and the family living in it. Most of the icy drafts were memories, and the few unpleasant times we'd had were dwarfed in my mind by the satisfaction of having a home of my own. My sons were enjoying school, Boy Scouts activities, and sports. They spent most weekends at the mink ranch, working for their grandfather and being spoiled by him the rest of the time. He cooked their favorite foods and taught them to shoot clay pigeons with his shotgun. They fished, wrestled, hunted wild game, and raised a garden together. The chief and I had weekends to ourselves, but the peaceful times were only an illusion.

Chapter Eight: Dark Times Return, 1973

THE CHIEF WAS ASKED to be the speaker at a volunteer firemen's fundraiser dinner/dance, and I went along. Country square dancing followed the dinner and his speech, but he didn't know how to square dance and must have felt insecure and embarrassed. Even though some of his friends guided him through the "allemande left," "grand right and left," and "swing your partner" calls, he suddenly left me on the dance floor with no partner, which ended our set's ability to continue. I saw him get his jacket and walk out of the building, so I commandeered a couple from the sidelines to take our place, grabbed my jacket, and ran after him. It was twenty degrees and snowing, the wind howling. I barely caught him as he sped out of the parking lot, but I ran along the side of the street in my high heels and cocktail dress until he stopped and let me in the car.

At home, the chief ordered, "Get out and unlock the door."

I expected him to hand me his key and leave the headlights on so I could see, but as my feet hit the ground he gunned the motor and drove away. Earlier, as he watched me put only a lipstick and comb in my evening bag, he had assured me that he had a house key and I wouldn't need my own keys.

It was 20 degrees and the wind was swirling snow around my feet as my little cocktail dress blew up around my hips; my legs were freezing. Panicking, I started to cry, and the tears froze on my cheeks. I had no gloves or hat, but I was thankful that I did have on my mink jacket. I pulled the collar up, huddled in the corner of the porch, and then decided to search for an unlocked window; there were none. No one was home, and it was storming so violently I couldn't see the highway or the twinkling lights of the nearest neighbor's house, a quarter of a mile away. Then I remembered that the pass-through for the wood box next to the fireplace had no lock on it. I set my handbag down and gingerly picked my way through knee-high drifts to the back of the house. I had just filled the wood box, so I had to pull the wood out first in order to crawl through it. The door was four feet off the ground, and I was only five feet tall. I looked around and spotted a big chunk of wood that had not been split. I rolled it over to the wood box door, climbed onto it, and began to pull the stored wood out onto the ground. Finally, thinking I would freeze to death, I managed to climb through the dirty, dusty, spider- and cobweb-filled wood box and into the living room. I brushed the sawdust and dirt from my lovely mink jacket and then collected old clothes, a warm jacket, boots, my regular pocketbook, and my car keys. I prayed that the car would start and that it would make it up the driveway, through the growing drifts. I went to my dad's house.

I thought my dad would be horrified, but, like before, he proved to be old-school. He asked, "What did you do to piss him off and make him abandon you?"

Of course I said, "Nothing," and that was the absolute truth.

There were no safe houses for abused women in the seventies, because at that time the popular thinking was that women loved to be abused, especially if it happened to them multiple times. Most people thought the women asked for it. Back then, bystanders ignored abusive situations, unwilling to get involved. My dad fit into that category. He harbored my sons and me, but he always returned me to my abuser.

The frequency of abuse increased to every few months, and then to every few weeks. The Chief succeeded at controlling me, making me feel guilty, and isolating me, one friend at a time. But this wasn't enough for him. He started on my young sons.

There were confrontations. I can't refer to them as fights, because I made sure I kept my mouth shut. The beatings weren't as bad. I call them beatings, but perhaps, in all fairness, they involved just shoving and an occasional black eye or broken rib for me; or a push, verbal berating, or slap for my sons when the chief deemed it appropriate.

We had a riding lawnmower with a brush-chopper attachment on the front and a sulky on the back. Andy had learned to mow with it at his grandpa's house, so he was the one who used it at home. The chief hated mowing and physical work in general.

One day, as Andy was mowing, a stone hit the old house's wooden siding. It did no damage, but the chief felt the act should be punished, so he barreled off the porch, grabbed my fourteen-year-old son, punching him, and kicking him. I screamed and tried to intervene. As punishment, I got a black eye and had to sleep in the guest bedroom for a week. I told my dad about it, because he was now my only lifeline. His take on it was, "Teenage boys need strong discipline."

Dad invited the boys to spend even more time with him. He was their escape, their sanity, their self-esteem. However, in retrospect, he let us all down in a major way. I believe that he visited us nearly every evening in an effort to protect us. He started to visit for dinner, helped me prune the vineyards, and became a major presence in our lives. His age, his upbringing, the demands of his lady friend, and the way the world was at that time kept him from doing or saying more.

The next time the chief tried to knock Andy off the lawnmower sulky because of some perceived transgression, Andy was ready. When the chief came at him like a locomotive, Andy braced his feet on the sulky and flipped the chief on his butt. When I arrived on the scene, Andy was straddling the chief on the ground and blacking his eyes. I can't tell you how proud I was of my son. I just stood there, grinning and thinking, *good for you, Andy. That SOB is getting a taste of what it's like to have black eyes.* The chief took two weeks' vacation time until his black eyes healed.

Most of the chief's anger and control attempts were aimed at my older son, but I was not immune, either. When I look back, I believe he acted the way he did because he was mentally ill and had control issues and poor self-esteem. Maybe he was jealous because my boys were exceptionally great kids. Andy was an A student, and when he graduated from high school, he won several awards and scholarships. One of the scholarships was for Grove City College tuition. Another was from a county medical group, because Andy's original aspiration was to become a doctor.

Larry, my younger son, was also an A student. He participated in sports and music, worked the same schedule as his brother, and also took a part-time job at a local grocery store. The more the boys achieved, the more controlling the chief became. The highs and lows of family life were punctuated daily by new demands and control from my second husband, who wanted an heir.

The chief wanted me to have another baby—his baby. On many occasions, he would tell me that I was a wonderful mother and that he would be honored if I bore his child. He would come up behind me while I was cooking, put his arms around me, snuggle me in the neck, and say, "You're the sparkplug in this family. You're such a great mother. Without you, none of this would be here." At those times, I was happy, because I felt loved and successful.

I was too close to the situation to see that my income sustained my family, paid for our home, put my sons through school and college, and allowed us a few luxuries. However, the truth was that I was enabling the chief to be financially and morally irresponsible. I was working at least two full-time jobs and a couple of part-time ones, as well as cooking, cleaning, and trying to be a good wife, and I was exhausted. His paychecks went toward a new car each year and his $400 suits, which he justified with the fact that he was an investigator, speaker, and chief of police. When I questioned his spending habits, he explained that he had to have expensive shoes, ties, shirts, topcoats, and more to complement the different hats he was forced to wear.

On March 3, 1975, there was another firemen's dinner/dance. The chief was the speaker. He insisted that I buy myself a new dress, get my hair done, and look my best at his side. During the intervals between the outbursts of rage and control, he was a good husband. He was a bright, successful man, one of the best criminal investigators in our area. He constantly reminded me that he was a professional, not a laborer.

Because I loved the farm and needed to pay living expenses, and because my boys were involved in our town and school, I forgave him when he sent flowers after every abusive incident. I was afraid that I would lose all the things I loved if I divorced him.

Many times, I was proud to be at his side in public. I enjoyed my roles as secretary and police matron for his department, because I was on the front line of investigations and happenings in our small town. We attended State Chiefs of Police events, dinners, and conferences. I met important people and knew inside details about criminal activities in our area. I took depositions and typed up minutes of meetings. I ghost-wrote articles from the chief called "Chief Topics" for our local paper. I was happy, needed, and important to him and our community. I was asked to serve on several boards of directors, and I chaired the American Cancer Drive in our town.

I bought the new dress and attended that banquet with the chief on a blizzard-filled night just one year after the first disastrous episode at the firemen's dinner/dance.

We sat at the head table at the local Moose Club. The chief spoke; we ate; we danced. The evening ended on a happy note. I had noticed that he'd had several mixed drinks, as he usually did, plus a couple of beers. He seemed capable of driving, so we started to head home, but first some of his patrolmen said they needed to talk to him privately. He had that conversation but didn't reveal what it was about. I didn't ask.

That evening, I had danced with the chief and enjoyed jitterbugging with him. We'd sat at a table with the mayor and some village board members, and the conversations had been lively. I had danced with the mayor, a couple of board members, and a fellow farmer, who loved to polka. The chief said it was great public relations for me to dance with others when I was asked. He also danced with some ladies. We had fun and arrived home in great spirits. I took my mink jacket off and hung it over a kitchen chair as I walked across the kitchen.

When I passed him, he lunged at me, grabbed me by my lovely new hairdo, and slammed me against the refrigerator. His fist connected with my solar plexus and then with the left side of my rib cage. He bashed me again and again against the refrigerator and slapped my face and head. My glasses flew across the kitchen counter and broke in half, and he blackened my left eye. Finally he stopped and hissed through clenched teeth, just inches from my face, "If you don't get pregnant and have my baby, I'll find someone who will. Do you understand?"

He let go of me, and I crumpled to the floor, sobbing. I already knew that I was pregnant with his child. I'd been waiting until we got home before I told him. I lay shaking and shivering on the floor for a long time. He calmly left to party with his patrolmen, as had been arranged when they spoke to him privately at the Moose Club.

The boys were away that weekend, so they didn't know what happened to me. I told everyone that I'd slipped on the ice and fell against the cement porch floor, broken my glasses, and gotten a black eye. I was afraid I would lose the baby, the farm, and my ability to support myself if I told anyone the truth.

Our friends said, "Yeah, we know, he beat the crap out of you," and they laughed, thinking it was a joke. The chief just smiled and said, "Yeah, right."

The first problem with my pregnancy came when I announced that the due date was my younger son's fifteenth birthday. The chief was angry instead of pleased, because he wanted his child to have his or her own, individual birthday. It was a tense moment, but eventually the chief was delighted with the fact that I was pregnant. He insisted that I spend my hard-earned money on a new wardrobe for myself and a layette for the baby. He insisted on long car rides, even though they made me deathly motion sick, and I begged to stay home. There was a six-month period of abuse-free living.

My oldest son was about to go off to college for his freshman year. About a week before he left, I set the kitchen table and prepared an evening meal, and we all sat down together, as was our daily routine. We were having some of the first sweet corn harvested from my garden that summer. The chief got up and walked to the stove to get the salt and pepper. On his way past my chair, he slapped me across the face, lifted me up by the front of my maternity dress, and punched me in my six-months-pregnant belly. He leaned in close to my face as I hit the floor and screamed, "Dumb bitch. You're a useless piece of shit. You can't even put the salt and pepper on the table."

When he straightened up Andy was all over him. He knocked the chief right out the back door and followed that with his fists. He was on top of the chief as the chief hit the ground on his back, but that soon reversed. The chief was screaming threats of arrest, murder, beatings, and more. Larry was on his way out the door to help put the chief in his place, but I grabbed his arm and steered him out the front door as I yelled, "Get out of here. Go hide. He'll kill you both if he can."

Larry ran for his life as the chief momentarily lost the upper hand over Andy. I yelled, "Run!" Andy ran, pursued by the chief, who was screaming more threats and curses. I grabbed my car keys and was ready to defend myself and my unborn baby, but the chief jumped in his private police car and tore up the driveway, looking for my beloved sons. He was in uniform, with his gun in its holster.

I jumped in my car when the chief was out of sight and spun gravel all the way up the driveway. When I hesitated at the road, I spotted Larry in the brush across the road. I yelled, "Get in the car, now! We have to get away before he comes back. We have to find Andy. I think he's hurt."

Larry ran to the car, got in and said, "I saw Andy running down the road. He's probably going to get help." We left the immediate neighborhood looking for Andy. I was afraid the chief would find us, but he was intent on searching the village. I thought Andy would make his way to my dad's house.

That's exactly what my son did. He ran through the woods and fields until he got to the home of his high-school science teacher. The teacher observed the blood and bruises, listened to his frantic description of the events, and then took him to his best friend's house. The friend begged his mother, my maple-syrup cohort, Peggy, for her car keys with no questions asked.

She recognized the anxiety in her son's voice and gave him her keys.

He took Andy to his grandfather's house, and soon after that, Larry and I arrived. Dad took one look at my black eye and torn dress and loaded his shotgun. Finally he acknowledged what was going on and realized that it was not my fault. He dialed the sheriff's department and gave the phone to me. I asked to speak with the sheriff himself and pleaded, "This is Chief Black's wife. I need help. The chief hit me and beat my older son. We're at my father's farm, and we're afraid. Please, please help us."

He calmly said, "Now, Mrs. Black, I'm sure it isn't a matter of life and death if you're away from him and safe. I suggest that you speak with the mayor, because this is an internal matter for your local town officials to handle. If things aren't resolved by morning, call me again."

My belief at that time was that the police community was a closed society; they stood in solidarity and protected their own.

The next day, the chief called me, apologized to each of us and to my dad, and said that he'd had a stressful day at work and that the pressure of dealing with criminals and lawbreakers was the reason for his bizarre behavior.

I went home, and my bruised, sore belly healed like the family rift, slowly. For worse, not better, we were still a family, and I was pregnant. The pattern continued, with flowers and a few months of abuse-free living.

I gave birth to the chief's much-wanted son on Larry's fifteenth birthday. He insisted on attending natural-childbirth classes, and he was my coach throughout the birthing process. When the baby was born, the chief was proud, eager to take him everywhere and show him off. He assumed that I would quit my partnership in my family's mink ranch and stay home with our son.

Robert was born in the middle of our mink-harvest season. Quitting was not an option, and besides, I really loved my work. I skinned two hundred mink on the day I delivered my son, and I went back to the skinning job in a heated building when he was forty-eight hours old. I had hot running water, a bathroom and kitchenette, and a crib waiting for him. I took the baby with me in the morning and cared for him throughout the day. I nursed him, so there were no bottles to prepare. I just fed, changed, and watched him sleep and grow while I worked. When you're self-employed, you have that option.

The little guy grew and developed on a normal schedule while Andy attended college a hundred miles away and Larry finished high school.

My marriage was far from ideal. The chief was still controlling and abusive. I had thought that having the baby would help him grow and change. He had hit, shoved, and beaten me; broken my ribs and glasses; and blackened my eyes. He had aggressively attacked my oldest son. He had verbally abused my middle son.

One snowy day, the chief came home for lunch when school was closed and Larry was home. Our 35mm camera and slide projector were on a projection table in the center of our living room, because we had watched family slides and enjoyed popcorn the night before.

Larry picked up the camera and was looking at it. The chief strode across the living room, grabbed the camera, and backhanded Larry across the face, screaming, "How does it feel to be a fucking failure?"

I thought I was going to collapse and my mind hibernated. Then my self-preservation mode kicked in, and I grabbed Larry as the force of the slap knocked him off-balance. I steered him upstairs, toward his room. We had not seen this behavior in almost three years, since the baby was born.

That was not the end of it. Robert was three years old now, still sleeping in a crib in an upstairs bedroom, just down the hall from the bathroom and his brothers' rooms. Andy was away most of the time at college, where he was safe from the chief's violent behavior, but Larry was home every night after his job at the corner store. He was in and out between school activities, working at the mink ranch, and in the grape vineyards. He was conscientious, serious-minded, and well-liked by his peers and teachers. Soon after the camera incident, the local American Legion selected him as their Boys State representative.

The week came for Larry to go off to the Boys State Convention. The chief, little Robert, and I helped him pack, and we took him to the bus. The chief seemed genuinely proud of him—after all, when the newspaper printed the announcement, it listed him as Larry's dad.

The chief was the third generation of his family to serve in the United States Marine Corps. He served two four-year terms. When he was honorably discharged, he went into police work, soon becoming the chief of police in a neighboring town. Then he took the position of chief of police in Westfield. Therefore, when Larry returned from the convention, he enthusiastically described all the Marine Corps-type activities he had experienced at Boys State. He was so proud to be able to relate his activities to the chief, his father figure, from whom he'd always sought acceptance. We helped him carry his luggage upstairs and then put Robert to bed. We left Larry alone to take a shower and sort out his dirty laundry.

I was in the kitchen, fixing us all something to eat, when I heard a terrible thump, a muffled scream, and a lot of commotion. I thought Robert had fallen out of his crib. I ran upstairs to find that the chief had broken in the bathroom door, grabbed Larry from the shower, while he was washing his hair, and begun to beat him. The chief, still in uniform, had cornered Larry behind the bathroom door and was pounding his face with his fists. I screamed, grabbed the chief by his uniform shirt collar and necktie, twisted, and pulled with all my might. His fists were still flying in midair. I screamed for Larry to run, get in his car and get out of there. The chief was still struggling, and my 95 pound body was no match for his 190 pound, anger- driven power. I pushed with all my might, heard Larry spin gravel in the driveway as he was leaving and I ran out of the bathroom, slamming the door shut on my way.

I thought that if I grabbed little Robert and had him safely in my arms, the chief wouldn't hit us and I could grab my car keys and escape. I got the baby and made it to the top of the stairs when the chief's fist slammed into my back. I grabbed the railing, took the steps three at a time, got my keys, and was nearly out the door when his fist closed over my shoulder. "Not so fast, bitch. Where the hell do you think you're going? Nowhere, that's where. You'll leave when I say you can," he snarled. "Get into my car right now. I'll kill that cocky little bastard son of yours," he spat in my face as he shoved us out the door and into his car. We took a terrible high-speed ride over the hills to my dad's house. He knew exactly where Larry would find refuge.

I was so cold. My stomach was in knots. The baby clung to my neck and I to him. We never stopped at stop signs, and the back roads were gravel, so we skidded around most corners and curves. I was terrified that Dad wouldn't be home or that, if he was, he would get hurt or killed along with Larry. We screamed into his driveway, screeching to a stop so fast I fell against the dashboard. The chief jumped out of the car instantly and headed toward the back door.

Dad's house was a ranch made of Ohio sandstone with Andersen windows, and it was secure. Suddenly, one of the windows cranked open just a crack and the barrel of a shotgun came out. Larry yelled, "One more step, you fucker, and you're a dead man. You lay a hand on my mom or the baby and you're a dead man."

The chief stopped, unsnapped the strap on his revolver, and I thought it was going to be all over. Instead, he hung his head, fastened the snap, and returned to the car. He backed up and left. We rode home in complete silence, within the speed limit. I dared not breathe as I fought the urge to gasp and sob, counting my breaths to keep them even and not show fear.

When we got home, he said, "Put the kid to bed, and go to bed yourself." That was it. I did as I was told. I had used the silent ride home to plan for the next day, should we still be alive. All night long, I lay in my bed, thinking it would be the last night I would ever sleep with that animal.

Morning came; the chief went to work. In a panic and as fast as I could, I snatched Robert's clothes, my clothes, and whatever else I thought we might need. Within five minutes I had everything in the car and I was speeding over the hills to my dad's house.

The night before, Dad had returned home soon after we left. He'd taken one look at Larry's face, with the blackened eyes and swollen tissue, and called a friend who was a professional photographer. He had pictures taken of Larry's face. When I arrived in the morning, he dialed the sheriff. This time I didn't ask: I demanded that the sheriff himself show up at my dad's to look at the damage one of his fellow law-enforcement officers had inflicted on his own family.

As soon as Larry had filled out a deposition, shown the sheriff his wounds, and answered a lot of questions, he left in his car. I, too, was afraid the chief would come looking for us, so I took Robert and also left. When I sorted through what I had hurriedly gathered up, I realized I didn't have enough clothes for Robert. I called my friend Sandy, who had a little boy the same age. She loaned me clothing and diapers. Then I called my friend Sherry. I was afraid to stay with either her or Sandy; the chief would look for us at their houses. Sherry knew a woman in Frewsburg who would let us stay at her house until I could find a safe place to go. That angel was an early version of help for abused women. While I was at her home that day, she let me use her phone to call my dad. He said that soon after the sheriff left, he had called back and advised me to hide myself and baby, as the chief was actively and openly hunting for us with his gun. We hid with a ninety-year-old distant relative of mine. We had to hide for ten days.

Larry drove to Westfield with his black eyes and swollen face. He went right down Main Street, from one business to the next, showing every merchant in town his face and telling them that their chief of police had done that to him upon his return from representing the town, school, and American Legion at the Boys State Convention. Then he returned to my dad's, where they armed themselves and waited, thankfully in vain, for the chief to show up.

One of Larry's stops was the mayor's place of business. When I checked in with Dad, as the sheriff had requested I do, Dad said the mayor wanted me to contact him. The mayor asked that I come to his home and answer some questions about Larry's beating.

"I will come, without Robert, only if you have police protection for me and clear the meeting with the sheriff," I said.

"Oh, Gail, that's not necessary. I know the chief well enough to know he wouldn't try anything here," the mayor argued.

"Those are my conditions. Otherwise, I won't come, and I'll also call the state police," I countered.

"Okay, as you want. Be here at two o'clock," the mayor agreed.

When I arrived at the mayor's house, everything looked quiet. I asked where the police backup was, and the mayor just smiled and held the door open for me. There inside stood the chief.

I turned to run, and the mayor said, "You two need to work things out. I have the name of a marriage counselor you should see."

"No marriage counselor," I shouted just as a Westfield patrol car drove up and two officers jumped out. I had called them to be sure they would be there.

When the chief saw his patrolmen coming, he lunged at me, screaming, "This is family business. You have no right to drag it through the whole goddamned community, you dirty bitch."

The officers restrained him while I drove away.

Because of Larry's assertive actions, the mayor and the sheriff decided to furlough the chief for a few days, demand that he get psychiatric help, and keep an eye on him. It was decided that, while I hid, the chief would move out, take an apartment in the village, see a psychiatrist in Buffalo, and abide by an order of protection issued by the sheriff's department. I was allowed to return home, and Larry, Robert, and I were provided some surveillance and protection by the sheriff.

Chapter Nine: Optimistic
Forgiving, Business Compromise,
Disastrous Results, 1978-1980

TIME PASSED. THE CHIEF had regular appointments with the psychiatrist, who declared that his problems were his mother's fault, because the chief said she was an alcoholic. Attitudes and anger abated. The boys thought Robert needed his father, so at Christmastime, we allowed the chief to return to our home, but only after we had remodeled it so that he'd have separate quarters. We were to live in our house with divided, locked sections. The design was unique, because when Larry was away at school, the locks were opened, and the chief, who was humble and quiet, had complete access to our home.

My older boys were graduating from their respective schools. Andy was following his dream of working with computers. In the midst of his premed courses in college, he'd discovered that the medical field was not for him. He spent a year or so thinking he wanted to return to the mink farm and continue it for a third generation. Then one day he called me and said, "Mom, I've met a computer, and I know this is for me. I don't want to come back to the farm after all." He'd happened to be walking

123

by when his college was having a new computer delivered, and he'd offered to help unload the truck and carry the equipment into a large room. The computer, in 1978, filled that room. His fascination has never dimmed.

Larry was graduating from high school with many honors. He was going away to begin his freshman year at the same college from which Andy was graduating. He was anxious to get away from the situation at home, although we thought it had improved.

Robert was growing up every day. He had big blue eyes, a huge vocabulary, an insatiable inquisitiveness, and an extroverted personality. He loved to have his daddy, the chief take him to visit the waterworks, the sewer plant, and different manufacturing facilities in our town. The chief had mellowed and would wait for us when we came back into town each day from the mink farm. He would turn the Christmas lights on in the park as he saw us drive onto Main Street. Robert accompanied him in the patrol car when he led parades. The chief took us to zoos, museums, and amusement parks; he took us on picnics and took us shopping, albeit with my money.

The chief was a planner with some activity on the horizon like a carrot before a donkey. Amidst the apparent oasis of calm, however, the chief still simmered with anger over my farming career. The long struggle for my career independence and financial security was about to intensify.

———————————

Dad was now seventy-eight years old and still came to the mink yard every day, even though it was increasingly hard for him to walk. The mink industry had made some real advances. Cornell University had maintained a mink-focused experimental station for many years; during that time, they had conducted many research projects that enabled us to continue the demanding work well into my dad's retirement years.

The experimental station engineered a dry feed for mink, which resembled the rabbit pellets you'd buy at a farm store. The ingredients of the dry feed could be changed with the seasonal needs of the animals, and we were one of the first ranches to implement the system. We no longer needed to grind one ton of fresh meat, fish, and chicken byproducts and mix them with grain, eggs, and outdated, leftover dairy products pulled from grocery-store shelves. We no longer needed our huge Cummins engine-driven grinder; our two-ton bread mixer, which was connected to the grinder with a conveyor; or our sixty-six-ton walk-in freezer. We now received several twenty-ton tractor-trailer loads of dry bagged feed every month. We installed metal hoppers in every pen and filled them weekly or as needed. The labor decreased by one third. I handled most of it and took baby Robert with me.

As Dad grew older, his knees weakened, and his ability to work declined. One day, when my older boys were home in the summer, we were separating the litters from their mothers. We were putting each mink into its own separate cage. It was nerve-wracking, smelly, sweat-generating work. Each animal had to be vaccinated and moved with a separate pedigree to identify it. We had to handle them a lot using special gloves, because mink are vicious. The flies bit, too. In combination with the hot, muggy weather and the nose-stinging, musty smell of mink scent, tempers became short.

A disagreement began about how often the automatic hoppers needed to be checked. The boys' opinion differed from my dad's opinion. The conversation became heated, and Dad said, "For two cents I'd retire and quit the mink business."

In the miserable, humid, ninety-degree heat, with the flies biting and the young, cannibalistic mink shrieking, my nerves shattered. I slapped two pennies on a nest-box cover and said, "There you go. I'll farm grapes; they don't stink and bite and eat every day."

Dad and I went to the house to work out the details, leaving the boys standing in shock as a forty-five-year-old family business was dissolved. The boys were going to be free of the daily chores at last.

I had carried Robert in a backpack for the first three years of his life, and he'd learned to play with his toys in the back of my car which I drove from mink shed to mink shed as I worked. At least when I was working in the vineyards, he could go to daycare a few minutes away. The reduced workload was good for him, too.

The chief was thrilled that I was no longer a mink farmer but livid about my plans to enlarge my grape-farming enterprise. I was adamant about farming, because I loved the outdoors and having control over my schedule. I had no idea what lay ahead as I left the cocoon of our family business and plunged into the male-dominated world of grape farming.

OUR MINK-BUSINESS PARTNERSHIP HAD been financially successful, and when it was dissolved, I had a lump-sum payout, which I decided to reinvest in farming to avoid paying taxes on the gain. Against the chief's wishes, I bought another twenty acres of grapes. With the growth of the grape business, I needed my own tractor and equipment. Farming is risky, but I had money to invest, knowledge of agriculture, a work ethic, and a few years of fruit-farming experience under my belt from my work on the seven acres in front of my home.

I had money in the bank and a checkbook in my pocket. I loaded up little Robert and went to a Ford tractor dealership to buy a vineyard tractor and the equipment to chop the brush, pound the posts, spread the fertilizer, and spray the vines in my vineyards.

"What can I do for you today, little lady?" the man behind the service counter asked.

I said, "I have a list of equipment I need to buy this morning." I handed it to him.

He looked at it for a minute, folded it up, unfolded it, read it again, and, with a puzzled look on his old, weathered face, said, "Now what would a nice widdle wady want wiff a gweat big twactor?" He actually talked baby talk to me. I was more than insulted. It was more distasteful than the bank president telling me I had no business in farming.

I didn't dignify him with an answer. Instead, I snatched the list from his hand and marched out the door. How dare he speak to me like that?

We headed to the International Harvester dealership a few miles down the way. I waited patiently for twenty minutes before any of the men selling parts and equipment acknowledged me. Finally I said, "Excuse me? Could someone please wait on me? I have a list of equipment to buy, and I need pricing on it."

The clerks behind the parts counter and the customers propped up on the stools in front of it stopped talking in unison. They all turned and stared at me.

Finally one arrogant man said, "Sorry, ma'am." With a wide sweep of his hand, he continued, "All of these men are ahead of you. Your estimated wait time is about three hours." They all laughed uproariously.

I walked out of there, too. Robert was only three and a half years old, but I said to him, "It's a lot harder to spend good money than I ever dreamed it would be. I guess those chumps never saw a woman try to buy a tractor."

We travelled to the next farm-equipment store. I still had my list, and now I had an angry attitude to go with it. I stomped through the door and up to the parts counter and was surprised when the owner called me by name. "Mrs. Black, how can I help you today?" he asked.

"I need to buy a new tractor for my farm, and I need pricing and advice about some of the other equipment I'll need to take care of my grapes. I intend to pay cash, a check, actually," I said with a smile.

The old guy rubbed his hands together and grinned from ear to ear, displaying his gold front tooth. He slicked his silver hair back and licked his lips. The word "shyster" popped into my mind as he said, "Mrs. Black, you are one lucky lady today. I just repossessed a tractor, because the poor bastard who bought it couldn't make the payments. He only had it a few months. It's brand new. Tell you what I'll do. I'll clean it all up and deliver it to your farm, and you can try it out for a few days. I can make you one hell of a deal on it, seeing as you're the police chief's wife."

I hesitated because of the shyster thought and the fact that his body language wasn't reassuring, but I finally agreed. I handed him the list of attachments that I also needed, and he said he would put a Bush Hog brush chopper on it for me to try. At least this guy didn't laugh at me.

The tractor was delivered just before dark. I had a brand-new barn with an unblemished concrete floor. There wasn't even a tire track on it or a speck of mud. I had the delivery man put the shiny white tractor and chopper inside on the new floor. I couldn't wait until daylight to try it out. I planned right then to take Robert to daycare so I could have a good time with that pretty tractor.

The next morning, a big grin on my face, I pushed the door up. There on my brand-new cement floor were three distinct puddles of liquid: one was motor oil, one was transmission fluid, and one was still dripping from the radiator. The shyster thought he could get away with anything with this little lady, but instead I stormed into the house to the telephone.

Mirror saw my agitation and declared, "The deal was too good to be true, and he thought you were a fool, didn't he?"

I glared at Mirror as I dialed the dealership, vented my anger, and demanded they come and get the piece of junk. I worked like a man, and I felt I had earned the right to cuss like a man.

I drove to the last farm-equipment store in the vicinity, a Massey Ferguson dealership. Again, there was a long service counter with men lined up on stools. The parts men were thumbing through their catalogues, and the phone was ringing. The place smelled of oil and grease and cigarettes and maleness. Finally I heard someone say a familiar name, Emmett Devlin. That was a fairly unusual name, and I knew it from my childhood. When I was a child, a guy by that name dated my best friend's sister. I watched, and when a man answered to the name, I made my way over to him. "Are you, by any chance, from Jamestown, New York?" I asked.

He looked rather blank and said he was. "Did you have a motorcycle and date a girl just outside of town?" I continued.

He looked even more puzzled and said, "Do I know you?"

"I think so. I was the pesky neighbor. Your girlfriend's little sister and I used to tease you, and then later I roller skated with you at Midway Roller Rink."

"Are you Gail from the mink farm?" he asked.

"Yes, I am. And from what I can see, you're well known here and probably know a lot about tractors and equipment. I need your help and advice," I said. I told him about my struggle to buy the equipment I needed.

He called the owner over, introduced me to him, and said, "Gail is an old friend of mine. I want to see the proposal you work up for her before she agrees to it. I want you to treat her the same way you'd treat me." I had finally found one gentleman out of hundreds and a group of men at the Massey Ferguson dealership willing to follow his lead and teach me about the equipment I needed. The learning curve was steep, but soon I learned to call the tractor by its initials, MF.

The chief's recurring anger emerged one morning when he repeated something he had screamed at me during our first year of marriage. "You're nothing but a dumb farmer, you don't know enough to be anything but a dumb farmer, and you'll never be anything but a dumb farmer," he yelled as he left for work.

I had a new Massey Ferguson tractor all fueled up, with a brush chopper on the three-point hitch, and my little boy had been delivered to daycare. It was a warm spring day, and the brush trimmings I had pruned and pulled from my grapevines were in the center of the grape rows, waiting to be chopped and mulched back into the soil. I had a whole day to get used to the new equipment, and I was hoping I'd have time to mow around the vineyard to clear away some of the overgrown bushes at the edges so the air could circulate better in the grapes. Soon it was late afternoon. I had a neat farm, and I was on the last cut down the nine-hundred-foot east side.

As I turned to make the last cut back to the road before I started home, I saw the chief's private police car racing down the freshly cut grass. He slammed on his brakes and barked, "Do you know what time it is? It's five o'clock, and you haven't even picked Robert up from daycare. Get the hell home right now and get my supper." He spun his wheels and did a donut in the new-mown grass.

I was furious. I was dusty, dirty, tired, and now angry, too. I rammed the tractor into high range and third gear and roared back toward the road in a rage of my own. I didn't see a half-buried railroad tie under some vines in the thick brush. One end stuck up at an angle, and the front wheel hit it, instantly stopping the tractor as the wheels spun to climb over the obstacle. The force of the impact threw me off-balance, and I slipped out of the seat and down the side of the tractor with only my left hand on the wheel and my left knee around the gear-shifting knob. The motor was roaring, the back wheels were spinning, and the deadly chopper blades whined with imminent disaster. I slipped farther and nearly lost my grip on the steering wheel as my unbuttoned, loose shirt dragged on the ground in front of the back tire and the machine moved forward onto it. The rotary chopper was spinning at full speed, and I was sure someone would find me chopped up like the brush when my shirt dragged me to the ground.

I used all my strength to pull myself back up onto the seat. The shirt ripped free of me and I was able to use my left hand on the steering wheel and my left leg, which was caught around the gear shift to gain control of the tractor. I was shaking violently with the realization of how close I had come to death. My dad's words, "Haste makes waste," rang in my ears. I suddenly understood why farming is one of the most dangerous occupations in the United States.

I thanked God, picked up my boy at daycare, and went home to fix supper. The chief appeared to be unconcerned, almost disappointed, when I told him what had happened. I knew I should not have let him upset me.

The next morning, the chief left for work as if nothing had happened. I was surprised, but not prepared for his early return from work that afternoon. I had finished my shower and was doing my hair and getting ready to pick Robert up from daycare. The bathroom door was locked but not properly latched. Suddenly it burst open, and a red-faced chief charged through in full uniform, gun belt and all. He grabbed me by my hair, threw the blow dryer onto the counter, pushed me onto the floor, and unstrapped his gun belt. He pulled my hands behind my back and handcuffed me. At first I thought he was just fooling around or that it was some kind of game or joke. Then he threw his uniform on the floor and proceeded to rape me anally. I screamed, but there was no one to hear. He kept yanking my head back by my hair. He grabbed my breasts so hard they became swollen and bruised. When he finished, he said, "There, bitch. That's what a dumb farmer is good for, and that's all a dumb farmer is good for." He calmly washed up, put his uniform back on, took the handcuffs off my wrists, and went back to work.

I lay there shaking, unnaturally cold, literally sweating with fear, in terrible pain, and bleeding. I was curled into a tight fetal position and couldn't stop crying. There was no one home and no one to help me. I was so ashamed that I couldn't have called for help even if there had been someone to call. I remembered that I needed to pick up Robert from daycare, so I prayed to God to help me, crawled over to the bathtub, and managed to get in. I ran the water until it gradually got hotter and hotter. I washed and scrubbed myself, but I couldn't get clean. The water turned red with blood from my wounds. Finally I got out, dried off, applied first-aid cream, dressed, and went after my little boy. It was so hard to walk. My whole body was bruised and sore; it refused to move normally. My face was swollen and red from crying, and my wrists were raw from trying to get free of the handcuffs to defend myself. My legs were bruised from where he'd used his knees to hold me down.

The chief didn't come home for dinner. He had a village board meeting to attend and was in the middle of an investigation. I fixed dinner for Robert and left a foil-covered plate of food for the chief in an effort to avoid more beating. After a story and Robert's prayers, I went to the guest room, braced the door, and crawled into bed, where sleep was a welcome relief. My last thoughts were that I was "nobody" and a "dumb farmer" and that I deserved to die.

In the middle of the night, the door crashed open. The chief pulled me from my sleep by the hair of my head, dragged me to the stairway, and sent me flying down the stairs into a crumpled ball of humanity on the floor of our front hall. He followed that by lifting me up by my hair and punching me in the belly. He yelled, "Don't you ever leave me cold leftovers for my supper, you bitch."

I was directly below Mirror, but Mirror was silent, reflecting only my broken image.

Robert didn't wake up, thank God. My already aching, bruised body was now broken, too. I'd heard a rib crack. The chief threw the plate of food on top of me and went to bed after slamming and locking his bedroom door.

The terror was back. I finally crawled back upstairs and into bed, but I was afraid to sleep. I planned how I could leave and hide again.

The next day, the chief went to work as normal as could be in his uniform, freshly laundered and pressed from the dry cleaner. As he entered his office, one of the bank's alarms went off. He dashed out the back door of the police station and ran across the parking lot to the bank. One of his patrolmen had gotten a radio message from the sheriff's department about the alarm and also arrived at the bank. They entered with their guns drawn, only to find that it was a false alarm—and the chief crumpled to the floor with his first heart attack. He refused an offer to call an ambulance and insisted on coming home.

The patrolman put the chief in the car and brought him home, pasty white, short of breath, and needing help to get to his chair. The patrolman helped him remove his gun belt and loosen his tie and suggested he go to the emergency room. Then he looked at me and said, "What the hell happened to you?"

Before I could answer, the chief said, "She fell down the stairs last night while I was at the board meeting and working on that investigation. When I got home, she was lying on the floor in the front hall. I had to put her to bed. I probably stressed my heart when I carried her."

Even then, his mind control wouldn't release me; I was completely brainwashed.

Chapter Ten: Sorry the Chief Didn't Die, 1980-1982

I SPENT THREE WEEKS sleeping on a couch at an Erie, Pennsylvania hospital while the chief recovered from open-heart surgery.

One night, the nurse said he had improved significantly and would be moved from intensive care to a private room. She suggested I go home.

I had not had a bed to sleep in, a shower, or regular meals for three weeks. As I drove, I wondered how a loving God could let the chief live to beat us another day. I hadn't felt sad when the doctor told me he might not survive the four bypasses and the massive, irreversible damage to his heart. I felt guilty immediately and replaced the negative thoughts with hope that this health scare would change his personality and behavior.

I was overjoyed to be going home, where I could see the kids, but I was also so tired I couldn't keep my eyes open. I fell asleep at the wheel, waking up in the nick of time when I crossed over a boulevard and dropped off the curbing on the wrong side of the road. It was two o'clock in the morning, and no traffic was on the road.

A few weeks later, the chief returned home, and I nursed him back to health. He had a special diet and exercise program and lots of follow-up appointments. He had issues with depression, blood pressure, and cholesterol, but he cooperated and improved.

My friends and family suggested divorce, and I considered it, but I had not taken my wedding vows lightly; I'd meant it when I promised "in sickness and health, till death do us part." Instigating a divorce when my husband was desperately ill, both physically and mentally, was out of the question.

The conflicting facts of our situation bounced around my mind like rubber balls: the brutality he inflicted, his ill health, and the responsibility of my vows. What if the circumstances were reversed? How could I desert him under those circumstances? I couldn't. I had failed once at marriage, and the thought of another divorce was devastating.

One day after the chief returned from the hospital, a neighboring farmer flagged me down. "Hey, Gail, got a minute?" he asked as I slowed to turn into my driveway.

I rolled the window down. "What's up, Chuck?"

"I know it's none of my business, but is everything okay with the chief since his surgery?"

"He's struggling with depression, but the doctors say he's progressing on schedule. Why do you ask?" I replied.

"You know I'm out here every day right now, working on my irrigation system, and I can't help but see and hear stuff that happens on your side of the road. I think you need to know that the chief meets the school bus every afternoon when Robert comes home from kindergarten. I kept hearing the little guy scream 'No, Daddy, no,' so I paid attention. The chief hides in the grapes, and when the bus is gone, he barges out with a stick or his belt and switches Robert all the way down your driveway. At first I thought maybe Robert had done something to piss him off, but certainly not every day. Sorry to have to tell you, but you need to do something about it."

He told me this as I returned home from working yet another job, which I'd taken so I could pay for the increased expenses caused by the chief's illness.

I was devastated. He had never attacked his own little boy. I asked questions, and the neighbor assured me that it happened every day.

With this knowledge fresh in my mind, I confronted the chief. He apologized, said it wouldn't happen again, and begged me to forgive him and to take care of him through the rest of his recovery. He seemed sincere, so I learned how to cook a special diet for him, helped him with his exercise and walking program, dressed his incision, and helped him up and down the stairs and into and out of bed. He was quiet, humble, appreciative, and a great actor. He would stop in front of Mirror, cry, and say that he saw himself as a big green frog. I felt sorry for him.

I heard Mirror say, "Don't you dare feel sorry for the bastard. He's getting a little bit of what he deserves, and don't you forget that."

I changed my lunch hour, started meeting the school bus, and, with my boss's permission, took Robert with me on sales calls every afternoon. I thought my boy was safe and that things would be okay.

Winter came, and I thought the chief was recovering well; he was mellowing from his ill health, even talking about going back to work. Then, one evening, I walked into the living room, and when he spoke to me, I couldn't understand a word of the garbled speech. I took him back to the hospital and cardiologist. They admitted him, did an angiogram, and determined that he had suffered a stroke. The nurse brought him back to the room, and when she left, I walked over to the bed. He gasped, "Get the doctor. I'm having another heart attack."

I ran out of the room in a panic, screaming, "Come back! He's having another heart attack. He's turning blue and can't breathe."

In a matter of seconds, the room filled with medical staff, and a nurse began doing chest compressions to bring him back to life. Moments later, another nurse attached electric-shock equipment and gave the signal, and his body jerked violently as he began to breathe. I was shoved into the corner and witnessed the whole event while trembling uncontrollably.

Further heart damage had occurred because of an allergic reaction he'd had to the dye in the angiogram. The doctor reported that only 7 percent of his heart was undamaged and told him to apply for complete disability.

Larry came home for the holidays, and he and I left Robert with the chief for a couple of hours while we went Christmas shopping. When we came home, the chief met us at the door and said, "You better go upstairs and see what's wrong with that kid of yours. I told him to straighten up his room, and he just played, so I spanked him. Now he says he can't breathe."

Larry and I looked at each other with horror in our eyes. We flew up the stairs and found Robert lying on his bed, gasping for breath. Larry sat him up and held him.

I said, "Breathe, breathe, easy now," while I rubbed his back. His breathing slowly returned to normal. He clung to Larry and gripped my hand, sobbing, "I didn't mean to do anything wrong. I tried to pick up my toys. Daddy hit me in the back. I fell down. Daddy hit me again, and I couldn't breathe, so he threw me on my bed. Then you came home." He cried and cried and cried. We vowed to never leave him alone with the chief again.

In February, I invited another couple, Don and Carol, to watch the Super Bowl with us. The men were in the living room, watching the game, and Carol and I were in the kitchen. Six-year-old Robert was playing with his new Hot Wheels race-car set on the living room floor. He stood up and ran between the TV and the chief. The chief jumped out of his chair, grabbed a two-foot piece of orange Hot Wheels racetrack, and began slicing the air with a *whip whoop* sound as he tried to hit Robert. He kept screaming, "Get the fuck out from in front of the TV screen, you stupid little bastard!"

I ran into the living room and scooped Robert up, and the chief turned on me. He cut my jeans and my flesh three times between my hip and my knee with the lethal plastic racetrack. My girlfriend already had Robert's snowsuit and my coat in one hand and her car keys in the other. Her husband struggled to restrain the raging chief as she pushed us out the front door and into her car. She took us to the mayor's house.

The mayor's wife listened to the succession of events. She knew the history and had suggested several times that I divorce the chief. That night, she said, "Gail, you need to shit or get off the pot. This keeps happening. Are you waiting for him to kill you or one of the kids?"

She spoke angrily, but her harsh words came at the right time, and I recognized them as the truth. My friend took me to my dad's house, and the next day I visited a local attorney and filed for a divorce.

My conscience was bothered. My husband of 13 years was gravely ill, needed a special diet, exercise, and care; was housebound; and couldn't work anymore. How could I desert someone who thought he looked like a big green frog? But how could I stay with a bastardly beast that beat his own little boy? I felt guilty, but my first loyalty and responsibility was to my young, defenseless child.

My dad was adamant about me pursuing a divorce. So were my girlfriend, the mayor, and his wife. My older sons were completely supportive and told me that sometimes it was impossible to win. Sometimes you could do nothing to protect yourself and those you love who couldn't protect themselves. I had support from those I loved.

The lawyer I hired propositioned me. He suggested that I meet him at his cottage and that we listen to music and dance while we discussed my case, so I turned him in to the county bar association. My boss called the attorney for the business where I worked and explained that he had personally witnessed an abusive situation when the chief had hit and shoved me in the parking lot outside his office. The attorney found me a group of lawyers in Buffalo who specialized in divorce. They assigned a young, sharp, female attorney to my case.

The mayor, village board, and sheriff's department met with the chief to discuss and implement his retirement. They insisted that part of the deal was that he rent a house in the village and move out of our home. His patrolmen arrived with him soon thereafter and took everything we owned out of the house. They dumped my clothes on the floor and took the dresser and other bedroom furniture. They took the dishes and the silverware, the drapes and the linens. When I returned home with Robert, the house was bare; even the food was gone. The only room still intact was Robert's.

My friend Carol, who had rescued us on Super Bowl Sunday, bless her, was with me. I sobbed, "I can't see how we can survive. I'm working as hard and long as I possibly can." I was out of control and couldn't see things realistically.

Carol, who was tall, strong, solid, and kind, put her arms around me, rocked me, and said, "Gail, be thankful. You have your house, your little boy, your family, and your farm. You have your health, you're safe, and, finally, you have an order of protection." I realized that she was right as I stood in my empty house.

Again, these were the right words at the right time, and I smiled through the tears. Carol went home and then brought back soup, crackers, and an electric Crock-Pot, along with plastic bowls and spoons. After we ate, I put my little boy to bed, locked the doors, and slept peacefully on the living-room floor, with a fire in my fireplace. The next day, I changed the locks again.

My dad and his lady friend, Freddie, arrived at my house. Freddie said, "I have a lot of extra stuff I don't need. I brought it all to you." She and Dad carried in TV tables, an overstuffed chair, and some curtains. They unloaded dishes, silverware, and groceries. I bought a used stove and refrigerator that day, and we were good to go.

Now that my care-giving role had ended, I had more time for work. I had taken a part-time job driving a school bus; I had gotten licensed as a real-estate agent and a notary public; and I was farming thirty acres of grapes by myself. Estranged friends returned and offered help and support.

I had regular meetings with the Buffalo law firm, and the first appointment with my new attorney went well, but she said she needed a $5,000 retainer. I went to my farm-lending agency and borrowed the money "for operating expenses." I felt that it was a deception in a way, but I couldn't operate my business under the old circumstances. The lawyer sent me home with a questionnaire examining my marriage, the abuse, our financial history, and more. She wanted detailed information.

My older sons came home for a long weekend to help me gather information for the questionnaire. My dad joined us, and we found a babysitter for Robert. We spent an intensive seventy-two hours, with little rest, filling out the forms, referring to detailed financial records I had kept for tax purposes. I had believed that the abuse was somehow my fault, so I had kept a journal throughout the thirteen-year marriage.

I took the materials to my attorney on Tuesday morning. She thumbed through the thick sheaf of papers and said, "Wow, this is a lot of information. It will take extra time to examine it, and I'll need another $1,000." Dad loaned me the money.

Meanwhile, the chief had used some of his severance pay to buy an airline ticket to visit his sister, where he spent nearly three months. I was free from fear and completely buried in managing the spring work in my vineyards, working the part-time jobs, taking care of Robert, and dealing with the law firm.

February turned to March, and March marched by. In May, I heard that the chief had returned to town and that my attorney had the divorce papers served on him. I was afraid there might be repercussions.

Chapter Eleven: Evil on My Shoulder, May of 1982

THURSDAY EVENINGS, A BABYSITTER or my dad looked after Robert so that I could drive to Jamestown with three other women from Westfield to roller skate. It was great exercise and my only social activity. My life had become routine and was free from stress and abuse. At the rink, a man approached me with some papers and asked me for identification. I handed him my driver's license, and he proceeded to serve me with a countersuit for divorce.

My friends were surprised and worried, but I wasn't; I'd expected the process to get nasty. As I read through the papers, however, I became terribly alarmed. The chief was using his disability and ill health to justify his suit for half my farms, alimony, and full custody of Robert. He claimed that he deserved to have custody because he was home full-time and I had to work. He claimed that he needed the alimony and was entitled to half the farm because he was disabled and ill and had contributed half the labor. His labor contribution was sitting on the porch and watching me work.

I began to shake and cry. There was no way that I could lose my little boy, but I couldn't stop working, either. If I lost half my farming operation, I couldn't afford to live. If I had to pay him alimony, I might as well go on welfare. I was scared.

My attorney was not encouraging. She said that because he was disabled and home all the time, he would, in her opinion, be favored in family court. I was too sick to eat. I was too sick to think straight. She didn't think any evidence I provided or any witnesses I suggested would matter. I was prepared to lose everything.

━━━━━━━━━━━━━━━

The third week of May rolled around. On Wednesday, I was chopping brush with the tractor and Bush Hog in front of my house. I didn't have to drive the school bus that day, so I had started early with the vineyard work. As I worked up a grape row, toward the road, I saw a car back up and stop. One of my real-estate sales peers jumped out and waved her arms frantically. I thought maybe one of my listings had been sold.

When I stopped and jumped down off the tractor, she said, "Oh, Gail, I don't know what to do. I'm pregnant, and the baby isn't my husband's."

I stood there feeling stupid and confused. I had enough troubles of my own.

She continued, "Can you help me? I have to get an abortion, and I don't know how to do it." She was crying.

I said, "Okay. I don't know a thing about abortion, where you get one or even how it's done, but come on down to the house, and we'll talk about it." I didn't know her all that well in the first place and was surprised that she'd asked me for help.

I made coffee, and Larry came into the kitchen for his breakfast. He asked what was wrong with my friend. She gave me a sidewise look and proceeded to tell him all about her problems.

I grabbed the phone book and said, "Let's look in here and see if there's a place to call." There was no listing under "abortion," but it said to see "birth control." Under "birth control," there was an 800 number, so I dialed it. While I waited for an answer, I said, "It's a little late for birth control when you need an abortion."

The call went somewhere in Georgia. When an operator answered, I told her I had a friend who needed an abortion and that we needed some information.

She replied, "Honey, you don't have to pretend it's your friend's problem. This is a confidential call. What's your zip code?"

"Look, I really do have a friend sitting here. Her name is Martha." I gave her my zip code.

She said, "Oh, you're in luck. There's an abortion clinic right in your town, at your local hospital." She was so cheerful, a regular little Miss Suzy Sunshine.

I said, "I'm going to put my friend on the phone. Please give her all the information. However, this is a small town, and there's no way in hell she could go there, because everyone in town would know it in two minutes. What else do you have?" I handed the phone to Martha.

There was a clinic in Buffalo, an hour away. It would cost $350, and they would accept cash; the appointment was scheduled for six o'clock in the morning on Saturday, only three days away. When Martha hung up, she said, "Thank you, Gail. I knew you'd help me. My boyfriend is also married, but he agreed to pay for the abortion." She left to find him and finalize the arrangements. I went back to work in the vineyard.

It wasn't long before Martha came down the driveway again in a swirl of dust. Not surprisingly, her boyfriend had reneged. He said he couldn't get the money on such short notice and that he had plans with his wife on Saturday. My friend was beyond consoling. She begged me to take her and to loan her the money.

Larry stood behind her and nodded. He said, "Mom, if you take her, I'll babysit Robert. My girlfriend is coming from Buffalo anyway, and we can watch him for you." His generous offer was rooted in sympathy for this crying, desperate, middle-aged woman.

I agreed. Martha said she would tell her husband that she and I were going shopping and would be gone all day. On Saturday, she arrived at my house at five o'clock sharp, and we left for the abortion clinic. This was all new to me. I was curious, and glad to think about something other than my own troubles.

We were greeted in a clean, professional office. We were the first ones there, and my friend was seen immediately. A few minutes later, the nurse came to get me; my friend had requested that I join her. That was the last thing I wanted to do, but I went in.

Martha was crying. "I want to go home," she said. "They're going to suck the baby out of me into a bottle, like an IV bottle. I'll have to see it. They call that procedure vacuum aspiration. Get me out of here, now!"

My wild sense of humor and my desperation to get the mess over with kicked in. I said, "Okay, we'll go home. I can do that for you. I just got a new Rainbow vacuum cleaner."

Everyone gasped in horror. They hurried me back to the waiting room, which had become a depressing scene. It was filled with little girls, or so they seemed, some looking as young as ten or eleven. Most were black or Hispanic, and most were alone. I never wanted to experience anything like that morning again. I knew I could never go through such trauma. Yet I also knew that most of those girls could not go through a pregnancy and parent a child on their own, physically, financially, or emotionally. I believed that the right of choice must be given to each individual pregnant female and that more education of our youth was necessary.

The thought of going home to face certain divorce, upset children and disgrace in the community was too traumatic for Martha. Following the procedure, she was sick and bleeding profusely. We got home around four o'clock. It was May 29, 1982, much too warm and beautiful outside to waste the day on such a hideous experience. My friend was too ill to enjoy the weather or to go to her own home. She could not explain the excessive bleeding or the pain to her husband, so I covered her with a blanket on my couch, where she immediately fell asleep. She wasn't expected home until after nine that night anyway.

While I went about getting supper ready for my family and recovering friend, I felt a tug on my shirt. It was Robert. I scooped him up and set him on my hip just as the phone rang.

I answered and the chief said, "I want you to bring Robert and come up to my apartment for supper. I have it all ready."

I replied, "I can't do that tonight. I have company, and I'm just about to put our supper on the table."

The chief had visited me unexpectedly on the Wednesday afternoon my friend had made arrangements for her abortion. We sat on the front porch and discussed the divorce in a civil manner while Robert was at school. He seemed to understand my point of view. He repeatedly asked if I would consider changing my mind and why we couldn't just go forward living apart, and I expressed my views honestly and calmly. He left without incident.

"You can bring Robert and leave food for the others, can't you?" he now asked.

A young part-time patrolman had called me the day before and cautioned, "Stay away from the chief, Gail. He's acting weird." I was surprised by the call, but the young man was a high-school friend of Andy's. I had forgotten about the call until I heard the desperation in the chief's voice.

"No, I have company from out of town, and I can't leave. Maybe we can come for supper another time."

"I said I want you to come up here and bring Robert right now. I said *right now*," he yelled. I refused again, and he said, "What did I ever do to deserve this divorce, anyway? Tell me that."

"You were down here just last Wednesday afternoon, and we went over all the reasons while we sat on the porch." I said.

"Well, tell me again. I want to know what I ever did that was so bad that you have to have a divorce. Tell me now," he demanded.

His voice was rising in agitation, and I was getting frightened. I repeated that we had discussed all the issues just a couple of days ago, but he wasn't satisfied. He shouted repeatedly that he wanted Robert and me to come there immediately for supper. He screamed, "The table's all set, and supper is on the stove."

When I still refused, he demanded answers to his questions again and again.

Finally I shouted, "Okay. I'll tell you what you did to deserve this divorce. I already told you on Wednesday, but I'll tell you again. You blacked my eyes. You broke my glasses. You broke my ribs, and you beat me and abused me in terrible ways. That wasn't enough. You beat up Andy and Larry, and now you've started on an innocent, helpless little boy—your *own* little boy. I can't stand by, be married to you, and let that happen. If I do, I'm just as guilty of child abuse as you are."

He was quiet for a second, and then he spoke softly, saying, "Can you hold the line a minute?"

I heard a click that I thought was him setting a pan on or off the stove. Then I heard a muffled thud, like he'd dropped something. Then there was a louder thud and then something like hammer taps on a nail or wall. I said, "Are you there?"

There was no answer. I jiggled the button on the phone, but the line was open and silent, and I couldn't get a dial tone. I was holding Robert. A few seconds went by, and suddenly I knew what I had heard.

I ran out the front door and threw Robert to Larry. "S-U-I-C-I-D-E," I cried.

Larry asked, "What did you say?"

I spelled "suicide" again. I grabbed Larry's girlfriend's arm and screamed, "Come with me. The phone doesn't work. His receiver is off the hook. He didn't hang up, and I can't dial out."

Larry yanked her back and said, "*No*, don't go." Then he tried to block me from leaving and said, "I don't want you to go up there."

I tore my arm loose from his grip and screamed, "I have to. He's my husband."

I tore up the driveway and pulled onto the highway right in front of a tractor trailer. Jake brakes thundered and rumbled, and I'll never know how that big rig avoided hitting me as it laid black marks down the pavement. Frantically looking for a phone, I drove across the road to the nearest neighbors' house, but they weren't home. In my shock, I drove out onto the highway again toward the next neighbor's home, going the wrong way, against traffic.

My neighbor heard horns blowing and came out her back door to investigate the noise just as I screeched to a stop. I almost knocked her down her cellar stairs as I ran to get to her phone. I dialed the police department's number that I knew by heart but when the officer answered, I couldn't speak. I mouthed the words, but no voice came out. I was in shock.

My neighbor knew something was terribly wrong. She took the phone and said, "Gail Black is here, and she can't speak." She gave me a little shake, handed the phone back and commanded me to talk.

My voice returned and I told the officer, "Meet me at the chief's apartment. There's been an accident, and I think he's dead."

I tore out of my neighbor's house and headed toward the chief's apartment.

In the meantime, Larry was afraid that the gunshot I'd heard was a hoax. He believed that the chief was going to shoot us all if I went to his apartment. At that moment, a motorcycle came down the driveway, and the driver asked for me. My son told him briefly what was happening and asked him if he could look after Robert.

The stranger said, "Sure. You got any fishing poles around here?"

Larry pointed toward the barn, and the man headed off with Robert in tow. Meanwhile my sick friend on the couch was oblivious to the situation and slept on.

Larry was terrified that I would be killed, so he and his girlfriend arrived at the chief's duplex at the same time I did. Larry blocked my way to the back door. "You can't go in there, Mom," he yelled. "I don't think he's dead. I think he'll kill you. You can't go in there."

"I have to. He's my husband."

"No, you don't. Where are the police?" he asked. We struggled and wrestled. We were both in shock and unable to think rationally. Finally he said, "Okay. I'll go in."

The possibility of what could happen to Larry put terror in my heart. I said, "No, no. You're right. Go get the firemen, and I'll find a phone to call the police again."

We each left. I ran across the back lawns of the village until I found a woman in her yard. I was so upset that I didn't recognize her, even though we belonged to the same women's group and she had been a guest in my home many times.

"There's been an accident with a gun over there where the police chief lives. I called for help but no one showed up." I told her.

Her husband was listening from the porch and said, "I'll call the police again for you," and hurried into their house.

I ran back across the grassy lawns just as Larry returned, accompanied by the local volunteer fire department, the local police, the sheriff's department, and the state police.

Emergency personnel assembled on the lawn and formed a plan. The young officer who had warned me not to see the chief would go in first, because he was the officer on duty. All the other policemen concluded from my description of my phone conversations with the chief, that he might not be dead. They felt it could be a setup.

The young officer was nearly as upset as I was. He had gone to the wrong address before he called for backup. The chief was one of their own, so all the agencies responded.

A tall, rugged state policeman asked, "Do you want to go in with us, Mrs. Black?"

"I don't want her to go in there," Larry protested.

"Yes, I do. I'm going in," I insisted. I was third in line, right behind the sheriff and the part-time patrolman, both of whom drew their guns. The young officer dropped his gun on the sidewalk just outside the door. As I watched, it seemed to me that the gun spun in slow-motion circles on the ground. They broke the door in, and we saw the chief on the floor in a pool of blood. Brain tissue, hair, and blood splattered the walls, ceiling, refrigerator, table, stove, and curtains in the little white kitchen.

The state policeman right behind me proclaimed in an authoritative voice, "Now there's a message for you." He picked up the chief's service revolver from the floor and ejected just two bullets from the cylinder. The rest were lined up on the kitchen table, all in a row. He explained to the other officers that the two bullets remaining in the gun were for me and little Robert. He put his arm around me, and as he ushered me to the door, he said, "You're one lucky little girl that you didn't come here. I hope you noticed that no supper was waiting on the stove, and the table wasn't set for dinner."

All I saw was the river of blood I had to step over on my way out.

Halfway across the lawn, I passed out cold on the grass. Larry and his girlfriend picked me up just as the coroner asked, "Mrs. Black, where do you want us to take the body?"

My legs were as limp as the grass on which I'd been lying. My mind was murky, but I answered, "He always wanted to be cremated before sunset on the day he died."

The coroner made a note on his tablet and walked away. The kids helped me into their car and asked me where I wanted to go.

I managed to whisper through my tears, "I have to tell the chief's mother. I have to tell Robert. I need to get to a phone. Take me to my friend Carol's."

When Carol saw me at her door, she immediately said, "What's the matter?"

"The chief just shot himself. Mom needs to use your phone," Larry said quietly.

"Jesus. When? Where?" Carol's husband asked. While Larry gave them the grave details, they helped me into the house and gave me two shots of straight whiskey followed by three aspirin tablets. Carol hugged and held me. I was caught somewhere between racking sobs and thanking them for the whiskey and aspirin, and asking to use their phone to call my mother-in-law.

The phone was dialed for me and placed in my hand. Nellie answered immediately and recognized my voice when I said, "Hi, Nellie. I have some terrible news. Is George there?"

"Yes, he is. What's the matter, Gail? Are you all right? Is Robert okay?"

"We're okay. Your son is not. He just shot himself in the head, and he's dead."

There was a pause while she repeated what I'd said to her husband, George. Then she gave a deep, audible sigh and said, "Thank God. George and I don't have to be afraid anymore. He won't be pushing me down the stairs and pushing George around. We'll be right over. Do you need anything? Oh, yeah, Gail, you need to know that we know he beat you. We were on the front porch years ago, the first time at the first family picnic you ever had in Westfield. You're lucky he didn't kill you. We'll be right there, honey."

Larry and my friends reassured me that I was indeed lucky to be alive and so was Robert. They helped me into the car, and I headed home to tell my little boy that the daddy he loved, the daddy he thought was perfect, was dead. I prayed all the way home that I could find the right words.

When we drove down my long driveway, I saw the motorcycle parked by the house. "Whose motorcycle is that?" I asked.

"It belongs to some guy who said he met you at the roller-skating rink the other night. He said he was going by on his way to visit his sister in North East, and he just stopped to see if you might like a ride on his bike. I think his name is Cappy. He's watching Robert for me," Larry said.

I couldn't place anybody named Cappy from roller skating. But as I walked across the lawn toward the pond, where he was teaching my little boy to fish, I remembered skating with him briefly in a mixer skate. He had asked my name and where I lived. I was bewildered by the fact that he was there by the pond with Robert. I walked up and said, "I need to speak to Robert in private."

"I know. I'll be right here if you need anything," he said, reaching for Robert's fishing pole.

Just then Robert got a bite. The tip of the pole dipped down and started to bob up and down. "Yank it. Yank it hard," Cappy firmly but quietly commanded. Robert yanked, and the fish came out of the water and flew over our heads onto the grass.

Cappy turned to Robert and said, "Go with your mom. I'll take care of your fish. It's your first fish ever, isn't it?"

"Yup. Wow, Mom, I caught it all by myself!" My six-year-old son was beaming.

"That's great, honey, but I need to talk to you over by the woods," I said.

As I started to lead him away, he asked, "Can we cook it for supper?"

I said, "Not tonight, sweetheart." My voice wavered, and I felt off-balance again.

Cappy said, "I'll help you cook it, Robert. It's your first fish, and you need to eat it, right?" Then to me he said, "Your older son told me what was happening. I know you can't deal with this, so I'll just stay and help out any way I can."

I nodded and kept walking until I disappeared with my little boy around the end of the vineyard by the woods. I knelt down, took both his hands and looked at him at eye level. The tears overflowed. I could hardly form the words I needed to say because of the choking knot in my throat.

"Robert, I need to tell you something."

"What, Mommy?"

"There was a terrible accident a little while ago. Do you remember when I left?"

"Yes, Mommy, I do. Larry left right after you did, and Cappy came, and we went fishing. Why are you crying?"

"Robert, your daddy had a terrible accident with his gun. It went off and hit him in the head. He's gone to heaven to live with God."

"When is he coming back, Mommy?"

"He isn't ever coming back. No one could fix what happened."

"Am I going to go with him this weekend to the Parents 'n' Partners picnic?"

"No, honey, Daddy has already gone to heaven. You won't ever see him again. He was hurt really badly, and he died. I'm so sorry." A sob escaped me. I hugged my boy to my heart and wondered why life was so unbearable.

He let me hug him for a minute, long enough for me to get him wet with my tears. Then he said, "Can I go watch Cappy cut up the fish now?"

"Sure," I said, and he scampered off to clean his first fish. He had no real understanding of what had happened.

I crumpled onto the ground between my grapes and my woodlot. I was suddenly so cold, so tired, and so out of control of my life. What was I supposed to do now? What should I do next? Then Larry appeared. He helped me up and walked me back to the house and the confusion that was to follow.

As I neared the house, Martha, my real-estate friend, ran toward me. The abortion in Buffalo had been a horrendous ordeal, but now I hardly remembered it. She wrapped me in her arms and cried, "You don't deserve this. You helped me all day long. You saved my life and my reputation. You didn't deserve to have this happen. How can I help you?"

Before I could respond, I was surrounded by my dad, Freddie, my mother-in-law, and my friends Peggy and Carol. They were all talking at once, and it sounded garbled and mixed up to me. Suddenly, all I could hear was the gun going off in my head. It stopped me cold and still. Then I heard the first replay of the phone call complete with the clicks and thuds and no dial tone. I thought I was losing my mind. My hands flew to my head and I started to scream to drown out the noise going on in my brain. Someone helped me into the house and gave me another drink. More people surrounded me including my sister, the mayor and his wife, and Andy and his wife. Everyone was asking questions all at once.

My coworker said, "I'm going to call my husband and tell him I can't come home until tomorrow. I'll stay and take care of you. I'm going out to gather some burdocks before it gets dark. We all need something to eat, and I know how to cook them." She disappeared out the kitchen door with a paring knife in her hand.

Just then Cappy and Robert came in with another fish they had caught in Lake Erie. It was a sheep head, which no one usually eats. Cappy announced that he was going to clean it and that he and Robert would cook the two fish for their supper.

The whole scene seemed bizarre. The rest of the crowd declined food and just went on drinking. Someone said I was so lucky that the chief was dead. At that point, Cappy grabbed Robert's hand and steered him toward our grill on the porch. "I'll keep him out here to help me cook, and then I'll put him to bed. Don't worry about him, Gail. I'll take care of everything."

Somebody asked who Cappy was, how I knew him, and what his last name was. I answered, "I don't know. The man roller skates, I guess. I don't know his last name. He showed up on a motorcycle, and Larry asked him to take care of Robert. That's all I know." Right then I thought he must be an angel sent to protect Robert from the pain.

Everybody wanted to know about the chief's last phone call. They made me repeat it over and over, and each time I cried. I drank more whiskey and got really drunk. Soon everybody was talking about what the state trooper had said about the bullets. Then my coworker brought in the burdocks and began to bread them and cook them with garlic.

The mayor, who, in addition to being our family friend, was also our insurance agent, suddenly stood up and said, "I just thought of something. Where's the chief's life-insurance policy, Gail?"

I didn't even remember he had one. The mayor said, "Remember, Gail, about two years ago, when you were doing estate planning, just before the chief's open-heart surgery, I talked you both into taking out life insurance?"

"Yes, now I remember. The policy is in the metal file cabinet in my bedroom. It's locked, and I don't know where the key is. The chief couldn't find it either, and because the cabinet was heavy, he didn't take it when he moved out."

The mayor looked at my two older sons and said, "What do you say, boys? Let's break it open. I need to look at that policy."

Andy and Larry were feeling no pain, and neither was the mayor. They disappeared into the bedroom. We heard some metal-on-metal clanking and a couple of crashes, and then out they came with the policy. The mayor took it into the living room to read. We were all quiet. Soon he whooped and said, "Great news. The suicide clause expired ten days ago. I think the policy is good."

I felt sick. "I don't give a good goddamn about money. I don't even want to think about it. I just want this gun to stop going off in my head," I screamed.

Nellie said, "Okay, everybody. The party's over. Gail, just remember that this was the ultimate abuse the chief pulled on you. Remember, he's dead. He can't do anything more to hurt you. Thank God you and Robert are alive. He might have been my son, but he was a son of a bitch to me, to George, and most of all to you and your boys. Thank God he's dead. That's all I've got to say. Come on, George, let's go home. We'll come back tomorrow. Call if you or Robert need me, Gail."

My dad added, "She's right, folks. Gail needs to sleep." He hugged me and said, "Freddie and I are going home now, too. We'll be back in the morning. You have Andy, Larry and your friends to look after you. Call if you need me. I love you. Goodnight."

Soon everybody was gone or in bed; only Cappy and Martha were still in the kitchen. We ate fried burdocks, a weed that grows stick tights, or burrs, later in the summer. Martha had peeled and cooked a huge batch of the tender, delicious stalks. My friends insisted I take several aspirin and sent me to bed. Robert was fast asleep.

Sleep came instantly for me when the light went out. It was nearly three in the morning, and my children were all safe and asleep upstairs. Martha was snuggled up under a blanket on the couch, and the angel named Cappy was bunking in the lounge chair in the living room. The house was quiet and peaceful at last.

The scream that had the dog snarling, growling, and running frantically from door to door awakened all the humans in the house except Robert. He slept on peacefully, innocently.

The scream came from me. The nightmare started with me telling my yet-to-be-conceived granddaughter to never say wedding vows, because once you say "I do" and commit to those common vows, "for better or for worse, in sickness and in health, till death do us part," divorce is impossible. If you are honest and sincere when you make those vows, you are trapped in whatever hell befalls you, even if the hell is not your fault. As I was warning her hidden face, the phone rang in my nightmare. I heard a replay of the conversation just before the click, bang, thud, and pounding sounds. Then I could see the bloody pattern of brains and flesh that stretched all the way to the ceiling above the wall phone in the chief's little white kitchen. I turned to run and fell over the chief's body. I slipped and fought to keep my balance in the pool of blood on the floor. I grabbed the stove to steady myself, and my hand slid off the top, trailing bloody finger prints down the front.

The scream I let out was piercing; it sliced the quiet, peaceful, liquor-induced, sleepy darkness into lightning bolts of wakeful reality. I began to shake and sob. I was cold and wet with sweat.

My eyes hurt from bulging open to search for reality, sanity and an escape from the terror of the nightmare.

Instantly, warm arms wrapped around me, a blanket was laid across my shoulders, my daughter-in-law's soothing voice reached my ears, and both of my older sons gave me tender hugs, reinforcing that it was just a nightmare.

Cappy grabbed my pillow and blanket and said, "Come on out to the living room. We'll all camp out by the fireplace and keep the nightmare from coming back." I was exhausted, and sleep came again as I rested in the midst of those who cared for me.

In the coming days, weeks, and summer months, that nightmare invaded my conscious and subconscious mind when I was awake or in deep sleep, according to its own will. I never knew when it would overpower me or to what degree it would take control.

I was at the deepest, darkest blackest point of my life. The day that had started with my friend's abortion had ended with my husband's suicide.

CHAPTER TWELVE: FIGHTING MY WAY TO SANITY, SUMMER 1982

SUNDAY, MAY 30, 1982, was the first day that I was a widow. I awoke when the group of well-meaning friends and neighbors began talking in my kitchen. Around that time, two local policemen and a clergyman arrived. Cappy was busy making breakfast for Robert, and my coworker had recovered enough to go home to her unsuspecting husband. My older kids weren't up yet.

The topic of discussion was a memorial service for the chief. He had been baptized at a local church a few days before his premeditated murder/suicide attempt. The clergyman was asking questions about his life achievements, and the two young policemen were filling in the glorified details. Peggy and the chief's cousin were planning the reception following the service.

I was pouring a cup of coffee when the phone rang. I answered it in the laundry room adjacent to the kitchen and discovered that it was the chief's sister in Florida. She had received word of his suicide and called to blame me. Her whining, incessant voice assaulted my fragile state of mind. "Gail," she said, "I'm sure you're aware that the divorce proceedings that you initiated caused my brother to kill himself. I hope you're happy about that. You've never been a decent wife to him. I know you left him cold food to eat when he was working overtime on investigations. I know a lot of things. He was here for several months, and we talked a lot. You can just blame yourself for his death."

I bent over the washing machine and rested my head on my left arm so I could wipe my tears on the sleeve of my sweatshirt. I listened to her blameful punishment for a few minutes and then replied, "I don't suppose the chief showed you the pictures of Larry's face after he beat him." "I bet he didn't tell you he broke my ribs several times or that he chased little Robert viciously with a two-foot piece of plastic Hot Wheels track or—"

"You all deserved everything you got," she interrupted me as she screamed, "but my brother did not deserve to die like he did."

"People are here planning his memorial, and I have to go. I'm sorry you're upset, but..."

"Upset? You bet I'm upset. My brother is dead," she continued hysterically. "He was going to sue your ass off, get custody of his son, and take your farm, and you deserved it."

I couldn't take any more. The language that vomited out of my mouth, with the volume turned all the way up was heard loud and clear in the kitchen by the clergyman, the policemen, the relatives, and many of my most prestigious neighbors. I began to sob uncontrollably as the chief's phone call began to replay again in my head.

The laundry room door flew open, and Cappy came in with Robert. "Gail, my brother-in-law took my motorcycle and left his car for my use," Cappy said. "You and Robert don't need to be here for this circus. Let me take you to my cottage on the Alleghany River in Pennsylvania for the day. I'll look after Robert, and you can get some rest. When all this calms down, I'll bring you both home. Come on, now," he urged, taking my arm. There was not a sound from the crowd as we walked out the door.

The policemen stopped me and asked if they could pick up the revolver that had been issued to me as a police matron. The coroner had given me the chief's service revolver at the scene of the suicide, and it belonged to the police department, too. When I gave them both of the revolvers, I felt like I'd been fired from the police department. I was relieved to be rid of the guns and the job. That was the first moment I fully comprehended that I was no longer married to the chief of police. I felt thankful.

As we got in the car, I said to Cappy, "I'm glad he's dead. I don't have to be afraid any longer."

When we arrived at Cappy's cottage, Cappy showed me his guest room and took Robert to pick up turtle eggs along the river. I fell asleep instantly and woke up only when supper was ready. We went home at eight o'clock, and my house was quiet and empty.

Cappy said, "You'll be okay now. The memorial will happen soon, and then it will be over." He squatted down so he could talk to Robert at eye level. "You're quite a young man. I'm glad I could see you catch those fish and find those turtle eggs. You take good care of your mom, will you?"

"Yes, sir," Robert answered.

Cappy got in the car and drove away. It was the last we ever saw of him. In the confusion, we never found out his last name. I added him to my angel list.

The memorial service took place that week. The young policemen came to see me when they heard that I didn't plan to attend. They thought it was important for Robert to remember that his father had been respected, and they encouraged me to be at the service for his sake.

Andy, Larry, Robert, and I stood in a reception line and shook hands with over three hundred police officers from all around New York State and northwestern Pennsylvania. Many of them spoke of the successful investigations Chief Black had led. The men who'd worked for him recounted his exceptional leadership. An American flag was folded and presented to Robert. When I saw how straight and seriously he stood and how solemnly he shook hands with each officer, I realized that he needed to be proud of his daddy no matter what the circumstances were. I let that belief guide my tongue on many occasions.

My older sons and I couldn't feel remorse or grief. It was unbearable to sit through the eulogy, knowing how he had abused us all. The chief's mother sat beside me and simply shook her head, as though protesting the words. At the end, she put her arms around me and said, "We'll be okay now."

Robert was at daycare when the undertaker brought the cremation ashes. Larry was home, and he and I spread the ashes near the edge of Lake Erie. When I picked Robert up that afternoon, he was carrying a bag filled with Popsicle-stick crosses that his day care class had made to show sympathy. We didn't tell him about the ashes; he was only six years old. He hopped out of the car with purpose in his movement and announced, "I have to hang these crosses up in the woods for my daddy." He picked the exact spot where we had sprinkled the ashes, out of ten acres of woods and a thousand feet of lakefront, and hung those crosses all around the area. We realized we had a lot of uncharted roads yet to follow.

It was a long struggle to move from the deep pit of despair to any kind of normal life. I was no longer afraid of abuse, but I struggled with guilt over the suicide. Soon, however, I got some positive surprises, and I had supportive friends to guide me through the haze of shock.

A few days after the memorial service and the scattering of the ashes, my anger overcame me. I was beginning to realize the seriousness of my situation. I was in debt for the $6,000 I'd borrowed for a divorce I no longer needed. I had funeral debts. I had a little boy to parent. I was too upset and stressed to keep up with the vineyard work. The chief's final conversation kept replaying in my head. I just wanted to sleep.

The mayor called and said he was bringing insurance papers for me to sign and that he wasn't sure the policy was good. Peggy, my maple-syrup friend, showed up at the same time to check on me. We sat together with tea and discussed the events of May. The mailman knocked at the door and gave me a registered letter in a large, thick manila envelope. I signed and opened it while my friends were there and found papers from my attorney in Buffalo. A cover letter explained that they had read the entire file and had never encountered such a complete and documented accounting of abuse. They were appalled by what I had suffered and by the chief's countersuit demanding half my farm, alimony and custody of Robert. Because of the severity of the case and the chief's suicide, they were sending a refund check for the full amount I had paid them. I couldn't control the tears as I realized I could give the borrowed money back and use what savings I had for counseling for Robert.

The mayor stood up abruptly and demanded to know where the chief's ashes had been scattered. Peggy, the mayor, and I walked to the edge of the lake, and I pointed out the ashes, some of which were still on top of the ground. He asked us to please go back to the house and allow him a few minutes there alone. Soon he came in smiling and said, "I'm sorry, ladies, but I had to take care of something out there. The chief came to me a few days before he ended his life and told me what he was going to do. I took him out for lunch, talked about how hurtful such an action would be to Robert, and pointed out everything he had put you through, Gail. He assured me that he hadn't thought of all that and promised he wouldn't do it. Then that's exactly what he did." The mayor pounded the table with his fist. He looked Peggy and me in the eye and said, "I had to piss on his ashes. I'll probably need to do it again and again. I listened to all that shit at the memorial service, and all I could think about was seeing firsthand what he did to his own family. Don't judge me. It was something I just had to do."

As soon as my guests went home, I ran to the maple tree by the lake, found the ashes, and followed the mayor's example. It was a weird kind of revenge, and it felt good.

During the week following the chief's death, several merchants from the main street of our town told me he had visited them to apologize for various problems he'd had with them. I also learned that he had systematically paid all his bills.

Our plumber came to the door and said, "Gail, I need to tell you something disturbing. I had to make a plumbing call at a deserted local campground before their season started, and when I drove in, there was Chief Black with a female friend, naked in his car. Don't ever shed any tears for that bastard. If you or your boys need anything, don't hesitate to call. My wife and family are always there if you need company." He was nearly in tears when he left.

An old high-school friend and her husband offered to spend a couple of weeks of their vacation catching up with my vineyard work. It was a wonderful, generous offer, which I accepted.

The mayor, Peggy, and I realized that the chief's final act was not only a planned murder/suicide but also a well-orchestrated event intended to make a lot of people feel guilty. The chief managed to have the last word, the final say, committing nearly the ultimate abuse with no possibility of retribution. My friends reminded me that the silver lining in the horrific event was that no one would hurt my children or yank me out of bed by my hair and beat me ever again.

It truly surprised me that I had such friends, because I had been isolated during the abuse. These friends were sincere and always ready to help. I had God, too, and I asked Him daily how He could have let this atrocity happen to me.

Each time I came home from taking Robert to daycare and pulled the curtains, attempting to disappear from the world, Peggy arrived. She demanded a house key and intercepted those dark times regularly in the following weeks. She marched in, yanked open the curtains, and ordered me to get up, stop crying, go out in the sunshine, and go on living. She told me to pray. She sent her clergyman to visit me. The mayor called daily and took care of all the paperwork involved with settling the estate. My friends were worried and in constant communication with me. Dad and the boys visited often.

My work was my escape and my salvation; I worked until I was so tired there was no question about sleep. I immediately sought counseling, and it reinforced the fact that the suicide wasn't my fault. I didn't pull the trigger.

Larry went off to the Marine Corps Officer Candidate School at Quantico. Robert went back to school and time passed slowly. I returned to my real-estate job but found that the sympathy offered by my clients was more than I could handle. Every time someone told me how sorry he or she was, I burst into tears, and the replay in my head would begin. I tried to work for about a week and then quit. I'd been wrong when I thought my problems were over; there were even more hurdles to leap.

A few days after Robert returned to first grade, the school sent home a notice that IQ tests would be administered. My little boy was having nightmares and acting out, and he wasn't in a normal state of mind, so I called the school and requested that his test be postponed until the fall semester. They insisted that he be tested. When I suggested that I would keep him out of school that day, I was told that he would take his test the next day he attended classes. Even a call from his pediatrician wouldn't dissuade them from administering the test.

Of course, when the results came back, I saw that he had failed miserably. The school declared that he was borderline retarded. I reminded them that he was in no state to take tests. At Peggy's suggestion, I brought in his report cards, which were all above average. Nothing I said made any difference. He passed first grade, but I received a note about his IQ test that said he would be placed in a resource program for retarded children. It was too much to comprehend. I made appointments for both of us with my counselor.

One of the counselor's recommendations for our recovery was that I find activities in which we could both participate. In the newspaper, I found an ad for a picnic at a ski resort to organize a political campaign for a new county executive. All we had to do was show up with a dish to pass. I made potato salad, loaded Robert up, and away we went.

Most of the participants were adults, but there was a sprinkling of children. Robert soon made connections, borrowed a bat and ball from the bartender, and organized a softball game. I was sitting by myself, watching him, when a warm, friendly girl approached me and said, "Hi! My name's Miss Wendy. You're new at these meetings, aren't you? We're glad to have you. I'm the party chairman's wife, and I just saw that little boy over there go to the bartender and get a bat and ball. Would you look at the softball game he has going? Is he your son? He sure is friendly and resourceful. I never saw all those grownups play any games at any of these functions."

When I got a chance to answer, I said, "Yes, he's mine. He's great. Too bad his school doesn't see any value to his IQ. My name is Gail, and his is Robert. We came to fill some free time and find a way to help your campaign."

We shook hands, and she sat down beside me. With a puzzled look, she asked, "What do you mean about the school? Did he recently take the state IQ test?"

"Yes, he did, and I'm quite upset about it—but I'm sure you aren't interested. They said he had an IQ of less than 80 and that he was borderline or mildly retarded. Meanwhile, he got above-average grades and passed first grade, and he's been reading since he was four. They're going to put him in a resource room in the fall, and I can't do a thing to change it." I touched her arm. "I didn't mean to bore you. It's just that on top of his daddy's suicide in May, we didn't need this. I can't seem to shut up about it."

"Are you Chief Black's widow?" she asked.

"Yes, I am."

"I'm sorry. I heard all about it," she said softly. "I'm interested in your little boy. I work for the City of Jamestown school system and administer all their testing. Why don't you bring Robert to me for three weeks of summer school and thorough testing? I can test him in many ways—verbally, written, with pictures, and more. I'm a psychologist, and when I finish, there won't be any doubt about his IQ or many other factors. What do you say? There won't be a charge. You help us with this campaign, and I'll test that young man. From what I've seen here, I believe he's exceptionally bright. He should never have been tested so close to his father's traumatic death. It will be my pleasure to help him," she added. "That boy is a long, long way from being retarded." She gave me the date and time for the testing and then left to rejoin the crowd.

I watched her walk away. She was neatly dressed in a checked shirt, jeans, and cowboy boots. She was so pretty that heads turned; everyone seemed to know and like her. With her infectious smile and outgoing personality, she made it her business to speak to everyone there and find out personal things about them. She was a real asset to her husband, the campaign chairman for the next election. She moved among the picnic tables and ended up on the softball diamond, where she bent down and spoke to Robert as he was pitching. He smiled up at her and then waved at me.

At the end of the organizational meeting, we were assigned the job of handing out flyers at a supermarket twice a month. Robert loved it, and he looked forward to the summer session with Miss Wendy.

Appalling as it was, numerous men in the community felt duty-bound to visit me. They arrived with disguised agendas. Some were professionals who offered their services, along with offers to take care of any physical needs I might have as a widow. Three were neighbors who offered to help with the grape work, wood cutting, gardening, and equipment maintenance in exchange for some home-cooked meals and personal time. Nearly all of them were good, churchgoing, married men, and it was sickening.

I told the counselor about the men. He assured me that it was not unusual and that he understood their concern and desire to help me. "If you ever need to talk about this when my office isn't open, feel free to call me. Here's my private number," he said. I wondered about his agenda and, for the hundredth time, if I was sane.

One day at the grocery store, the cashier told me that she and her husband had started a new business selling ultralight airplanes at a nearby airport, and she invited Robert and me to attend an open house. It was something to do, so we went. The airplanes were colorful and looked like lawn chairs with wings. As we walked around the half-dozen displays, a tall, nice-looking man approached us and suggested that Robert stand just outside the hangar and watch the runway—one of the little planes was going to land soon. Robert ran to the doorway, and the man demonstrated the mechanical workings of the ultralight, explaining that no license was necessary to fly one. He told me to push one over to the doorway.

"How much does one of these cost?" I asked as I pushed.

"Anywhere from a couple thousand to five thousand—talk to the lady named Jenny. I'll show your little boy how easy it is to take off. It's airborne in fifteen feet."

He turned the electric start key, and a motor like a snowmobile engine sputtered to life. He winked at me with one of his big blue eyes, and the little plane started to roll. Another one landed, and yet another took off. Jenny told me the man was Stew. By the time he came back, I had agreed to buy an ultralight airplane. Before we left, I learned that the little plane would be delivered to my farm in several pieces and that Stew was the mechanic who would assemble it. I also learned that I needed to mow a nine-hundred-foot landing strip beside the vineyard. I arranged for Stew to advise me about where I should mow. I was given several papers outlining rules, laws, and instructions for how to start and fly the airplane. I smiled, anticipating the challenge and fun the pretty plane would bring into my life.

It had been only a few weeks since my husband's suicide, and later, when I looked back on that evening, I understood that I was not in any mental condition to undertake such a project. At the time, the complexity and danger of flying an ultralight airplane didn't matter, because life didn't matter; I had a subconscious death wish. We met with Stew and another pilot, mowed the runway to his specifications, and hired a guy to add a storage area for the plane to the back of my barn. Before Stew and his friend left the day we planned the runway, they asked me if Robert and I would like to go to a local amusement park. They had extra tickets. We went and then stopped for dinner on the way home.

Stew's pilot friend, Mickey, came by to check on our preparations for my solo flight. We watched a couple of sunsets, had a few cups of coffee, and soon were dating. In three weeks, when the plane was delivered, Stew and Mickey were there to assemble it. Robert and I had been busy picking up rocks and stones from the runway, and we were excited about flying the little plane. The instruction sheet said there could be no wind, so I bought a wind meter. Then we were ready.

Just as I was about to sit in the seat and start the motor, with the two men to instruct me, the wind came up, and we had to wait. The men got busy, and I got impatient. One evening, when there was absolutely no wind, I decided I had waited long enough, so Robert and I headed for the new hangar.

I said, "Robert, you sit here on the rock and watch while I fly this pretty thing." We rolled the little plane out to the runway, and I strapped myself into the seat.

I was sure I could do it. Stew and his friend, both experienced pilots, had told me to take it up to four hundred feet, level off, go once around my farm, and land from the far end of the runway, going toward the barn. The instructions had explained that the altimeter would tell me how high I was. "No sweat," I called to Robert as I taxied away from the barn and down the runway. Stew had told me that flying an ultralight plane was like operating a snowmobile and that when you rolled the handlebar grips back toward you, the plane would climb. When you rolled them forward, it would level off. It sounded pretty easy.

I started the engine, revved it up, took my foot off the brake and let it go full speed ahead with the handle bar grips rolled back toward my body. The plane roared forward, and within fifteen feet, I was lying on my back, rising fast. I was looking straight up, defying gravity, going high into the sky. The wind was in my face as the little plane raced upward. The sun was still warm that evening and I felt exhilarated as I climbed, passing birds on my right. Up, up and up some more, I went not daring to look down. I was headed toward the railroad tracks that bordered my vineyard and suddenly the whole contraption shot up faster than before. After I passed over the tracks, still climbing higher, it dropped dramatically, taking my breath away. My whole body was rigid, and my hands were welded to the controls. I finally forced myself to look down. The barn looked so small, and the vineyard was disappearing behind me. I pulled the left handlebar, and the plane banked left. I flew back over the railroad tracks, bouncing again because of the thermals no one had mentioned.

I hardly dared look down at the gauges, but when I finally I glanced at the altimeter, I was still climbing, I was amazed to see that I was at eight hundred feet—four hundred feet too high.

"Shit! What the hell am I doing up here, anyway?" I screamed against the wind and the whine of the Japanese engine. I forced myself to look down again and knew I had to level off. Even the birds were below me, looking smaller every second. But each time I rolled the handlebar grips forward, the plane felt like it was going to nosedive and crash.

Finally, by sheer willpower, I brought the nose level and began a gradual descent. I was up nearly a thousand feet. I was too high in the air, I was high on the adrenalin of fear and I had to land.

Then I noticed the crowd of people in the road in front of my farm. They had run down from the nearby ice-cream stand to watch the plane, and Robert had joined them. "Shit!" I yelled again, dreading the prospect of having an audience. "Everything that goes up has to come down. I have to land this damn thing, or gravity will do it for me."

I had to circle several times before I was down to four hundred feet and could start the approach to my landing strip. My heart pounded as I repeated aloud what the instruction book had said: "Down, down, down, pull the nose up, set it down easy, and then roll the handlebars forward to keep it down."

The plane bumped onto the runway but was moving really fast toward the barn. I applied the brakes with all my strength. The crowd was running toward me, but I didn't mind because I was down smoothly and safely and I was exuberant. I coasted up to the hangar and barn, shut the engine off and unstrapped myself. I stepped out like I was a returning astronaut coming home from a successful mission.

Robert was grinning from ear to ear as he said, "Can I try it now, Mommy?"

We pushed it into the hangar and waited for another windless night.

One windless evening, I decided to fly inland ten miles. I had studied the topography map and knew there was a nine-hundred-foot elevation to the top of the escarpment on my way to the airport where I had bought the ultralight. I climbed the nine hundred feet, but suddenly there were high-tension electric-transmission lines and poles directly in my path.

"Oh, my God," I screamed. "Do I fly under them or over them? I have to do something, quick!" I decided to make a steep banked turn to the right, climb to an even higher altitude, and go over the wires. It worked and I successfully landed on the grass strip a few minutes later. The touch-and-go practice was perfect, and I flew home, put the pretty little plane in the barn, and went in to Robert and his babysitter.

I had four perfect landings, including the first one, then ten mediocre bounces. Sometimes I couldn't keep the plane from bouncing, because I weighed only ninety pounds, and no one had told me to put sandbags on it. In my first bad crash, my wing clipped a grape row as I veered off my landing strip and tipped over into the grapes. I was sick when I saw the torn fabric on the purple section of the rainbow wing. Stew and Mickey came over the next day and said they would fix it.

Around that time, a man who had purchased an ultralight that was similar to mine didn't survive a downdraft when he flew it in the wind. The incident was a wakeup call regarding the risk, but when I was up in the air, I was free from all the mental replays and pain of the chief's suicide so I ignored the message.

The next time I landed inappropriately, I came down too hard and too fast, buckling the ultralight's frame and bending the wheels. The engine was in the back and escaped damage. That landing was the hardest and hurt the most. My whole body ached for days, but when the wind ceased to blow, I couldn't resist the challenge. Flying was an ego boost and set me apart from almost everyone I knew.

I misguidedly sought positive attention from the local population, who gathered on calm nights and stood with shaded eyes to watch me soar with the birds. I was euphoric. Every time I landed and walked in the door unscathed, that damned Mirror would scoff, "I see you still think you're superhuman. You're an accident waiting to happen, girl."

The last time I flew, Robert waited on the rock by the barn. I flew a bit farther north and west and finally headed for the end of the runway from a slightly different direction. Somehow, I came down fifty yards too soon, in a field of heavy red brush and blackberry bushes. I did miss a big pond, to my credit. The plane hit the brush and tipped up on its nose with the motor still running. With the plane in that position, gasoline started leaking from the cap on the tank. The seat had bent in the crash landing, and I couldn't reach the safety harness to unfasten it. Gasoline was dripping on me, all over the framework, and near the motor behind me. The key to shut the motor off was out of reach. My hands began to shake. They were cold and stiff from the evening air, and I had trouble manipulating the seatbelt when I finally found it amid the tangled framework. I thought the plane was going to catch on fire any second but I finally got loose, crawled out from under the twisted frame, found the key and shut the motor off.

I had to slither on my belly on a deer trail under heavy brush to get to the end of the runway, where I saw my little boy dragging two old folks toward me.

I could hear him screaming, "Hurry! My mommy crashed her airplane, and she's dead under it."

The old man yelled, "Thank God you're all right." Everybody was out of breath.

I grabbed Robert and hugged him as he ran into my arms. "Mommy, please don't fly it again," he pleaded.

"No sweetheart, I won't," I promised as I gave him crushing hug after hug.

I got the tractor and mowed down the red brush and berry bushes, tied a rope to the airplane, and pulled it back to the barn. My next chore was to call Jenny and tell her the wreckage was for sale. Within a week, a man bought it for nearly as much as I had paid for it, even though it was bent and broken.

Once the wreckage was loaded onto the flatbed trailer, I had the check in my hand, and the new owner was driving away, I felt a cold shiver. What had I been thinking? Robert stood as close to me as he could get, and I hugged him tightly. I was so thankful to hug my little boy as the plane was hauled away, with my body in one piece, unharmed.

My dad had often recited a little rhyme to me: "For fear of taking risks in life, I've missed a lot of fun. The only things that I regret are those I haven't done." He also used to repeat the common adage, "If at first you don't succeed, try, try, try..." He'd add the word "try" infinitely. I was absolutely glad I'd experienced the thrill; I'd had some success and lived to tell about it. A strange pride welled up inside me. I had lived through the challenge, but I vowed I would never do anything so dangerous again, as long as I had the future of a precious little boy in my hands.

Chapter Thirteen: The Disaster of "I Do," Fall of 1982

THE DECISIONS I MADE in the first few months after the suicide were influenced by the effect they had on the mental replay of the suicide.

Mickey had been busy at the air field where he demonstrated flying ultralights and worked as the chief mechanic. Summer was their busy season and our time together was sparse. As summer waned and glorious fall colors appeared, he surprised me with a lovely engagement ring. The suicidal replays had disappeared during the summer filled with flying, dancing, dining and roller skating. Robert was always excited to see him when he visited and, obviously, I wasn't thinking clearly.

Mickey told me he was going to prove his love. He quit his full-time job of many years, saying he could be more useful helping with the grape growing. I'd been successful on my own and questioned the decision, but, in the end, it was a relief to have help with the heavy labor.

My husband-to-be thought that getting married by a justice of the peace at the airport where we'd met, under the wings of an ultralight airplane, would be perfect. We were married six weeks after we met.

For a number of years, I had volunteered as the local cancer-drive chairperson, supervising volunteer workers. I organized the commercial drive and personally visited all the businesses in my community. Soon after the pilot and I got married, I began the cancer campaign for that year.

When I called on a local business one day, I hemorrhaged badly. The owner's wife bundled me up and delivered me to the emergency room, but the doctor on call couldn't stop the bleeding. He admitted me and called the surgeon of my choice, who was a roller-skating friend.

I soon found myself in the recovery room. The surgeon said, "You're really lucky. As I opened you up, your appendix burst. You'll need bed rest and can do no hard physical activity for at least a month. That means no work, no roller skating, and no lifting."

My husband came in a few minutes later. My mind was still foggy from the anesthesia, but I clearly heard him say, "Gail, I want you to know that I can't do anything to help you when you come home from the hospital unless you put my name on your property deed."

Bells of warning started ringing and clear enlightenment flashed in my head. There had been red flags and suspicions, but I still felt disbelief at what I was hearing. He repeated it, as if he wanted to be sure I understood. New words waltzed around with the ones I remembered from my accident ten years earlier: added together I heard them singing, "You're hurt, can't work, husband number three is a greedy jerk." I understood completely.

Three times, three marriages, was not a charm, but experience was knowledge, and the answer came easily and much more quickly than the other times. I said, "Okay. As soon as I'm able, I'll call my lawyer." My voice was groggy, but my mind was wide awake and sharp.

When he left, I made plans to meet with my attorney. When I married this guy, I'd forfeited my late husband's social-security benefits. What had I done? Only a few days before I landed in the hospital, my new husband had gotten angry because I had one of the mental replays and ended up crying. He had pushed me against the stove and said he'd had enough of me feeling sorry for myself and he didn't want to hear any more. It had been only about six months since the suicide, and I couldn't help the replay attacks. Now it was clear he had married me for my money, my farm, and the chance to quit his job; he felt no love, concern, or sympathy for me. I got the picture clearly as I lay in the hospital.

When I was well enough, I saw my attorney and told him what was going on. He said, "He married you under false pretenses. You need an annulment."

Before I left my attorney's office, I had signed the paperwork, but I also needed my husband's signature. The attorney suggested that I call him and ask him what it would take to get that signature.

I made the call saying, "You know I am at the attorney's office. I have a question for you. Will you sign an annulment agreement?"

He yelled, "What are you asking me to do? I thought you were going to put my name on the deed this morning. I can't believe this."

"Believe it. I want an annulment. It's obvious that all you wanted was to quit your job, lie around the house, and get your name on my property. I want out. Will you sign the annulment agreement?"

"Come on home, and we'll talk about it," he demanded.

I calmly answered, "No, I'm not coming home until you sign. What will it take to get your signature? The papers are ready right now."

"An annulment means this marriage never happened, right? Let me think. I sold my car, and now I'm driving one of yours. If I sign, I won't have a car, so I need a new car. I quit my job to help you, so I need money to live on. I need to rent a place to live, and I need a security deposit. Can we negotiate this?"

"Just give me a figure, and my attorney and I will decide if it's fair. Otherwise, I'm prepared to take you to family court. It's up to you. Why don't you make it easy on yourself and name a price. You married me for money, and now's your chance to cash in."

He named a price, the attorney nodded agreement, and I got money from the bank across the street. The annulment papers were signed on the sidewalk in front of the attorney's office. I drove home, feeling like a failure. The words "divorced, widowed, and annulled equal freedom, not failure" popped into my mind. I wondered how many other kinds of abusers there were besides religious tyrants, men who beat their wives, and gigolos.

CHAPTER FOURTEEN: CAN'T STOP
LOOKING FOR LOVE, 1983-1986

I WAS WORRIED ABOUT Robert and the ramifications of our difficulties, and I couldn't help adding up the horrific experiences we had endured. We had survived the suicide, trouble with the school, another marriage, a serious operation, and an annulment. Just as we adjusted to living by ourselves, my dad had suffered a stroke and spent months recovering in my care before he could return to his home. I was too busy to question why I was still sane, if I was.

Two old friends materialized and helped us in our journey through those dark times. I had known them for a long time, but now they moved to center stage in our lives.

Way back when I was twenty-six and living at my dad's house, I worked as a cocktail waitress at the Elks Club in Jamestown, New York. I met a girl who was the cocktail waitress at The Vikings, a Swedish club in Jamestown. We often worked together when the two clubs held joint events. Seven years younger than me, Sherry was a vivacious, perky redhead with a quick wit and friendly smile. She spoke some Swedish and understood a lot of it, because that was her heritage. I spoke no Swedish, so she took the orders, and I ran the drinks where she told me to. We developed a wonderful lifelong friendship.

We were both single and adventurous. I had a pickup truck, and she had a snowmobile when snowmobiles were a new invention. We'd load her machine on my truck and participate in all the races we could find. We were the only women who raced, and we usually beat the men. We double dated, compared notes, took guys for rides on the snowmobile, and enjoyed dumping them in snow banks far from the starting point.

Sherry was one of the first people to arrive at my house after the chief committed suicide. She, like Peggy and the mayor, kept a close eye on me. She had married and she and her husband, John, invited me to spend every weekend with them and their children. She and I had not waitressed for years, but had stayed close friends. John and Sherry went dancing every Saturday night. They always asked me to join them, and when I couldn't find a babysitter, they would provide one.

John was older than Sherry and me. He was a rugged man; he was a man's man who owned a drilling rig and drilled oil wells in northwest Pennsylvania. He didn't mind having two ladies on his arm, and Sherry made sure he danced with me now and then when I didn't have a partner. No jealousy or competition existed between us. We were supportive and proud of each other's successes and progress in life.

It was Sherry who'd found the safe house for Robert and me when the chief was hunting us with his gun. It was Sherry who'd loaned me diapers and cash to survive those first few days. It was Sherry I always wanted to see and with whom I wanted to share any news. The feeling went both ways.

I spent a lot of weekends at John and Sherry's house after the suicide. They always had some single guy for me to date, but usually it didn't work out. One bright summer day, Sherry called in a panic. Her beloved John had suffered a stroke and was in a city hospital forty miles away. She wanted me to be with them. It was time for me to return their kindnesses and I was honored and happy to help in any way possible. It was wonderful to give back to someone after all the help I had received.

One day that fall, Sherry asked me to bring Robert to their house and help her take John to a hunting camp in central Pennsylvania where handicap-accessible hunting trails were available. A group of his friends wanted to help him get his deer that first fall after his stroke. The day was snowy, and the roads were slick. I worried about the driving, but after all they had done for me, I couldn't refuse. We packed up and drove the forty miles to their house, regrouped, and took John another fifty miles to the hunting camp. We took their two kids and Robert along.

While we were unloading John's wheelchair, hunting gear, and sleeping bag, all three kids fell through the ice covering a creek and got soaking wet. The cabin had a woodstove, but it had not yet warmed the place or dried out the dampness. We put them all in sleeping bags on various bunks while Sherry and I cleaned the refrigerator and kitchen and heated up the homemade vegetable-beef soup I had brought along.

Just as we were ready to sit down at the picnic table with John and his five friends, the door opened. A tall, handsome, clean-shaven giant of a man walked in wearing a camouflage hunting jacket and a red and black wool cap. I noticed his huge feet. He had on insulated hunting boots, which made them look even bigger than size 15. His size captured everyone's attention. Everyone but me seemed to know him. Apparently the leader, Bob spoke about the deer herd and the tracks he had seen in the state forest. He planned where each hunter would stand and who would participate in the drive to put the deer herd within John's shooting range on the handicap-accessible trail.

I was transfixed. My hands were motionless in midair and I know my mouth was hanging open. I couldn't feel myself drool, but I thought he was the most delicious looking specimen of a man I had ever seen. Before I knew it, he was walking out the door.

"Hey, wait," I yelled after him. He turned around. "You seem to know this area well, and you just said you've been hunting here for sixteen years," I said. "You're just the man to give me a tour."

I was so brazen that I embarrassed myself. He didn't bother to answer. He just looked at me, and believe me, I was a mess. I hadn't fixed my hair, changed my clothes, or put on any makeup. Then his face broke into a slow grin, and he held out his hand. I grabbed my coat, walked out of that cabin and climbed into his four wheel drive pickup truck. He drove me around for a couple hours, showed me deer herds, buck scrapes, his favorite hunting spots overlooking well-used deer trails, where he wanted his ashes scattered one day. He also told me he was within days of finalizing his divorce. He said he had two kids who were almost grown and that he never wanted any more; his, mine, or ours if we became friends.

Then he said, "Would you like to fool around?" I thought that meant kissing and hugging, but he had more on his mind. I declined.

Bob ended the tour by taking me to his hunting cabin and introducing me to his son and his soon-to-be son-in-law. Then he took me back to Sherry and John. The soup was all gone, but I didn't care.

I rode home in a fog. I couldn't think of anything but him. Sherry said I was twitterpated, which was a word my mother used for people who were infatuated with each other. She'd used that word a lot while using Mirror to watch my sister's and my behavior with boys on the couch as it reflected in Mirror who lived at her house back then.

As we drove away, Bob called, "I didn't get your number, but I can get it from John."

All the way home on that long, snowy ride, I wondered what would have happened if I had accepted his offer to "fool around." I was certain I'd never hear from him again. All I knew about him was that he lived in Pittsburgh, where he owned a construction business. Andy and his wife, Cindy, also lived in Pittsburgh and were expecting their first child in a couple of months. I wondered if he lived near them.

I resumed my normal routine and continued dating a less-than-satisfactory man, who was physically challenged in some important areas. He had named a part of himself Junior, and it truly deserved the name.

I was glad I'd helped Sherry take John for his week of hunting. Robert went back to school, and I continued with my vineyard pruning, which took eight hours a day all winter long.

A few days later, the phone rang one morning around seven o'clock. It was Bob, and he informed me that he was on his way from the Pennsylvania hunting camp to drop John off at his home. From there, he was driving to my house.

My mind raced 100 miles a minute. I needed a makeover, my house needed a makeover and I figured I had an hour at the most. To complicate matters, when I opened the front door to walk Robert to the school bus, I found a bouquet of roses on my picnic table. The card was signed "Junior." It said he missed me and would be stopping by soon. I stuck the roses in a bucket of water in the laundry room; they were too beautiful to throw away. Robert got on the bus, and I decided to put my tractor, which was parked in front of the house, in the barn. On the tractor seat I found another long-stemmed red rose. I threw it on the porch and moved the tractor to the barn; just inside the barn door was another dozen long-stemmed red roses. I put all of them in the bucket in the laundry room and closed the door. I didn't want any roses from "Junior" or the guy he was connected to.

I scurried around, cleaning up the house, and each time I passed Mirror, it looked back at me with raised eyebrows. I looked rough, needed to wash my hair and change my clothes, and I had only thirty minutes left. The phone rang again. It was the florist, announcing a delivery for me. I just knew it was more roses. "Can you be here in the next fifteen minutes?" I asked.

If the delivery was what I thought it was, the total rose count would be thirty-seven. I needed another bucket of water; because the first one was full. I opened the back door to get that second pail and found more roses, bringing the total to forty-nine. Junior must have had a wallet much bigger than his body part.

Every time I opened the laundry-room door, the house smelled like a funeral parlor. How could I explain all those roses to this new guy Bob whom I really liked?

Then the Mirror said, "Hey, it is such a wonderful problem to have. Just lock the damned laundry-room door so Robert doesn't open it when he comes home." Great idea, I thought. When the new roses were delivered, I put them with the rest and then not only locked the door but moved a table in front of it.

Sherry called to report that John had arrived home. She was surprised that Bob had said he was continuing on to my house. She asked how I felt about that.

"My God, Sherry, I've got problems. Do you remember Bubba, the guy I've been dating?" I asked.

"What a loser. Clearly you're desperate, if you're dating a guy named Bubba with a little friend named Junior," she laughed. "I thought you told him to take his awful beard and his reconditioned cars for a hike. Why do you ask?"

"If Bob left there already, he's due here in about twenty minutes. Bubba said he was going to come and see me soon, and today I've found forty-nine long-stemmed red roses around this place—all of them from Bubba and his little friend Junior. And yes, I told Bubba all those things. Do you think I should call him and threaten to have him arrested if he shows up?" I asked.

"That or shoot out his tires when he starts down the driveway. No, wait—he couldn't leave if he had flat tires. Yeah, you better call and make him understand he isn't welcome. Bob's too nice a guy to risk losing for some jerk like Bubba."

"Okay. I gotta do what I gotta do," I said.

Bubba wasn't happy to hear that I hated long-stemmed red roses; I told him there had better not be any more of them—or any more of him. Before he hung up, he said, "Honey, you better check your pickup truck, your car, and your mailbox before you stop thinking of me. I get the message, and I won't bother you no more."

I ran from the house to the truck and found another dozen roses, another dozen in the car, and one rose with a big bow on it in the mailbox. I put them all in the laundry room. Just as I got it all sealed up again, Bob arrived at my front door with a bouquet of *yellow* roses; I was thrilled to have them and I put them in a vase on the table in front of the laundry-room door.

Mirror said, "That's a cool move, Gail. The yellow ones smell just like the red ones. Talk about camouflage. You're a master of aroma deception."

Robert was at school that morning, so I suggested that I give Bob a tour of the area. We drove northwest along the Lake Erie shoreline to the Dunkirk harbor. The day was frosty cold, with diamonds sparkling in the new snow and trees dressed in what appeared to be white gowns covered with shimmering rhinestones.

It was a zero-degree day, and the pier in the Dunkirk harbor was glazed with ice. The break walls were pillars of snow, and waves were frozen in motion, gleaming against the bright blue sky. The morning sunshine was a distinct contrast to the slate grey, open water with steam wafting upward. I moved the truck slowly to a parking spot and let it coast to a stop.

Two fishermen stood at the edge of the pier, each with a foot braced against the low railing. One of them got a bite just as we slipped and slid toward them. He'd landed a steelhead trout that was close to forty inches long. Bob made his way precariously to the edge to see the fish and marveled at the open water in the harbor.

The coal-fired power plant discharged enough hot water daily to keep a portion of the harbor free of ice. Trout and salmon migrated to that warmth and were easy to catch that winter. Bob wanted to fish, so we drove back to my house for my fishing gear and returned to the fishing hole. We caught our limit in just an hour, and I cooked fish for supper that night.

After supper, Bob was about to leave for Pittsburgh when a banner came across the television screen announcing that the New York State Thruway was closed due to lake-effect blowing snow. The other major highways going south and west to Erie, Cleveland, and Pittsburgh were also shut down. A school in a neighboring town was designated an overnight safe haven for travelers.

I already had a wood fire in the fireplace to augment the gas furnace. The house was toasty warm, Robert was asleep in bed, and we were having so much fun we hadn't noticed the howling wind and blowing snow that had snuffed out the rest of the world and allowed us to snuggle in front of the fire.

I said, "Well, that settles that. You can't leave, so I'll get you some pillows and blankets, and you can camp out here in the living room and keep the fire stoked."

"Sounds good to me, babe. Sorry to overstay my welcome, but it doesn't seem to be my fault," he said with a big smile and a wink.

As I walked through the front hall, Mirror whispered, "Yeah, yeah, yeah. You always luck out, and he called you 'babe.' Just remember, if he calls you 'babe,' 'honey,' 'sweetheart,' and so on, he can't call you by the wrong name. Think about that, babe!"

I went to the kitchen for a bottle of my homemade elderberry wine, two wineglasses, and some crackers and cheese and returned to the living room just as Bob came in the front door with an armload of wood for the fire.

"I have to go to my truck before I can settle in; I have some great Conway Twitty music. We can listen to it while we wait out this storm."

I went to the kitchen again to get an ice bucket, and when I passed Mirror, it commented, "You lucky dog. How did you manage a blinding snowstorm, a fire in the fireplace, wine and cheese, music, *and* a handsome man, all sequestered in your living room for a whole uninterrupted night?"

"Perfect, isn't it? Here's the thing, Mirror," I said. "I don't want to hear another word out of you. Do you understand? If I do, I'll throw you out in the storm and destroy your interference." I threatened as I hung Bob's snow-covered jacket over my reflection. Happiness and love peeked through my fog of loneliness, and I was hoping for some stress-free time. However, another challenging situation loomed, and I was rapidly hurtling toward more conflict. It was like one battle just followed another in my war of life.

Chapter Fifteen: Trouble at School, 1983

Although Robert had satisfactorily completed second grade just after the first anniversary of his father's death, he was placed, for the second time, in a special-education class with children with limited learning abilities. When I complained, I was told that he was hyperactive and disruptive in class and needed to take Ritalin.

As a rule, I don't even take aspirin when I have a headache. I had never given anything but a multivitamin to my son, and I certainly was not going to drug him so that incompetent, unfair school administrators could take the easy road. In all fairness, Robert had been active and talkative after his daddy died, and he seemed to get even more animated as time went on. He was a handful even at home, and I wanted to figure out what was causing the behavior change—not mask it by drugging him.

I was summoned to a meeting with the principal and the committee on the handicapped where I was given an ultimatum. I asked for some time to determine what was causing any hyperactivity or problems. I was told that, without my permission, they had sent Robert to the school psychologist, who had diagnosed the problem as hyperactivity, or ADHD. The school principal said I had to give him the Ritalin.

I emphatically refused the idea several times and said I would contact my pediatrician. The grade school principal said Robert was no longer welcome in the school unless he took the Ritalin.

A few days later, I was again summoned to another meeting. Around a boardroom table were the psychologist, my son's teacher, the principal, and the five-person committee on the handicapped. I was supposed to be seated at the end or foot of the table. I was so clearly outnumbered, and I felt that this was an attempt to bully me. A woman entered, and it was announced that they had chosen a mentor for me. They explained that she would listen to the facts and decide for me just what course of action I should take.

When I said, "There's no need for her to be here. I'm quite capable of making my own decisions," they sat up straighter in their business suits.

In a fake sympathetic manner, the principal said, "If that's the way you feel, but we all know that you're not in any condition to make competent decisions because of your husband's suicide a few months ago." The mentor tried to put her hand on my arm in a friendly, intimate gesture. I moved my chair away.

My son's teacher stood up and thrust a spelling test in my face. She said, "Gail, how can you explain these two spelling tests, on which your son scored 100 on the first and only 10 on the same test the next day, which had the same words?" Then she repeated the drill with two math tests that had been given on successive days, which also had conflicting grades.

I looked at the papers and wondered why she wanted me to explain something that had happened in school, when I was not present. Finally I said, "Don't ask me. You're the teacher. Did you lose control of the class the second day so that a distraction was created?"

189

The principal said, "You're out of order. The teacher is a professional, and we were just trying to find out what caused the discrepancy."

I felt outnumbered and manipulated, weary and worn down. I said, "I'll give him the damned Ritalin."

They produced a prescription on the spot, with the dosage at 10 milligrams. I went directly to the drugstore, filled it, and took it home. The next day was Saturday, and, as directed, I gave one pill to my son. Within an hour, he was running and screaming throughout the house. He jumped from the couch to the coffee table to the fireplace hearth to an end table to the floor and then climbed on top of the TV and jumped off. This bizarre behavior persisted all day and all evening, and his energy level never diminished. Bedtime came and went; I had to stay up all night, listening to him talk and scream and run wildly without stopping.

When he finally slowed down and his activity level returned to normal, it was Sunday afternoon. It had been over thirty hours since I had administered the dose of Ritalin. I flushed the rest of the pills down the toilet and filled the empty prescription bottle with baby aspirin.

I was summoned again the following Friday for another meeting with the committee and my mentor. The teacher opened fire on me by saying, "Look at this. Your son got 100 on all his spelling papers and all but one of his math papers. Aren't you glad you decided to be sensible and give him the Ritalin? He was no problem in class this week."

I should have kept my mouth shut and continued to give him the aspirin instead of the Ritalin. However, when the mentor gave me a conciliatory pat on the shoulder, I couldn't contain myself.

"He took only one Ritalin, on Saturday, and he couldn't stop moving or talking for thirty hours. It was like an overdose of caffeine. It was terrible. We didn't even go to bed, because he couldn't stop moving, jumping, running, and screaming. It didn't quiet him—it charged him up. That's what the damned dope did," I screamed.

The teacher pounded her fist on the table and shouted, "I knew we should have administered the pill to him in the nurse's office every morning. I asked him each morning if he'd taken his medicine, and he said he had. Now, Gail, who's telling us the truth? Did you tell Robert to lie to us?"

I was on my feet, boiling mad. "Robert always tells the truth, even when it's not to his advantage. That's why I gave him aspirin instead of Ritalin. I knew you would ask him if he took his pill, so I wanted Robert to *think* he was taking the medicine. He doesn't know how to lie. It's incredibly awful that you're his teacher again this year." I glared at the principal's pet teacher.

At Christmastime, the art teacher started a card-making project. A little boy in Robert's class walked up to him and said, "Ha, ha, Robert. You can't make a Christmas card for your daddy, because he blew his fucking brains out."

Robert replied, "You say that once more about my daddy and I'll gouge your eyes out." He held his blunt, two-inch-long children's scissors up in a threatening manner.

Robert came home crying as he told me what he had said and done. Then he continued, "I told Jason that Daddy had an accident. I miss him, Mommy." I held him and explained that sometimes people say horrible things; but, even so, he could not threaten anyone with scissors.

I said, "Robert, just walk away. Go tell the teacher or another adult, and let them handle it."

I called the school but couldn't get through to the teacher or the principal. Jason repeated the taunt a second time in the cafeteria. Robert doubled up his fist, smashed Jason's lunchbox, and told me he glared at Jason saying, "I told you my daddy had an accident!"

I called the school again, spoke with the principal, and was told, "I've already heard about the cafeteria incident from the staff, and I've concluded that you need to buy Jason a new lunchbox, and that Robert needs to apologize for his aggressive behavior. Otherwise, keep him home, where he can't hurt anyone."

I bought the lunchbox, thinking it might end the whole ridiculous mess. On the way to Jason's house, I asked Robert why he'd smashed the lunchbox instead of just walking away as I had suggested to him.

"Mommy, I was in the cafeteria, and we can't leave until the monitor tells us to get in line. I wanted to smash Jason in the face, but I smashed his lunchbox instead. The teacher got mad when I said I'd gouge his eyes out, so I hit the lunchbox so I wouldn't hurt him. Why does he keep saying stuff about my daddy? It makes me so mad!"

We walked up to Jason's front door. Suddenly I realized that this golden bully boy had political connections and family members who had been arrested by Robert's daddy.

"Ring the bell, Robert, and when you see Jason, just say, 'I'm sorry,'" I instructed my seven-year-old son. "Just hand him the new lunchbox and we'll turn around and leave."

Jason's mother answered the door. Before either of us could say anything, she snatched the new lunchbox, said, "Good. You're a stupid little fuck," and slammed the door in our faces.

In the car, Robert said, "I didn't even see Jason to say I was sorry. Why was his mommy so mean?"

I stopped the car and looked directly at my son and explained, "Not all families live by the same principles that we do. Jason and his mommy should have accepted your apology and shook your hand, and Jason should have been made to understand that what he said to you was wrong. He should have apologized to you a long time ago. You used good thinking skills when you

hit the lunchbox instead of Jason's face. You shouldn't have to endure mean comments and insults from a bully, and I'm proud of you for standing up for yourself. You took the high road by not hitting him. That's more important than bullying and hatred."

Robert threw his arms around me and said, "I know, Mommy."

The third time this happened with the same bully, the school summoned me for another conference. I was no longer a tiny, newly widowed, easy-to-intimidate pushover. I had Bob, a handsome new friend who was 6'2" and not one bit afraid of the school staff. I took him along to the conference.

The teacher opened the comments by saying that she and the committee had been right in their opinion that Robert needed medication. She went on to say, "Now, as we predicted, he's dangerous to the other children. He attacked a boy in his class with scissors"—little, blunt children's scissors—"and threatened him by saying he'd gouge his eyes out. He destroyed the boy's property in an act of hatred in the cafeteria. The most recent incident involved Robert describing what the boy's mother said to him when he replaced the smashed lunchbox. He used vulgar language, and we all know she wouldn't say such a thing to a child. He clearly needs medication and special classes. I rest my case, Gail. He's out of control and I will not have him in my classroom."

Pounding my fist on the table as I stood, I asked, "Do you have any idea what made Robert react like that?"

She replied, "Why, not a thing. He just jumped up and thrust the scissors at the boy's face. Then, a few days later, he smashed Jason's lunch box. Now he's used the F-word in front of the whole class. He needs Ritalin, just like we said."

Bob unfolded his huge frame and said in his Pittsburgh drawl, "No disrespect, ma'am, but I questioned the boy after you called Gail, and he said that another little boy—a teacher's son and the grandson of a politician, I believe—made some inappropriate remarks to him about making a Christmas card for his dead daddy. What do you know about that?"

"That's a lie, an outright lie," the teacher yelled.

"Well, we took the liberty of calling the art teacher and lunchroom monitor at home, and they both said Jason told Robert he couldn't make a card for his daddy because of the suicide. Did the art teacher and monitor both lie?"

The teacher pounded her fist on the conference table and yelled, "I don't care what that innocent little boy said to your kid. Your kid cannot threaten anyone with scissors or destroy anyone's personal property."

Bob said, "We don't want him to threaten or hurt anyone, either. But you need to understand that we don't want him to be bullied or intimidated by anyone. You don't seem to be able to control your class enough to prevent that, or seem smart enough to recognize it. So I'll tell you what I told Robert. If that boy ever says such a thing to him again, and if you interfere when he attempts to defend himself, he should kick you in the shins, run to a phone, and call me. I'll deal with you myself. Let's go home, Gail. This meeting is over. It's not just the kids who are out-of-control bullies here; it's the whole damned place."

We took Robert out of school and spent Monday through Friday in Pittsburgh with Bob, who lived on the edge of the elementary-school playground. I enrolled Robert there. I quit the school bus driving job and came home each weekend to take care of the farm. Peggy checked the house and picked up my mail. It was a difficult decision, but necessary for Robert's self-esteem and education.

I went to the principal, who had supported the unprofessional teacher, and requested that Robert's scholastic records be sent to the new school. The principal said he'd send the complete file.

The new school was large, with a graduating class of over five hundred each year. Several elementary schools made up the district, and the records from home didn't find their destination until springtime.

Robert walked across the playground every day to get to school. After he'd attended for about three weeks, I was summoned for a conference. I thought there was a problem and I prepared myself for some sort of difficulty. It was a long walk across the playground, and I felt like I was going to an execution.

The new teacher, a plump, middle-aged woman with kind eyes, met me with a friendly handshake and a big smile. I immediately felt she was a friend, not a foe. "It's a pleasure to meet Robert's mom," she said. "Thank you for coming in. You have such a nice, bright little boy."

After making several positive comments, she said, "I have a couple of questions. Can you help me understand what kind of school system Robert is coming from? His records haven't arrived yet. On the first day of school, I seated him in the middle row, second seat back. He looked at me with those big, beautiful blue eyes and asked me if I was sure he could sit with the rest of the children, right in the middle of the classroom. I told him of course he could, and I explained that I wanted him to be where I could see him in case he didn't understand something. He said that in his old school, the teacher made him sit in the back corner of the room, all by himself. Second, when we go outside to play, he stands right beside me. I told him he could go play with the kids, and he said, 'Oh, no, my old teacher said I was dangerous and that I had to stand by her. I wasn't allowed to play.' What in the world was going on there?" she asked.

I told her about Robert's father, the suicide, the aftermath of the IQ testing, and all about the bullying. She was incensed. She said he was a bright, normal little boy who was great socially with the other kids.

She was instrumental in having a news reporter from a nearby city paper come to interview me at the school while I provided homemade grape juice from our farm for everyone. I presented a slide show about our grape farm and demonstrated how to make grapevine wreaths and baskets. The program had the desired effect, and Robert made more new friends. What a difference in school districts.

His behavior was much improved, but he was still active and extremely talkative. He passed all his classes, and for two and a half years we traveled home every weekend to take care of my farm.

While I lived in Pittsburgh, I continued to follow the advice about finding things to do to stay mentally and physically active. I worked construction every day with Bob.

I signed up for an evening creative-writing class at a nearby college and the professor was a published author who wrote detective stories and travel articles for several major publications. She asked what had motivated me to move to Pittsburgh, and I shared my background. She said she wanted to write a travel article about the grape industry and Lake Erie. She accompanied us to western New York one weekend and commented that Robert talked a lot and pointed out that he was more active when he ate artificially colored candy and ice cream. I noted her observation but didn't really pay a lot of attention to it.

It became necessary to move back to Westfield to take care of my farm. I enrolled Robert in the troublesome school system once more, where the persecution and difficulties were instantaneous.

We coped with it, discussed it, and didn't see any alternative until I visited my dentist. Of course, my dentist insisted on speaking to me when my mouth was numb and full of cotton rolls, tools, and his fingers. "How's your boy doing in school?"

he asked. "I hear a lot of horror stories about the teacher in question."

Before I could attempt a mumbled reply, he continued sarcastically, "A lot of times I've often wondered if Mrs. Professional Teacher just had to have a whipping boy to cover up her inadequacies in the classroom. I bet it went just fine in that school system you found in Pennsylvania."

I nodded.

He seemed to enjoy having the floor, and he continued to elaborate. "Twenty-two other parents couldn't take the undeserved support that awful teacher received from the principal and school board. It made them want to puke and now they drive fifteen miles one way every day to get their kids a decent education and a fair shake."

Now he was drilling my tooth. My mouth was stretched open so far I couldn't even mumble. He took the opportunity to enlighten me further. "I'm so glad you came in today," he said. "I've thought about calling you, because I heard from some of my other patients that Robert is back in school here. I also heard a lot of horror stories about the old gang of politicians' kids and grandkids finding new, secret ways of picking on your boy. Did you know that?"

I knocked his hand away from my mouth, sat upright, and screamed, "What did you just say?"

He looked shocked and sympathetic as he continued. "I didn't think you knew. Ask around, and if you confirm what I just told you, call me—I'll give you a name at the school they found for their kids."

When I got home, I asked Robert about his treatment at school, and he said, "Same old stuff, different year."

One of Robert's classmates, a boy whose mother often worked in my vineyards, was severely burned, and we went to visit him when he got out of the burn unit. He said to Robert, "You need to get out of our school, Rob. The kids blow their noses and put the dirty tissues in your desk. They take your homework out of your desk and throw it in the wastebasket while the teacher's out of the room and they distract you."

Robert confessed to me, "I didn't want trouble with the teacher, so I didn't tell you. The teacher thinks I'm not doing my homework because I can't ever find it, even though I know I put it in my desk. She calls me a liar when I say I did it. I didn't want to tell you because this is a new teacher, and teachers are always right, you know."

Only a day later, the troublesome principal called and said, "Robert is disorganized and never turns in his homework. He's a distraction in the classroom, and his stories about doing his homework make the other kids laugh until the teacher loses control of the class. Unless you're willing to let the school administer Ritalin, he's no longer welcome here as a student. The school board agrees with this decision, and there will be no discussion."

Bob and I went to see the school that had welcomed and was successfully educating the other twenty-two exiled students. The principal told us that he was chairman of the committee on the handicapped in our county. He pointed to a book in the middle of the table, which contained the rules and guidelines for labeling children with ADHD and other learning disabilities. He turned to a certain section and put the book down, saying the book was only for the committee. Then he winked and said he needed to make a phone call and would be gone for twenty minutes. We read the pages. We knew that Robert was talkative and active, but he did not fit the profile and should not have been labeled.

The kind man told us he would welcome my son in his school. He looked at the scholastic records I had from Pennsylvania and Westfield and said he thought Robert would be a wonderful addition to their student body. We shook hands, and I paid the small tuition. I began to drive a total of fifty-two miles a day to transport Robert to his new school.

It seemed that the more friends and contacts I made, the more people with helpful insights came forward. Their interest and support were comforting.

Soon it was Martin Luther King Day in 1984, a school holiday. My former creative-writing teacher from Pittsburgh called and said, "Gail, turn your television on. There's a program about kids with food allergies, and the kids look and act like Robert when he's hyper and talkative."

Robert's new teachers had assured me that he did talk too much. I turned the TV on and listened to Dr. Doris Rapp, a renowned pediatric allergist and an expert on the effects of food allergies on children. She said allergies to milk products were the worst culprit; children with such allergies had a lack of attention, were unable to perform their work at an acceptable level, and appeared to be hyperactive. The children on the program who were experiencing these reactions behaved exactly like Robert.

She said that if a person has a food allergy, it is usually to a food he or she either loves or hates. She recommended taking all dairy products away from the child for three days and then giving them back in large portions, and said that milk was the most common culprit. Robert loved milk, ice cream, and cheese; she had my full attention. If the child was allergic, his or her eyes would swell, ears would turn red, and cheeks would flush; he or she would exhibit hyperactive behavior and would be unable to read, write, or do simple mathematical exercises in a consistent manner.

I immediately threw away all the dairy products in our house. For three days, I let Robert have juice and pop, but no dairy. After the first day, when I picked him up after school, his teacher came all the way out to the car. She said, "You should take Rob to the doctor. I don't think he feels well. He just sat in his seat, did his work, and didn't talk."

After the second day, she said, "If you didn't take Rob to the doctor, you better. Today the teacher next door asked if he was absent, because she couldn't hear his shrill voice next door in her room."

After the third day, she really got on my case. "He's acting really strange," she said. "He's quiet, his writing is completely legible, and he got 100 on all his papers—even the spelling words the first time they were given. The art teacher and the gym teacher think he's sick, too."

I told her we were experimenting with something new and that I would let her know what we found out. On the way home, I bought Robert a big ice-cream cone and gave him a glass of milk as soon as we got home. Then, as Dr. Rapp had suggested, I gave him paper and a pencil and a spelling test with ten words. He wrote the first one pretty well, but by the fifth one, his writing wasn't legible. After number eight, he threw the pencil, tore the paper, and pounded his head on the wall. He ran upstairs to his room, screaming, "I can't do this. I hate you. Why are you doing this to me? My ears are on fire, and my face burns." He started to sob as he lay on his bed.

I gathered him up in my arms and soothed, "At least we know what's wrong. All the trouble is not your fault. I love you. You're a good boy, and you're really smart. You're just allergic to milk."

He looked up through his tears and said, "I know, Mom."

At our first appointment with Dr. Rapp, she gave Robert a complete physical. Then she took a detailed history of when the problem started, how it had progressed, and all the difficulty with the school system.

One of the things I loved about Dr. Rapp was that she tested her patients and then had a lab in her office facility make up treatments for each patient individually. Robert had multiple allergies to food, dust, molds, trees, flowers—everything except green beans and cherries. On his new regimen, his school and social interactions showed marked improvement.

Life was easier, my work schedule returned to normal, and I caught up on my farm work.

Chapter Sixteen: Expanding the Farming Business, 1986-1993

On a sunny summer afternoon in 1986, while Bob was in Pittsburgh visiting his family, a neighbor, Mr. Ray, drove down my driveway and told me I needed to buy his picking business. I thought he was way out in a left grape field. "I don't want your grape picker. It's all I can do just to keep my forty acres of grapes growing and the equipment I already have greased and running," I remembered saying as I shook a wrench at him from under a tractor.

"Come out from under there, and listen to me. I'm going to make you an offer you can't refuse. You have too many acres of grapes to pay someone else to pick them," he continued as he stood there peeking under the tractor at me.

I slid out and wiped my greasy hands on the rag hanging out of my back pocket. While I was at it, I wiped some mud off my chin. "What don't you understand? Can't you see that I'm working at capacity here?" I said. "I'm not interested, period. You couldn't offer me any deal I'd even want to hear. And why do you want to sell the business, if it's so great?"

"My wife is sick. She needs to get off the farm and stop the work and worry. She said I should tell you we want you to buy the business. We could sell it to a lot of folks, but she's worked right beside me for years, and she wants you to have it," he said softly. There was sadness in his voice, and I instantly decided to listen.

"Okay. Lay it on me, the whole deal."

"Gail, we'll sell you the harvester, two John Deere tractors, three wagons, fifty-two one-ton picking bins, and a Massey Ferguson tractor with a Henry Loader so you can load the bins on the three trucks that are also included. We'll throw in a power washer and a five-acre grape vineyard and give you the contract to take care of and pick the grapes around our house."

I was flabbergasted. I explained my hesitation. "I don't know the first thing about the picking business," I started to say, but Mr. Ray interrupted me.

"My wife thought of that argument, and she said to tell you that we've already talked to our picking crew, and they've agreed to work for you for the next three years at least. They could run it on their own, for that matter. I'll see you through the first two seasons and teach you about the equipment and scheduling the picking contracts with the processors. We pick for twenty-one other farms, and you also get six custom farming contracts. My wife has watched you for the last fourteen years, ever since you bought the grapes in front of your house. She knows you'll work hard. We want only $42,000 for all of it. The harvester alone is worth that."

"I have to think about it. Let me get a cup of coffee and let the shock of the offer settle on my busy brain for a few minutes. Please come back in an hour or so, and I'll give you an answer," I said.

I went in for the coffee, and Mirror was waiting for me. "You left the front door open, and I heard that. What an offer. How could you even think of refusing? You already have the Carhartt coveralls and the good old boys at the grape harvesting plant will never guess you're a woman when you pull that cap over your head. Go for it."

I called my farm-lending institution, briefly outlined the offer, and asked if they would lend me the money. I had become credible in the farming community, so unlike the banker I had to coerce to buy the first grape vineyard, they had confidence in me and said the check would be in that day's mail. They didn't even ask me for collateral. I planned to use the money I made harvesting other people's grapes to make the payments.

Bob returned the following week. "Babe, I'm delighted that *we* own a picking business. I'll operate the harvester."

Mirror heard him and whispered, "It's not your picking business, asshole. Your name is not on the titles or the loan. In fact, I doubt you could even get a loan for a farm business." I looked sharply at Mirror, who continued, "Look out, young lady. I smell something rotten." Mirror made me wonder where this greedy assumption of ownership would lead.

CHAPTER SEVENTEEN: MORE SCHOOL PROBLEMS, AND BACK TO HELL, 1984-1989

AFTER THREE AND A half years of successful education and wonderful school experiences with many new friends, the Chautauqua School District announced that it could no longer accept any of the twenty-two tuition-paying kids from Westfield. The Chautauqua school's classes were full, and space in their junior and senior high schools was limited. We all had to go back to our own school district or find other options.

Robert and I made our way with caution and trepidation to speak with the high school principal about Rob's enrollment in Westfield. We reassured each other that at least we were not going to see the principal and teachers at the grade school. We assured each other that we had successful records from both the Pennsylvania and Chautauqua school districts. All his grades were passing, and we had letters of recommendation, support, and success from his teachers.

After presenting all of those records in a folder that also contained several newspaper articles about Robert's experiences in Pennsylvania and the science fair at Chautauqua, the principal said we would have to wait for a ruling from the school board.

A week went by, and the principal of the junior/senior high school finally summoned us. "I'm sorry to inform you of our ruling on your enrollment at Westfield," he said. "We've decided not to accept your records from Pennsylvania and Chautauqua. Those schools don't operate with the same professionalism that we demand and enjoy here in Westfield. We have to take you back, Robert, because you live in the district, but we have the right to insist that if you do come back into our system, you'll repeat seventh grade."

I felt my blood pressure and adrenalin rise and explode over the top when I stood up and said, "What the hell do you mean you can't accept this exceptional and complete record of Robert's accomplishments? Every single teacher he's known and worked with has written letters attesting to his exemplary behavior, high intelligence, and perseverance in achieving above-average grades while overcoming health issues. What is wrong with you people?"

"I'm truly sorry, Robert. This is *not* my decision or my recommendation. However, the Board of Education has made the ruling. If you don't repeat seventh grade, we don't have to accept you back into this school system." the principal said.

He was new in his position, and I could sense that he was troubled by the message he had to deliver. "If I were you," he continued, "I'd repeat seventh grade. It will be easy for you, number one; and, number two, you won't be exposed to the same old crowd you encountered here in your early grade-school years."

I had done some investigating and knew that if I asked to see Robert's records, they had to allow it. I stood up and said, "The decision is Robert's to make. I won't advise him. But at this time, I'd like to have him wait in your office—where he'll be safe, I trust—while you produce the file of his records from when he attended school here."

"Mrs. Black, it will take time to retrieve that file. If you come in tomorrow afternoon, I'll have it available for you," the principal said, standing to gather his papers.

"I have all day, today. I know you must have those records available, because you seem to have read them—you're new here, with no memory of Robert's history. I also know that by law you have to produce them. I will wait as long as it takes."

He shrugged, smiled, and winked as he said, "I'll see what I can do."

I felt that the new principal was at least fair and maybe sympathetic to our cause. I spent the waiting time mentally reviewing Robert's history with the school. In my purse I had a list of things to look for in the file. I knew that anything that was not true could be expunged.

Sure enough, the original IQ score and the notation that Robert was borderline retarded was the only IQ record in his file. The notes from his early grade-school teacher saying that he was dangerous to his classmates were there, but not a word about bullying was mentioned. A long letter describing me as a troublesome, uncooperative, and unstable parent who gave my child drugs was included, but it did not identify the drugs as baby aspirin. It was extremely difficult and upsetting to read the file. No report cards or grades were included. Anyone who read the file would get only the former principal's and teacher's points of view.

I returned the file to the principal when I went to get Robert. "I'd like copies of every paper in the file, please," I said. "You don't have to get them today; I made notes on what was in there. I'll pick them up when they're ready."

The principal said, "You sound like you know that legally we have to do that for you, is that correct?"

"Yes, it is."

"There will be a charge of twenty-five cents a page. Have you sought legal counsel in this matter?" he asked with a furrowed brow.

"I've spoken to my attorney in Buffalo, but I haven't given him a retainer yet. I've also spoken to Robert's pediatric allergist, Dr. Doris Rapp, in Buffalo. If Robert decides to come back to Westfield, I'll have a letter and file for you from her. He'll miss one day a week because of his allergy testing and treatment and will need a special aide to help him with the classes he misses. Dr. Rapp tells me that legally you have to provide that."

"Not unless you let us label him ADHD and give him Ritalin, which, I am told, was the original conflict between you and the school." The principal crossed his arms and looked confrontational.

"Shall I contact my attorney to clarify that, sir?" I asked.

"Let's not get ahead of ourselves. Decide if he's coming into our system, and I'll try to work with you if I can," he said, seeming to have a little change of attitude.

After considering the idea of repeating seventh grade, Robert concluded that the principal was right in saying he would be with a new group of students. His decision to take the principal's advice seemed to create a bond between them. The principal's support and guidance were valuable assets until Robert graduated.

The years swiftly passed; Bob spent much of his time pursuing his own interests in Pittsburgh; I took Robert for his allergy treatments every week and the rest of the time was used up on the farm.

———————————

The harvest season was nearly upon us, and I felt lucky that Bob was willing to get the equipment in good working order. I concentrated on contacting our customers, carrying out sugar-solids tests on the grapes, and meeting with the processors to agree on picking schedules.

The grape harvest got underway, and Bob became more disagreeable with every success Robert had. As Robert had gotten older, he had taken on more responsibility on the farm and worked long hours pruning the vineyards. He had also learned to operate the harvester and gotten his tractor certifications and driver's license; he loved to fill in for any of our harvesting crew who needed time off. One day, one of our harvesting-crew members, who had been working for us for years, called Bob over and said, "You know, Bob, you have a big ass, but it isn't big enough to sit on all the tractor seats at the same time. Why don't you let Gail and Robert run some of this equipment without hassling them?"

That angered Bob so much that he threatened to fire the man, who was seventy-seven years old and the best mechanic we had. I refused to let that happen, and there was a huge disagreement, causing us to miss our scheduled loads for that day.

We finished the harvest season before the processors closed their doors for the year. Robert successfully completed his withdrawal from allergy treatments and had a great senior year in school, complete with the Future Farmers of America convention in Kansas City and a class trip to Washington, DC. He was accepted into an agricultural program at Alfred State College.

The summer before he started college, Robert went to work for a local campground, mowing, cleaning bathrooms, escorting campers to their sites, and doing many other odd jobs. He spent the rest of his time working in the vineyards, but the tension between him and Bob did not diminish. Bob was always finding fault with him and asking me to choose between their opposing opinions. I was concerned about Robert's self-esteem and Bob and I fought often.

Harvest season faded into a memory, and cold wind and snow howled across Lake Erie once again, creating whiteouts on the highways and impassable driveways along the shoreline. A new friend appeared unexpectedly out of the storm.

Chapter Eighteen: Containerboard, New Friends, and Community Challenges, 1990-1994

I HAD BUNDLED UP for a trip to the grocery store, and the truck didn't want to crank over. Finally it started, I engaged the four-wheel drive for the dash up the driveway through four-foot drifts; clouds of snow completely obscured the path, and I tried to gauge where the wheel tracks were. I reached the road and moved into zero visibility. A few hundred yards down the road, a car was parked by the driveway of a house that was for sale. I slowed, wondering why the car had stopped, and as I did I saw a small young woman running and falling as she made her way through the drifted snow down the long driveway. I stopped, blew the horn, got out and yelled above the wind, "No one lives there. Do you need help?"

She followed her own tracks back toward me until I could hear her. "I was just passing by and saw the for-sale sign," she shouted. "I have to see this property, because I'm going to buy it. It's exactly where I'm supposed to be." I was shocked to hear nearly the same words I had spoken on that long-ago day when I'd found my home at Vinewood Acres. It had now been my home for twenty years.

"I live next door, a couple houses back. If you need anything, stop and see me. There's nobody down this driveway, just an empty log cabin, and it's locked. I'll check and see that you get out okay when I come back from town." I drove on.

A few days later, the young woman knocked on my door. "I'm the girl who was running down your neighbor's driveway," she said when I answered. "My name is Judith."

I made tea, and she told me her story. "I'm from Cincinnati, and I came here a few months ago to work at a factory in the next town. I live in the condos west of here, and I bought your neighbor's house the day after I saw you. I just know I'm supposed to be there," she explained, giving me a look that said she didn't expect me to understand. Someday I would tell her that this was exactly how I'd ended up in my home.

"Welcome to the neighborhood. When are you moving in?" I inquired.

"I already did. I don't have much, a futon, a few dishes, and my clothes. I'll furnish it as I go. It doesn't matter, because I know I'm supposed to be there. It's pretty isolated, so I'm glad you're over here. I hope we get to be good friends."

Neither of us had any idea how intense our friendship would become. I remember inviting Judith for dinner and a glass of wine. The friendship grew as Judith sought information on gardening, the trees and plants growing on her property, garbage pickup times, names of neighbors, snow removal, gravel for the driveway, contractors' names, and thousands of other things. She worried about having paid too much for the house.

A few weeks later, the local newspaper reported that a new factory was going to be built in our town. I called Judith.

"Did you see today's paper?" I asked.

"No. Why?"

"Because there's a new factory coming to Westfield and your property will increase in value. You didn't pay too much for it, so stop worrying."

"What kind of factory?"

"It's a cardboard-recycling mill coming from Canada."

"God, no, don't tell me that. Where will it be located?"

"It's planned for right across the road, on the other side of the thruway."

"That's awful. Do you think it's the one they called Dunkirk Containerboard?" she asked.

"They're calling it Containerboard. It's supposed to be a $210 million project," I replied. "It'll be wonderful. There will be jobs, and the economy will grow. Our taxes will go down."

"I'll be right over to see the paper. I have a degree in finance and development, and I worked in Beijing and with the redevelopment of Washington, DC, and New York City. See you in a minute," she said. Over a cup of tea, Judith explained that she had accepted a job as a financial planner at a local ink factory here because she was tired of traveling. She said that the cardboard-recycling mill would smell and discharge chemicals into the air and water, and she doubted that it would be pretty. She insisted that our taxes would only go up, no matter what the developers said.

A few days later, I loaded my new video camera into the truck and set out for Canada, where I planned to photograph the parent plant and model for this Containerboard factory. It took the better part of the morning to locate it. I drove around Ontario until I noticed a lot of cardboard and paper that had blown against the airport fence; then I followed the trail along the roadway and ditches for miles. Suddenly I spotted the factory, a large, square blue building. There weren't any "No Trespassing" or "Keep Out" signs, so I drove through the truck entrance. As I rounded the corner of the building, the factory's neat, clean appearance changed. Acres of bales of rotting, used cardboard were strewn about and loose pieces blew around the enclosure.

A plume of steam and smoke and an acrid smell billowed out of the back of the building. A man on a forklift was bringing bales of cardboard to the building. The temperature was twenty degrees, and I saw that the ground was covered with freezing black liquid when I got out of the truck with my camera to take pictures of the mess. I had to step from one frozen lump of cardboard to another to walk through the black gunk, which I later learned was called "black liquor," a byproduct or discharge from the paper-making process. The forklift operator posed and waved, proud to be in my video.

The smell was nauseating and musty and stung my nose. I took a lot of pictures as I watched the forklift operator stockpile the dirty cardboard inside the factory.

I couldn't believe that anyone would actually be happy to have such a mess in our pristine, beautiful, grape-growing town. When I got home, I invited all the town officials to my house to see exactly what was coming.

Meanwhile, Judith had obtained a copy of the Environmental Assessment Form (EAF), because I had doubted her claims about the huge number of trucks that would haul in cardboard. I also had doubted her claim that the factory would smell.

I read the EAF and could not believe that two hundred trucks a day would travel to Westfield from Canada, bringing used cardboard from the Canadian chemical industry to the new factory, where it would be cooked up and made into new recycled-cardboard boxes. The description reminded me of a witch's caldron, in which the chemical residue on miscellaneous pieces of cardboard would be cooked and discharged into the air and water behind our central school and rural hospital.

The EAF also disclosed that the same trucks would take the recycled cardboard back to Canada. I learned the definitions of the phrases "turnkey operation" and "green card," which indicated that most of the building jobs and employees would be coming from Canada. I learned that the factory was a highly technical, computerized operation. I expressed my concerns and fears to the town-board members, town supervisor, and mayor when they came to view my video.

The Westfield politicians and community leaders said I'd gone to the wrong factory. They said cardboard recycling was clean and did not smell. They said they'd been told that by our county-development leaders.

Judith and I found twenty-five other residents who were willing to read the EAF and related documents. After researching similar projects in other locations, we insisted on a complete environmental review known as an Environmental Impact Study (EIS), which, by law, would disclose all aspects of the proposed project, including both financial and environmental impacts on the local community. Our local politicians and officials in charge of economic development said an EIS was not necessary, because cardboard recycling was for the public good and, therefore, not subject to environmental laws. They said an EIS would cost too much money; they claimed that we needed the jobs and that they did not want to burden the company with that kind of expense.

There were too many red flags. Judith thought the paper mill promoters and the politicians with agendas were lying; I thought they were really defensive. I knew that the factory I'd photographed was, in fact, the model for the one they wanted to build here.

I went to a county legislative meeting, where I took the first privilege of the floor, because the Containerboard project was on the agenda. I spoke about what I'd seen, my video, and my fear that this factory would decrease property values, our standard of living, and our community's appearance and adversely impact our grape-juice industry.

Two days later, the development leaders announced that there would be a bus tour to see the parent cardboard-recycling factory in Canada for the elected officials; any leftover seats would be available to private citizens on a first-come basis. Judith signed up and made the list. They did not know her or that she was a friend of mine. She took pictures, which matched my video except that all the cardboard had been cleaned up from along the fences on the way there. The field of rotting cardboard now appeared neat and orderly, and the baled cardboard was nearly gone. The parking lot was an expanse of clean pavement, with nothing coming out of the pipe on the blacktop. Most of us clean our houses when we expect company, and that's just what the recycling factory did.

The bus-tour sponsors said I had photographed the wrong factory and that there was no smell or bad emissions of any kind. In essence, they called me a liar.

Judith and I got angry. We formed a Containerboard Watch Group with twenty-five other interested people to ensure that the truth was told and that an EIS would be done. The group met weekly or as necessary in my living room.

We learned that Canada would institute a freedom-of-information law on April 1, 1991, and we had our request on the minister of environment's desk on that day. It was granted, and we received a packet in the mail containing many incident reports. The ministry had told the company calling itself Containerboard to cease their polluting operation in Canada immediately. No wonder they wanted to build in our neighborhood—they had nowhere to go. The incident reports cited repeated pollution of a Canadian creek and lake with dioxin. The reports also detailed how pollutants were discharged via a pipe from the factory onto the parking lot, which was graded to a forty-two-inch storm-sewer drain that led directly to a creek draining into one of the Great Lakes. The reports concluded that the damage was irreversible.

Through the Freedom of Information Act (FOIA), we immediately applied for surface-drainage engineering studies from our local county-finance department, the development office, and every other agency that might have the studies. We were able to get surface-water and -drainage engineering studies and learned that the plant would discharge thousands of gallons of three-hundred-degree water with enough volume to scour the sides of the numbered and registered Spring Creek. That lovely stream meandered through my farm, carrying sparkling, clean, clear water to Lake Erie. The study said that the discharge would kill any wildlife therein and that the discharge would happen weekly and maybe more often. We knew it would forever change the pristine water. Our "small group," as the promoters began to call us, compared the studies we'd acquired locally with the ones from Canada. The only major difference was the final destination of the hot, polluted water, which was Lake Erie instead of one of the other Great Lakes. We noted that the point of the discharge into Lake Erie was smack in the middle of the best smallmouth-bass breeding area in the world.

We used the FOIA extensively and successfully with every agency in New York State that might have touched the project. Judith developed techniques that helped to prohibit state agencies from removing material from requested files. The more we received and read, the more concerned our small group became.

One day, a woman called me and said, "My name is Lois Gibbs. I understand you're having some difficulty with a company that intends to site a highly polluting company in your community. I'm calling to offer my assistance. Perhaps you recall hearing my name associated with the Love Canal." I was immediately on high alert because Love Canal was a large neighborhood in Niagara Falls, New York. It was famous because hundreds of families were relocated due to chemical contamination of their land. The area was fenced and abandoned for decades. Lois Gibbs led the fight to get justice for the sick families who lived there. I confirmed that I knew who she was, quickly outlined our problem, and requested all the help she could offer—then explained that we had no money. She gave me the name and phone number of a Canadian activist named Pat.

Soon arrangements were made for a visit by the activist's boat. She would bring her yellow tug boat from Port Maitland, Canada to Barcelona Harbor which lies on the northern border of the Town of Westfield on Lake Erie. Pat would pilot the boat named the "*NIMBI*," which stands for "now I must become involved," a play on the word "NIMBY," which means "not in my backyard." After completing a thirty-five-mile trip south, across Lake Erie, and through the projected point of paper mill discharge, she arrived amid television and newspaper reporters that our group had also invited. The event increased awareness of the environmental problems that might result from cardboard recycling in our town.

Several meetings with Pat ensued. She was instrumental in helping us find an attorney named David Seeger, who represented us *pro bono*. At first, Mr. Seeger was not interested in our case due to time constraints, but when I offered to explain the project over a special home-cooked, roast beef dinner, homemade apple sauce, bread and pies he agreed to hear our concerns. He ate, listened, nodded, ate, listened, and finally managed to speak when Judith and I stopped to catch our breath. By the time the food had disappeared, he had agreed to represent us in our pursuit of an EIS.

Mr. Seeger was a handsome, studious, conservative young man who dressed impeccably and possessed a quiet demeanor. He took all the paperwork we had accumulated and called a few days later to tell us that after reading the EAF, he was sure we had a case, and he would be honored to help us protect the clean water and air along the south shore of Lake Erie. He agreed to attend the first public hearing held in our local town hall.

On the evening of the hearing, I prepared another homemade dinner, and Judith organized notes and news clippings to add to Mr. Seeger's growing portfolio. She and I were a bit apprehensive about the reception we would receive at the town hall. When the meeting commenced, the town supervisor announced that everyone was welcome to speak except me. He said into the microphone, "Gail Black is represented by a Buffalo attorney, and he's going to speak on her behalf." He looked directly at me and said, "You will not take the floor at this meeting, Gail."

The first woman to speak was politically connected and in a position to gain thousands of dollars if she supported the paper-mill project. She hissed into the microphone to the capacity crowd, "I'm here to speak in favor of jobs and economic development in our community. I don't have to hide behind a high-priced, out-of-town attorney." Most of the people cheered.

The quiet city attorney leaned over to Judith and me and whispered "Doesn't take a rocket scientist to see that those two are assholes."

Mr. Seeger took the microphone next and calmly explained the legalities of and need for a full EIS. He then read the law concerning public hearings and reminded the town supervisor that he did not make the rules but that the rules were clearly spelled out in the law and everyone was entitled to speak at a public hearing if they chose to. Then he handed me the microphone. I told the crowd that I was not against jobs and economic development and that I only wanted it done safely, with full disclosure to the citizens of the community. Sparse applause spread throughout the crowd, but loud boos, chants, and catcalls exploded from the back of the room. The meeting was called to order, and a slightly more restrained atmosphere prevailed.

The predevelopment team moved forward with their plans to build the dirty, smelly factory in the midst of our three thousand acres of beautiful vineyards and gentle rolling hills close to the shoreline of Lake Erie.

Three years of public speaking, civil disobedience, drawing and distribution of cartoons depicting the effects of cardboard recycling, phone calls, meetings, and demonstrations followed.

Our small group was soon joined by a dozen more concerned citizens who were also disillusioned with political shenanigans.

Bob, who had so valiantly defended Robert and me throughout our school problems, was incensed and appalled by the project, as well as by the treatment I received at public meetings. Countless times, I felt his love as he physically stood between me and irate community members who believed they would get rich if the politicians and developers successfully located the paper mill in our town. Because he was not local, was not intimidated, and spoke out against the environmental abuse, especially to the fishing industry in Lake Erie, where he loved to fish, he took the brunt of the name calling. He was the person politicians and developers liked to blame for all kinds of perceived damage to the project. Local opportunists referred to him as "Gail Black's dumb dildo."

Some of the other people who joined our group when it met in my living room each week were bright, brave and committed folks. They were engineers, teachers, antique dealers, farmers, scientists, financial wizards, business owners, housewives, insurance brokers, fishermen, hunters, professors, office workers, attorneys and more. They came from as far away as Toronto, Canada and New York City, Cleveland, Pittsburgh, West Virginia and Washington DC, and each contributed expertise from his or her own circle of influence. Most of them found out about our battle from word of mouth. Financial contributions poured in from odd sources; these were usually cash, because the contributors were afraid of retribution.

Judith and I had each invested approximately $20,000 of our own money to the cause, in addition to the contributions. Our concerned-citizens group spent three years scrutinizing each page of each available document pertaining to the project, searching for environmental problems, financial inconsistencies, political back-scratching deals, and untruths.

We agreed unanimously that the project was ugly and needed an EIS. Our group's research indicated that the cardboard-recycling plant was a for-profit business, being built by a private company. We wanted the EIS to disclose to the general public all the ramifications of the project for our community and agricultural area. The project met several of the legal criteria required to mandate a complete EIS: it was a $210 million enterprise that drew and discharged over a million gallons of water a day from an international body of water; it was being situated on land that was a potential wetland, with a water table only six inches below the surface; and it included many more red flags.

The Containerboard Watch Group, as we finally named ourselves, decided to file a lawsuit to ensure that full disclosure was accomplished, enabling our fellow citizens to make an informed decision on whether this controversial project was acceptable in our community. We voted unanimously that the lawsuit would be for disclosure only, to uncover the unscrupulous principles involved; it wouldn't be for damages or costs. We agreed that suing for money of any kind would be punishing our fellow citizens, whose only crime was voting for the elected officials we felt were pursuing personal agendas. We paid all the court costs and all other bills with our own private funds.

When it was finally over, the fracas had consumed four years of my life. I'd been filled with fear when gunshots were fired into my mailbox and the nuts on my vehicles' wheels were loosened. Robert had been required to stand before his class while a teacher's aide announced that I didn't have a college education and discredited any facts connected with me or the committee as a whole. The brake lines on my grape-delivery trucks had been sawed in half, and terrifying messages had been left on my answering machine.

I will never forget the day we went to court with the lawsuit. An involved attorney confronted me on the courthouse stairs and said, "Well, Gail, if it's too hot in the kitchen, you better get out. You're going to lose today."

We won the lawsuit on all three counts in New York State Supreme Court that day; an EIS was legally required, and all the things we had disclosed were proven beyond a doubt. I hurried to catch up with the attorney as he practically ran down the stairs in the courthouse and said, "What's wrong, sir? Was it so hot in the kitchen that you're running out of there?"

The paper-recycling mill was never built in our town. Two hundred truckloads of dirty cardboard and paper did not arrive daily from the chemical industry in Canada; and trucks never had the opportunity to take recycled boxes back to Canada. Concord-grape vineyards within a radius of ten miles were able to continue growing, unaffected by the increased moisture that would have originated from the proposed plant. The school and hospital do not have to exist in a plume of chemical fallout from discharge stacks that would have been built at less-than-good-engineering-practice height. My farm would not be compromised by paper-mill discharges. We won.

People I had formerly called friends scurried from grocery-store aisles rather than speak to me, and any time a scapegoat was needed, my name surfaced. The town no longer needed me as a member on any volunteer boards or as chairperson of their cancer drive. They ostracized me completely.

Three and a half years of terrible, stressful experiences added to the tension already present in my ten-year relationship with Bob.

CHAPTER NINETEEN: THE
VIOLENT END OF BOB, 1993

ONE DAY, A FRIEND from Pittsburgh called and said, "Gail, if a woman calls and asks for Bob, tell her you don't know where he is. She's trying to find him. She's the reason for his divorce. She told me point-blank that she wants him back in her life."

"I don't think we have any problems between us, so why would I do that?" I asked.

"You just don't know her. Please listen to me, Gail. His family asked me to call you. We all love you, and we know what this woman is like. Just listen to us," she argued.

Sure enough, the "other woman from his past" called and asked for Bob. I told her to call back the next day, because I wanted to prepare him for the call. I couldn't imagine that it would cause problems between us. Since Robert had graduated and was leaving for college soon, things were better with us as a couple.

During the stressful years, Bob had insisted we buy a cabin in north-central Pennsylvania, and we often found time to get away. We didn't argue when we were in the quiet forest by ourselves. We spent early November there, celebrating the end of the grape harvest. We had purchased two snowmobiles and enjoyed being snowed in at our log cabin in the Susquehanna State Forest. Our unique cabin was on a private, fifty-acre piece of land surrounded by state forest and snowmobile trails. It was at the end of the electric line and had no phone service. It was three miles to the nearest highway and thirteen miles to the nearest grocery store. We spent all of Pennsylvania's big-game–hunting season there and always got our limit of deer for the freezer. Robert joined us, and we were all happy and having fun when we were there.

When I warned Bob that his old girlfriend was trying to find him, he just shrugged and said, "Makes no never mind to me. Let her try."

I answered the phone the following day and handed it to him, expecting it to be a cut-and-dry conversation, with him telling her how happy he was and that he was not interested. I stood right there, waiting for that to happen, but Bob began to smile, and his conversation got really animated and flirtatious. He asked her all about her life and family and gave her glowing descriptions of *his* grape farms. He never mentioned me or our relationship as he described *his* cabin in great detail, including exactly how to find it. The conversation went on for thirty minutes, and I was standing right beside him the whole time. He never looked at me, met my eyes, or acknowledged that I was present. He said good-bye, turned his back, and went outside.

I was hurt and wondered if the warning I had received was right. I worried about where this new situation was going.

I thought about the move I'd made to Pittsburgh nine years earlier, when we agreed that I would help Bob with his contracting business. He had scheduled three houses to build and several remodeling jobs. While Robert attended school, we also built two garages for his clients. I learned to drive his ten-wheel dump truck, and several times a month I made dangerous trips up a mountain to a stone quarry to haul stone for him. I drove his other construction vehicles to haul materials and run errands, did his bookwork and billing, and answered his telephone. In return, Robert and I had a place to stay. I bought the groceries and paid for all our own personal expenses. Bob agreed to help me on weekends on the grape farm whenever I needed a hand. That was sporadic, however, and many weekends he stayed in Pittsburgh instead of making the three-and-a-half-hour trip north to the grape farm.

I recalled snippets of conversations between Bob and me. Once he asked me, "What do you think about me closing my construction company permanently and moving all my tools and equipment to your farm?"

I answered, "That sounds like a real serious move. Does that mean a real serious commitment to go with it? Are we talking marriage here?"

I shivered as I remembered his reply: "Hell, no, babe, we're not talking marriage. Things are fine just the way they are. Let's not rock the boat. We've been shacking up for over two years and doing just fine. Besides, I already told you I don't want kids, and you've got Robert."

Looking back, I recognized that conversation as a defining moment in our relationship; I should have left him then. Looking back without the foggy view I had while I was in the dream of love, I wondered if Bob had been secretly executing a master plan for creating an easy, low-cost life for himself. He had avoided investing any money; parked his equipment on my farm, promising that it could be used if needed; and contributed his labor only when he felt like it. I hadn't seen it that way when he moved to my farm. I had justified the conversations and the exchange of a business partnership for a marriage commitment. In a way, I'd been relieved because of my annulment experience. However, I had also felt hurt and sensed a lack of respect from Bob, so I had asked "How will you make a living and pay your bills?"

"I'll have all my equipment and tools, and I can do odd jobs and home repairs when we get moved to your place in New York. Plus, I can help you. In exchange for that, and because I'll use my vehicles in the farming operation, I'll use the bulk gasoline from the farm tanks. We can include my vehicles on your insurance policy, and the rate will be lower because of the multiple-vehicle discounts you'll get. You can make just one payment instead of worrying about all my paperwork. If it makes you more comfortable, we could get some sort of business-partnership thing, but marriage is out. We've both been there and done that."

Being in love with the dream of love, commitment, and a permanent relationship clouded my decision. "You've done a lot of thinking about this, haven't you?" I asked.

Bob pushed his agenda. "Yup. Working seven days a week at two businesses three hours apart is hard on you, babe. I don't want to wear you out. I just want to take care of you."

We completed all of his contracted work, closed his business, and moved his tools, equipment, and clothing to my place. He kept his apartment building and the rent he collected from it. His office was also there, and he did not dismantle it.

During the three months it took to finish his work and move, I strived to avoid making another mistake. I visited a local attorney, expressing my concerns and describing my experience with Mickey, the pilot, and the annulment. I requested some options for protecting my home and business investments. The lawyer advised against marriage unless there was a prenuptial agreement, but marriage was not part of the plan anyway. His advice made me feel less rejected and more proactive. It helped me accept that forgoing marriage was not about being unwanted; rather, it was a good option.

The lawyer suggested a business partnership, which had been Bob's suggestion. At that time, I was not familiar with business entities, and I told him I would trust him to draw up the papers and protect my interests. When the task was completed, we signed the agreement, and I stored it in my safe. I felt really comfortable with the situation and smart for speaking to my attorney and protecting my assets.

Bringing my thoughts back to the present, I wondered why I was so upset and suspicious after Bob's long conversation with his old girlfriend, whom I had never seen or heard much about. She was in Pittsburgh; I was here; and Bob and I were committed business partners and lovers. What was wrong with me? I concluded that I must be jealous, and I believed that jealousy stemmed from poor self-esteem.

Bob was around and helped a little at the farm, but then he found it necessary to put a new roof on the Pennsylvania cabin and was gone with his work van for a couple of weeks at a time for most of the summer. This was understandable since I held the pesticide-applicator's license; I bought, mixed, and applied the chemical treatments to the vineyards and fruit trees. I was also busy pickling, preserving, drying, freezing, and canning the produce from our garden. We had planted an acre of potatoes and an acre of sweet corn, and I sold them by the road in a pay-and-take wagon. I hardly noticed he was absent.

When picking season arrived, he prepared the equipment but was unpleasant because he couldn't work on the cabin during the six-week harvest season.

After a few months of silence concerning the "other woman," the phone rang one day, and Bob raced to answer it. He said it was a neighbor at the cabin, calling about an emergency—he needed to go cut up a tree that had fallen on the roof. He was gone within twenty minutes. He returned a week later and was particularly ugly toward Robert. Later, I figured out that no tree had fallen on the cabin roof. I surmised that the "other woman" had fallen into his bed at the cabin.

The day after Bob returned, we began building a small bridge across a little creek so that we could haul firewood out of a woodlot. Bob and I were at the creek with our chainsaws and tools, and Robert was identifying broken posts that needed to be replaced in the vineyard. A misty rain started falling, and Robert came down to the creek to see if we were going to quit for lunch. He jumped across the creek and said, "Boy, it will be nice to have a bridge. Do you guys need any help?"

"You look like you're already soaking wet, Robert. Why don't you go into the house and put the leftovers in the oven to warm up while you dry and change your clothes?" I asked.

Without warning, Bob suddenly hit Robert with all of his six-foot-two-inch muscled strength and knocked him into the creek. Shocked, Rob picked himself up, only to be pushed and thrown onto the opposite bank, where Bob put both his knees and his full weight on Robert's chest and began to strangle him.. "I never wanted any part of you, you lazy little bastard," he screamed. "When I met your mother, I told her I didn't want kids or any part of you." The obscenities poured forth.

I jumped across the creek, picked up a shovel, pulled it back like a baseball bat, and was about to sever Bob's head from his neck when I thought, *No, I'll go to jail if I kill him.* Instead, I yelled, "I'm going to call the police!" and kicked him in the privates. He jumped back just enough for Robert to free himself. Bob lunged at him again, but Rob's knee found the spot I had only grazed, and Bob rolled off him and lay in a fetal position, moaning.

I screamed, "Run, Robert! Get out of here." I dropped the shovel and began to run in the opposite direction toward the road. It was about seven hundred feet to the highway. The nearest neighbor lived about a quarter of a mile away, and I had heard him running a chainsaw just a few minutes earlier.

I ran in that direction. Bob recovered and was running after me, closing the distance between us with his long legs; he had a hammer in his hands. At least he was chasing me, not Rob. I thought my heart and lungs were going to burst. I couldn't get enough air, I was running so fast.

As I got near the edge of the highway, a tractor trailer came into view. Bob obviously didn't want to be seen swinging a hammer in pursuit of little me, so he stopped until the truck passed. I waved frantically at the driver, trying to stop him, but he just waved back and kept going.

The noise from the neighbor's chainsaw had stopped. I was afraid I couldn't find him, so I jumped a guardrail the minute Bob stopped because of the truck. I fell, rolled and scrambled into the thick brush and berry bushes, where I found a large fallen sugar-maple tree. I crawled under the trunk, near the upturned roots, and hid. I couldn't catch my breath. I could hear Bob start into the brush at the edge of the road. He was screaming my name and swearing at me. I dared not cry or sob or breathe or move. I huddled as close to the wet ground as I could. Bob got really quiet. He was listening for me to make a move so he would know where I was. We had hunted deer for years, and I knew this was how he often stalked his prey. I tried to blend into my little hole under the tree.

Then a tiny songbird flew onto a branch directly in front of my face and sang the sweetest, softest, most soothing melody I had ever heard. I suddenly thought that if God loved that little bird, created it, and took care of it, he would certainly do the same for me. My heart stopped racing. I wiped my tears and peeked out just in time to see Bob waving his fists angrily as Robert sped past in the truck his grandpa had left him when he died. I knew Robert was safe, and I was hidden. I could hear Bob cursing as he made his way back to the creek where his tools lay.

I waited a while and then quietly snuck across the woods and brush to a cornfield that bordered my farm. I could see Bob carrying his tools, chainsaw, and jacket as he headed toward the barn.

My things were still on the ground by the creek. When I heard Bob move his truck from the house to the barn, I hurried to the creek, gathered my things, which included my car keys, and purposefully stomped to the barn, where Bob was loading tools into his pickup. With the key in my hand like a weapon, I lied, "The police are on their way. You'd better get your stuff and leave. Don't you bother ever coming back." I ran to my car and followed Robert down the road. I had inherited my dad's farm, and again, like many years ago, it was our haven. I met Robert there, and we contacted the police. We filled out an incident report, showed the police the bruises on Robert's neck, and signed an arrest warrant. Bob left the state before the police could serve the warrant.

Robert and I figured out how to change all the locks. I couldn't believe this was happening again. I was positive that stepparent relationships between men and boys could never work.

Bob called a week later to say that he was leaving me and that he was moving in with his old lover in Pittsburgh. He wanted to come to the farm to get his possessions. I asked when he was going to do that, and he told me he would let me know.

"Call me when you cross the state line, and I'll be able to get home from the vineyard by the time you get here," I advised him, knowing I would notify the sheriff immediately about Bob's arrival in New York State.

We had been together for over ten years and had lots of legal ties. I didn't shed a tear, but I felt crushed because it was a replay of the abuse I had seen between the chief and my older two sons. I was paralyzed with guilt and the inability to protect another child of mine.

I notified the sheriff's department of the approximate time Bob would be crossing the New York border. They followed him down my driveway, through the vineyards, and the arrest warrant was served the minute he stepped out of his truck.

Bob said, as good as a professional actor would have, "What's this all about? Gail, what's wrong, Babe? You know I love you."

What he meant was that he needed time to execute the dissolution of our General Partnership Agreement. I could read the fear in his eyes, not of me or the police, but of the effect the arrest would have on his plans to ruin me financially. He wanted to fund his retirement with the gain he would receive from the proceeds of our partnership.

The sheriff handcuffed him and loaded him into the police car for a trip to jail and an appointment before the judge. I noticed that the color photos of Bob's handprints on Robert's neck were in the folder with the warrant. The sheriff said he would call me as soon as Bob had an appearance date and time.

Robert and I both appeared before the judge and recounted the events leading to Bob's arrest. An order of protection was issued, a fine was levied, a stern warning to stay out of Chautauqua County was given, and a date for the removal of his possessions was set. The sheriff brought him back to my farm to get his truck. As Bob was driving away, he rolled his window down, called our dog, coaxed her into the truck, and drove away with her. The bastard stole my dog!

I apologized to Robert on our way home from court. "I've tried it all," I said. "I've been divorced, widowed, and annulled, and I even tried a live-in arrangement complete with legal papers, but nothing worked. I'm sorry, Robert. You deserve better, but I can't seem to get it right."

"It's okay, Mom. We're still here, and we're all right. We got through the Containerboard crap, and now we survived this guy. We're tough." He smiled. "How's he going to get his stuff? Are we going to pack it, or what?"

"There are a lot of arrangements to take care of, Robert. I've already called Mr. Seeger, the attorney who helped us with the Containerboard fight. He said he'd look at the partnership agreement and go over the process of ending it. The bad news is that Bob is entitled to a settlement. Mr. Seeger will explain it when I see him."

"What kind of a settlement, Mom? Why would he get anything? He didn't work enough to compensate for the food he ate, let alone for storing his shit and sleeping with you." He grinned.

We had a good laugh about our troubles; it was great that we had each other. Robert wasn't even out of high school yet, but he had a wonderful outlook on life's problems. He was a survivor even at eighteen years old. I, on the other hand, viewed myself as a failure as a mother.

The complications began to multiply. As I looked back to 1993 and reviewed the decade Bob and I had spent loving each other and building a life together, hindsight allowed me to see that he had always possessed a hidden agenda.

I reminded myself of some things I have always believed. It is impossible to change any event that happened a second ago or any time before that; in the present, we are only able to try to learn from those past happenings, and we can only plan for a future over which we *think* we have control. We can't force anyone to love us, and we can't make them behave as we wish they would. I also reminded myself that, as in all my past disappointing relationships, I'd been in love with the idea of commitment and unconditional love, not with the man with whom I was involved. And finally, I reminded myself that there is no crystal ball in which we can see others' weaknesses—or our own, for that matter.

Chapter Twenty: Hindsight Perspective, 1994

In My Hurt, Blame-Laying state of mind, I reviewed the red flags. Sex had been the first thing on his mind when we met at that hunting camp in Pennsylvania. He'd pursued his horny desire to my home and discovered my farming operation, a great place to pursue his love of fishing and hunting, and to enjoy tasty home-cooked meals, a roaring fire to warm the cold winter nights, and, of course, a willing and experienced bed partner. He'd told me immediately that he was not into parenting, his own children or mine, and would never want any children together.

Bob fully understood and applied the concept of "pet the calf to catch the cow." He'd treated my older sons well and reluctantly played the role of dad to Robert. As his agenda progressed, he'd avoided the permanence of marriage. He'd substituted a General Partnership Agreement for real commitment, advising me, convincing me, and steering me into a dubious legal snarl. He knew from his own past business experience that all actions of either partner become legally binding to both partners once such a partnership was signed. The attorney I had hired to protect my interests had failed.

The more I reminisced about the course of our years together, the more I recognized the pattern he'd pursued to follow his agenda. At first, he'd been overwhelmed with his good fortune. Our very first night together, when we were snowed in, he'd said, "I've been divorced only a few hours. Yesterday it was final. I never thought it would be so easy."

I naïvely asked, "What's so easy?"

He was about to go home, and as he walked out the door he said, "Finding a tiny little woman as pretty as you, babe. My ex-wife was just your size, but she didn't have a farm and live in paradise like you do. I'm a southwestern Pennsylvania country boy, and I never thought I'd find somebody who looked like you and had it all." All I heard was a compliment.

When we moved to his home in Pennsylvania, I'd thought it was for Robert's sake, and it did help him. However, Bob had been adamant about not selling the farm or making our arrangement permanent. He'd been more than willing to let Robert and me spend many weekends alone on my farm, doing whatever chores were necessary. He'd found reasons not to finish a bedroom for Robert in part of the warehouse where we had built an apartment for us. Instead, I used bales of cardboard boxes to section off an area for Robert to use as his room. We never had a closet for our things; we always just camped out. It was understood that I would work at his construction business in exchange for our place to stay so that Robert could attend school there.

As soon as he could see the end of his contract commitments, he was anxious to make a permanent move to the farm. He mentioned the partnership agreement and suggested it as the best option for our relationship. Long before I committed to his plan, his equipment arrived on my farm.

Just before the partnership agreement was signed, a neighbor offered me a sixty-five acre farm adjacent to my home. I had wanted the farm for fifteen years, but the ninety-year-old owner had never wanted to sell. When he died, his son said that the old man's will and accompanying instructions had directed him to offer me the farm, because the old man knew I loved the land and would take care of it. Bob advised me to wait until after we finalized the partnership agreement, saying, "Don't get too many things on the table all at once. Wait until we get through the legalities of the partnership before you buy that farm. The guy will understand." The trouble was, I hadn't understood Bob's agenda.

In the partnership agreement, his contribution was listed as "labor." His equipment was not included. When I asked about that, he said, "Babe, it will be sitting right here. You can use it any time you want to. What more do you need?"

The day after I signed the agreement, I withdrew money from my farm account and bought the new farm for the instructed price of twenty-five cents on the dollar of value. Bob invested nothing but smiled broadly at the closing, declaring, "I'll build us both some tree stands on those deer trails."

Another neighbor offered me the grape-harvesting business, and I bought that with my own savings, too. Bob invested nothing, but he was eager to have his butt on all the equipment and strut around like he owned it all by himself.

Not long after I bought the harvesting business, Bob decided that the thirty-acre grape farm where I'd built the runway and the ultralight-airplane hangar was too far away, too much work, and too many acres of grapes. He pushed me to sell it and keep the new farm, which was right next door.

I bought and sold business entities as I thought prudent, taking Bob's advice and opinions into consideration. I had no idea that each transaction took my assets out of my personal estate and made them subject to the General Partnership Agreement. The assets were now divided half and half with Bob, without my permission or knowledge. That is how the local attorney failed to protect those assets.

I suddenly realized in my reminiscing that all the events that took place during my decade with Bob seemed to weave a pattern, all with the purpose of planning my demise and him acquiring business property.

There were so many red flags. When my dad died, I inherited his farm a few miles away, as well as some money. Bob immediately wanted me to buy another piece of land adjacent to my home so that we could tap the sugar-maple trees that grew on it. I did so, but I used a business check instead of my inheritance, not realizing that the land was now half his, even though I'd paid for it.

Then he said, "Babe, you look so tired and stressed. You won the Containerboard battle, but you endured four years of hardship. You work so hard in the grapes and at harvest time. Let's take some of your hard-earned money and buy a little place to escape the work. There's a place over in central Pennsylvania with a rustic, heated, modern log cabin that would be perfect for us. You could get away and get some rest. Why don't you use the grape farm account and leave your inheritance alone."

I never suspected a plan or an agenda. The cabin was all that he said it was. I bought it with a check from the vineyard account and never considered the consequences because Bob pointed out that my inheritance would cover the risk. If I had used the inheritance, the property would not have been in his control, and it would not have automatically become half his.

Now, as I brought my mind back to the present, Robert wanted to know why I would have to provide a settlement to Bob when he hadn't done any reasonable amount of work, had never invested a cent of his own money in our General Partnership Agreement, and had only agreed to provide labor when it was sorely needed.

Mr. Seeger, my attorney, came over to explain it. I made a roast-beef dinner, complete with homemade bread and apple pie. It was a repeat of Mr. Seeger's first visit, when he'd agreed to help us with Containerboard, *pro bono*. This time, I expected to pay him.

When we finished dinner, Mr. Seeger pushed his chair back comfortably. He said, "I've examined your General Partnership Agreement, and I'm so sorry to advise you this way, but there's no alternative. You need to offer Bob a settlement before he takes you to court. I recommend that you offer him $170,000. Each transaction you completed with partnership funds, which we all know came from your own farm labor and income, became subject to partnership laws. You don't have a choice, legally."

He continued with his reasoning. Bob had been in my life for approximately ten and a half years. A reasonable yearly salary for a farm laborer or consultant at that time was about $20,000. Mr. Seeger had looked at the real-estate transactions that had happened during the business partnership, both the buying and selling of farm properties. After considering tax ramifications, he felt that the dollar figure he suggested was fair. He thought it was a cheap alternative for me and that Bob would accept it. Then he suggested that I take the amount I'd paid for the farm properties, the harvesting equipment, new tractors, and the cabin in the Susquehanna State Forest, appreciate them to current values, and work out a deal. I ended up trading the cabin for a lot of the value, giving Bob the proceeds from the sale of the farm with the runway and hangar. I paid the remainder in cash.

On the day Bob came to collect his possessions, Bob's own daughter, Mr. Seeger, and the migrant-labor family who worked part-time for me were all present to ensure my safety and see that only Bob's belongings left the farm. I handed Bob a cashier's check along with quitclaim deeds for property transfers.

As he took the paperwork, he towered over me threateningly and said, "I'm doing you a favor by taking a settlement, but I'll get the rest of what I've got coming." The threat was ominous and worried me. Then Bob drove away, back to the arms of his old lover, and the dust settled behind his retreating truck.

———————————

Bob's belongings left empty spaces in my house and barn, which reminded me of the ten wasted years. One by one, the people who had gathered to protect me and mine said their good-byes and disappeared up the driveway. I was alone again.

Mirror always got really quiet when times were tough and I made hard decisions. It was as if Mirror spoke to me only when I doubted myself. This time, Mirror said, "I know what's next. You'll rearrange the furniture to fill up the empty spaces. If you get your old body moving, your mind will follow."

I looked at Mirror and said, "Who the hell are you to tell me what to do? You just watch what goes on around here and reflect on it. All you have is hindsight, and we all know that's perfect, don't we?"

"Honey, I think I'm your alter ego. You know I always tell you what you already know is right, and right now you need to get busy and remember that the sun comes up again in the morning. You were in love with the idea of a relationship, not with that awful man."

I felt really old. I was in my midfifties and couldn't seem to keep a decent relationship going. As I aged, I felt my chances were fading at finding that elusive knight on a white horse. Finally, I realized that all I really wanted was an equal, honest companion.

Mirror said, "I know what you're thinking, and you *have* kissed a lot of snakes—no, maybe that's frogs or toads; whatever. Trust me: there will be another reptile along any minute."

I knew subconsciously that Mirror was right. I began to wipe up the dust left behind when heavy pieces of furniture had been moved. My mood improved as I thought back on my time with that reptile Bob and the Containerboard incident. A new chapter was just beginning. Maybe it would hold the key to understanding the reasons for my difficult life.

After Bob's departure, life and farm work continued, as it always had. Suffering from the loss of community respect over Containerboard and the trauma of ending the terrible relationship with Bob, I began to take stock of my situation.

The maple season had been successful, and I had turned my little maple operation into a potting shed. It had a gravel floor and a corrugated, translucent plastic roof. I had vegetable seeds and more started for my garden. The wood from the maple-syrup–making operation was still stacked along the sides, and the seed trays sat atop the woodpiles. On cold nights, I put water in the tiny two foot-by-six foot maple-syrup evaporator, built a little fire, and kept the shed warm for the germinating seeds.

Hard work was my salvation. Other hard times had taught me that if I was physically and mentally exhausted, I could sleep.

I was suffering a huge financial drain thanks to the legal fight over the paper mill and another gigantic loss over the business-partnership dissolution. My outlook on life was not optimistic, calm, or pleasant. I felt aggravated every time I walked into the house and saw Mirror hanging on the wall, doing nothing but looking back at me. I made a face at Mirror.

Mirror reflected the mean mood and commented, "Doesn't cost anything to smile in the face of adversity. I shouldn't have to remind you of that. It doesn't cost anything to be nice, either. You used to have a smile in your voice when you answered the phone, and now you just snarl. Get a grip on yourself. The world is still turning."

"You, know-it-all Mirror, piss me off. I don't need you to tell me how to behave. I know what to do. Leave me alone and let me pity myself in my poor, miserable, man less, single-parent, heavy-workload life. Just shut the hell up," I grumbled.

Mirror responded, "You're a lot like your dad. He used to say, 'Of all my father's family, I love myself the best.' You do know he was kidding. You seem to be thinking only about yourself lately. Just look me in the eye and smile; force your lips to curve up; then tell me you still want to roll around in self-pity."

I slammed the front door and went back to working on the seedlings. Then a member of the Containerboard Watch Group barged through the door. Stan was ten years younger than me and owned a popular gift shop. He was a licensed water and sewer engineer and had reluctantly become involved with the Containerboard opposition.

He said, "Gail, I'm here in the spirit of Christian brotherhood. I shoot from the hip. You used to be a nice lady, and everyone in town liked you. You were a lot of fun, but now you're just a bitter, mean, nasty old lady. Don't you realize that Containerboard is over, and we won? You need to do something positive with your life."

First Mirror, and now Stan. I couldn't believe this guy had the gall to come onto my farm and speak to me that way. He had seen, firsthand, how our local elected officials had persecuted me and then him for our opposition to their development plans.

Angrily, I said, "How'd you get in here, Stan?"

"I came down the driveway."

"Well, get the hell back up it, and don't come back." I shook my gardening trowel in his face.

I kicked an empty maple-syrup bucket, and then I kicked the shed door shut. I kicked open the front door of my house. I stomped right in with muddy boots and came face to face with Mirror, who said, "He's right, you know."

241

I gasped when I looked at the mean face glaring out of Mirror. I recognized the residue of bitterness that had been left by my personal problems and the unpopular fight over the paper mill. I forced a tiny smile, and it was infectious. I realized how ridiculous and useless my bad mood was. Then I picked up the telephone and called Stan's wife.

"When Stan gets home, please bring him back here," I said. "I need to hear what he thinks I can do to stop being a bitter, mean, nasty old woman. I'll make some coffee."

I had nothing to serve with the coffee, but I did have some ice cream. I looked in my canning cellar for some peaches or something to serve with the coffee. On the shelf, amid all the jars of fruit and veggies, pickles, and jellies, stood a bottle of strawberry fruit syrup I'd made the year before with my grandma's recipe. The sunbeam streaming through the basement window highlighted that syrup bottle like a bright yellow word in a sentence. I grabbed the bottle and served the syrup over the ice cream. Stan said, "Why don't you teach canning classes and show people how to make this?"

"Don't be foolish. It's just strawberry syrup I make from my grandmother's recipe," I said.

"But it's really good strawberry syrup. I bet ladies would love to learn how to make it."

We finished our coffee and our visit, but it was only the beginning of Stan's relentless heckling. He called me day after day to ask if I had written a business plan yet.

One of the lessons of my earlier life that had led me to the predestined and purposeful Containerboard fight and the beginning of my agritourism business was reading the book *Acres of Diamonds*, which had inspired me to see maple syrup and grape farming as diamonds to be mined in my own backyard. My eight-year membership in 4-H taught me cooking, preserving, and sewing skills. The mink farm gave me a work ethic and showed me the rewards of hard work. The grape- and fruit-farming endeavor was also key in preparing me to create my new business endeavor, even though I was reluctant to act on Stan's prodding. In fact, most of my life experiences seem to have been preparation for this business which became the Sugar Shack. Stan's suggestion for canning classes was the jumping-off point.

Examples of perseverance were everywhere in my family. My favorite grandfather became the successful president and chairman of the board of directors of Empire State Life Insurance Company in Jamestown, New York, remaining honorary CEO until he died at age ninety-five. His formal education ended with third grade. My difficult paternal grandmother farmed, produced maple syrup, and supported her family after she was widowed in 1912. My father built an extremely successful fur-farming business with only an eighth-grade education. My mother put herself through business school and held a steady job all through the Great Depression. My sister fought an incurable, disabling disease that should have killed her by age twenty-five; she beat the odds, stayed married for over fifty years, and lived to the age of seventy-five. She was an inspiration to all who knew her as she surmounted her handicap.

Stan and his wife persisted in their spirit of Christian brotherhood and called me every day to insist that I start canning classes. They polled their church friends and business associates to prove that there was interest.

Tired and uninterested, I finally said, "Look, guys, why don't I just make the damned syrup and sell it to people?"

Chapter Twenty-One: The Sugar Shack Is Born, 1994

THE SUGGESTION TO SELL my syrups pushed the couple to a whole new level of harassment. Calls came twice a day, and in weekly visits they suggested (they would have said "encouraged") business plans, starting dates, locations, and more.

Finally, I caved. I wrote a sketchy business plan in the form of a "to do" list. One day, Stan walked into my shed, where my little tomato plants had germinated and were growing. Cobwebs veiled the woodpiles, and chipmunks had taken up residence. I was watering the seedlings.

"You need to throw this old wood out, get rid of these plants, take down the cobwebs, and feed the chipmunks a little lead," he insisted. "Why don't you just do it, Gail? Make a sign, make some syrup, clean the place up, and install some shelves. Quit wasting your time, and get it done," he ranted.

That outburst made me mad as hell. I threw down the watering can, grabbed the old broom and vigorously swept away the curtains of cobwebs above the windows and in the rafters as he disappeared with a smug, self-righteous grin on his face. I gathered up the tiny plants and set them on top of the maple-syrup evaporator. It wasn't going to freeze in the shed again; it was April, and the ice was gone from Lake Erie, only a couple hundred feet away. Spring beauties and snow drops were blooming in the woods. I wouldn't need a fire in here again.

I surveyed the shed and decided the wood could be stacked outside the back door until next winter, and I moved it there—over half a cord of it. It took an hour of aerobic-style exercise. It seemed a shame to move it in, move it out, and then move it in again next year. I hated wasted movement and work! I grumbled, "Well, if it silences the well-meaning bearers of Christian brotherhood...," and I got it done.

I was tired and sweaty. I needed strong, black coffee, a rest, and time to think about this. I made my way to the kitchen, put the teakettle on, dropped my tired, dirty body into a chair as I pulled off my gloves, and knitted skull cap. I caught a glimpse of myself in the hall mirror and was shocked again by how miserable I looked. Haggard was the word.

While I waited for the teakettle, I looked out the kitchen window at the acres of grapes that needed to be tied, work that I employed my friends to complete. Before I could start the tying, I needed to finish the post pounding and trellis work. Why was I worrying about pleasing Stan and his wife when I really needed to put the post pounder on the tractor, fix the trellis, and weed spray the thirty-inch band under the trellis wire and around the vines? I had forty acres to cover before I could get the girls in to tie all the vines to the tight trellis wire. That was at least a week's work, maybe two, daylight to dark, with half an hour for lunch and dinner after dark, which would be a boiled hot dog or a piece of cold pizza. This crap about syrup was just that, crazy crap.

The teakettle whistled. I poured the water into the drip-o-lator coffeepot and got out the cup. While I sipped, I picked up the pencil and made a list of chores: chop the brush, pound posts, tighten wire, weed spray, and buy grape-tying supplies, including new tying aprons. Most important: bottle homemade Concord grape wine in cellar for girls' breaks. The friends who helped me looked forward to the wine breaks. We'd been tying and sipping for a good fifteen years, maybe more.

I stared at all the white space on the paper, and my hand began writing another list: check juice supply in cellar, find used ten-ounce Welch bottles, take labels off, sterilize all—including lids, figure out label requirements, get other supplies. Later, I referred to the list as my business plan.

What had Stan said? "Make some syrup, make a sign, clean up this shed, get rid of the wood and the cobwebs, and nail up some shelves. Do something positive with your life. Containerboard is over, and you won." That was it. I needed to figure out something for a sign. I added it to the list, and then I also added, "Curtains for the little windows and a sap bucket on that maple tree next to the shed."

I began to visualize a difference in the little board-and-batten shed, which had no insulation or screens and only a gravel floor. I could see it with curtains and the old chainsaw version of a chair my boys had fashioned from a huge ash tree that had blown down in the woods. Before I realized just what I was doing, I was on my way around the barn to the scrap pile I intended to burn. I spotted an old four-by-eight-foot sheet of plywood, its edges all broken and bruised. It was a full sheet that I had used to lie on when I changed the oil in the tractor. One side was fairly clean, and it would do for a sign. I heaved and tugged it out of the burn pile, over the bank behind the barn, and fought the north wind blowing off Lake Erie to get it into the barn again. Sure enough, an old gallon of white paint remained in the cupboard I had recycled to the barn when the kitchen was remodeled. A can of red paint stood next to it. The clean side of the board needed two coats of white; the dirty side needed soap and water first and then three coats. It took the rest of the day and part of the next to reclaim that plywood sheet. I got a yardstick and measured off some lines. With no artistic talent, I lettered the sign with, "FRUIT SYRUP, MAPLE SYRUP, SIX FLAVORS." As an afterthought, I added "FREE TASTING." The lettering was crude; the sign's edges were frayed; one corner was completely broken off. I asked out loud, after three days' work, "How will I hold this thing up?"

I needed strong black coffee again. As I drank I realized that I had a sign, the shed was now clean and while I had taken rests from the strenuous part of the plan, I had sewn little curtains for the windows out of pretty white fabric. I had found some ten-inch pine boards for shelving and cut them to the right length with my band saw. I had also found some scrap wood and made cleats to hold the shelves between the studs in the little shed. I had put a spiel in the old maple tree and hung an antique tin sap bucket, complete with a little peaked lid. I had wrestled the huge ash-tree chair into the shed. What I hadn't done was make any fruit syrup to sell, and I had not bottled any maple syrup to sell. I didn't even have those on my list.

I groaned out loud and indulged in a brief period of "feel sorry for Gail." Where were my kids? Why didn't I have a lifelong partner—a husband, a significant other, or even a boyfriend?

As I paced and grumbled, I passed that damn Mirror in my front hall. I swore it spoke to me all the time and it was brutally honest. "I can tell you why you don't have a man," it said. "It's because you're dirty, disheveled, and too busy. You never take a break, get your hair done, or go anywhere. Work, work, work, and more work is all you ever do anymore. You wouldn't know a beauty parlor if you fell into one. Your kids are hundreds of miles away, productive, successful, and still studying to make better lives for themselves. You jerk. They call you all the time, come to visit, and never ask for a thing. What's wrong with you? Count your blessings, stupid."

I looked directly at Mirror. I fluffed up my hair, which was plastered to my head thanks to the knitted cap I always wore;

then I grabbed my purse and applied a little lipstick. It didn't do a thing for my appearance. I promised myself that as soon as I made some fruit syrup, bottled some maple syrup, made some maple candy, figured out some sort of labels, researched the legal requirements for those labels, and figured out how to cover up the Welch name on the caps for the used bottles I had sterilized, I would make an appointment to get my hair professionally cut and dyed and styled instead of doing it myself.

I was tired again.

I needed coffee again.

I needed to cover up that damn Mirror.

With pencil and paper in hand, I descended the cellar stairs. I would really need that coffee to complete the inventory I intended to take. I sat down on the bottom step and felt thankful that I had this new cellar under part of the house. At least I had a place to preserve and store the fruits of my farming labor. Four years after the furnace had exploded, nearly burning down the house, I had insisted on putting a new cellar under part of the old place.

Now, I sat on the bottom step, looking at the finished cellar under the central part of the old house, and brought myself back to the task of counting the used ten-ounce bottles and the fruit juices I had canned. I realized I would absolutely need this clean, remodeled cement basement to complete the predestined plan. I already had a wonderful facility to use as a syrup factory.

I looked at the wall of canning shelves, filled with quarts and pints and half pints of apples, peaches, cherries, carrots, beans, pickles, jams, jellies, juices, tomatoes, tomato and apple sauces, butters, and chutneys that I had canned from my farm. I wondered how city folks survived. In addition, twenty quarts of venison on the top shelf reminded me of the deer I had shot and processed. I loved to can, preserve, and store nature's bounty. Bags of dried herbs hung from the soffit in my kitchen, and jars of dried apples, fruit leather, and maple candies waited on my counter. Scores of empty jars stood on the shelves and attested to how I lived on this wonderful bounty—all from the farm I loved and called home.

I filled a box with fifty ten-ounce bottles and carried it upstairs. I would put them in the dishwasher and enjoy my cup of coffee. In the cellar, I had a card table, an old gas stove, a canner, a jelly kettle, pot holders, and tongs for lifting the hot jars. Everything I'd need to start a syrup business was already on hand.

I assembled all the ingredients and tools to make the fruit syrups. By the end of that night, when I crawled up the cellar stairs to that same old door that had trembled and shaken on the long-ago January night when the furnace had burned up, I had the fifty bottles filled, sealed, processed, pasteurized, and sterilized. I was ready for labels. "Labels," I groaned. "Tomorrow and six more pots of coffee will take care of that."

On my way to bed, I walked right past Mirror, who said, "You should be out pounding posts in the vineyard. Look at you. You actually look better when you come in from the vineyard, all windblown and covered with mud."

I glared at Mirror. There I was looking back, even more despicable in appearance than usual. I muttered, "You and I know that for sure, but the phone won't ring every five minutes, and Stan's heckling will stop." I went to bed. I would have 50 unsold bottles of useless but delectable fruit syrup sitting in a shed in my side yard. I could always use them for Christmas gifts. Tomorrow I would have a sign, such as it was, at the end of my driveway, and I could get on with my life without Stan's meddling phone calls.

"Spirit of Christian brotherhood," I said in my prayer, "I try, God, to keep it civil with these people of yours. You and I both know they're crazy." I fell into an exhausted sleep.

Bright spring sunshine greeted me the next morning in April of 1994. I bounded out of bed and avoided the mirror. I drank two cups of strong black coffee and then headed to my office in a vacant upstairs bedroom. Soon I had the words "fruit syrup," "ingredients," and "weight" all lined up in PowerPoint. I printed, copied, sized, and adjusted the label design until it was adequate.

All the computer work I'd done for the Containerboard effort actually helped me with this label-making process. It didn't really matter, however, because nobody was coming, and certainly nobody was buying. I assured myself that I didn't need a business plan or any permits. After all, the Amish sold their stuff by the roadside, and I knew they didn't worry about such things. Why should I?

As the sheets of labels came out of the printer, I colored in the fruit motif with markers and taped the labels to the bottles. Then I cut small circles from fabric scraps and glued them over the caps to cover up the commercial printing. After a couple of trips across the lawn, all the bottles sat neatly on the shelves in my shed. I added two quarts and six pints of maple syrup, and it was done. The offerings were pretty sparse, but I thought nobody was coming anyway.

The beat up, used piece of plywood that I had recycled into a sign lay flat on its face in the gravel driveway in front of the barn. The only way to get it up the nine-hundred-foot driveway was to drag it. I found a roll of disgusting, rusty, number-nine trellis wire, hung it around my neck, and started the journey. My mailbox was attached to a twelve-foot-high wrought-iron post, which had once held a sign. I heaved and pushed against the wind and finally had the plywood upright against the post. I walked around and around with the rusty wire and twisted it together at the edge of the plywood to keep the crude sign from blowing over. I left the ugly mess of extra wire on the ground. It would be there only for a little while because nobody was coming. I planned to dismantle the whole project as soon as I proved to Stan that it wouldn't work.

My hands were freezing, the wind was still blowing, and it was only forty-two degrees, even though the sun was shining. It was ten o'clock in the morning. I could call Stan and his wife now and tell them (politely) to get off my case. I was hurrying down the driveway toward the house, mumbling, "That fixes that. I won't have to listen to those do-gooders anymore," when I heard the crunch of gravel under tires. A car coasted to a stop beside me.

An older gentleman rolled his window down and said, "Hi, I'd like to taste your syrup. By the way, what exactly is maple syrup?"

I stared at the old man in amazement. Was I dreaming, or was this a customer? I had put "free tasting" on the sign almost as a joke because I was so sure nobody would ever come. I had added "FREE TASTING" in big letters only because there was so much blank space on the plywood. I had no equipment to conduct a tasting session and no idea how to proceed. Looking back, I see that I had no formal marketing plan. However, a higher power and predestination had taken care of that.

When the man asked what maple syrup was, my natural response was, "Where in the world are you from?"

"New Zealand," he answered.

My next question was, "What brings you down my driveway?"

"I turned around because of your sign. I've always heard about maple syrup, and you have free tasting."

"Oh. Park your car over there, and come up on the front porch at the house. I'll bring samples out."

While he parked, I went to the kitchen for a spoon and a half bottle of extra Concord grape syrup. I also got the maple syrup that had been left when I had finished bottling.

He tasted and asked, "How do you make maple syrup?"

I took him out to my little shed, with its new curtains and the fifty bottles of syrup nobody was ever going to buy, and explained how the tiny two-by-six foot evaporator turned forty-five gallons of sap from the tree into one gallon of pure golden maple syrup as it cooked over a fire, for which I had cut and split all the wood during the last year.

He asked, "How do you get the watery juice out of the tree?"

I showed him the little tin bucket I had hung on the nearest maple tree and explained the tapping procedure and gathering requirements.

He bought a jar of maple syrup and a jar of strawberry syrup, thanked me, and then said with a sheepish grin, "I have a problem. Maybe you can help me. I'm a retired mathematics professor, and I'm on a world tour. I've just finished speaking at the University of Buffalo, and I have one day, today, to see the countryside. I'd really like to see water, mountains, and farm country. Is that possible? I have no idea where to go."

I got my own New York State map and a highlighter from the house and drew him a route from my farm on the cliff edge of Lake Erie south along the old French and English Portage Trail to the north end of Chautauqua Lake; then south to Allegany State Park for the mountains and the Allegany River, returning to Buffalo through farm country, including some cattle farms with rolling hills and fields being cultivated for crops. He could do it in one day and fly out of Buffalo International to Ukraine. The topography maps I had studied during the Containerboard crisis had given me a wonderful background for providing such tourist information.

He drove away after a handshake that conveyed sincere appreciation. I had no idea that I'd just given my first maple tour and tourist information, or that I would repeat the drill thousands of times in the next two decades. I thought about calling Stan and his wife but decided to put it off for a few days.

I didn't want to admit that I had actually had a customer. It was probably an isolated incident.

A couple of days after the New Zealander's visit, I was making real progress with the post pounding and trellis work in the vineyards. I was working near the driveway, and, late in the morning, I realized I had not eaten breakfast. The old John Deere two-cylinder tractor was quite eye-catching, with the belly-mounted post pounder sticking up ten feet in the air. Cars often slowed on the Seaway Trail just to watch the pounder drop on top of an eight-foot locust post, moving the post into the ground a foot at a time. I was tired of entertaining the traveling public, so I drove the equipment down the driveway and parked it in front of the house. A peanut-butter sandwich and a tall glass of milk were foremost in my mind. I heard a car horn just as I took the first bite. When I looked out the window, expecting the mailman with a package, I saw that it was a car with out-of-state license plates. So much for the cold milk; I took the sandwich with me.

"Hi there! Where are you from?" I asked.

"We're from Ohio, near the Kentucky border. We saw your "Johnny Popper" and wondered what that thing sticking up ten feet in the air is for?" one of them answered. Two couples got out of the car and circled the tractor.

"We all work in a John Deere factory, and we've never seen a machine like that," another said.

"It's a post pounder. A local grape farmer invented it," I answered.

"Could we see it work?"

I nodded, crammed the sandwich into my mouth, and climbed onto the tractor. They stood back as I maneuvered the tractor and wagon full of new posts into a row of grapes. My "post checker" was own invention, made from an old tent pole. I drove up the grape row and jousted with the posts. If one waved back at me, it meant that it was broken at ground level and needed to be replaced. That method was much better than walking all the rows and pushing on the posts to see if they were broken. Sure enough, the second post up the row was broken. I stopped and detached the trellis wire with my staple puller. Then I pulled and pushed and got the old post loose, heaved it onto the used-post side of the wagon, and wrestled a new, heavy locust post into place.

Over the years, I had devised a method of holding the post erect and in place while I stretched to reach the hydraulic levers and operated the pounder with my other hand. It was a dangerous maneuver; the stretch was awkward and put my body in range of the heavy steel plate when it dropped onto the post to drive it into the ground. I risked injury because doing this myself saved the expense of hiring someone to assist me. I learned that when you weigh only a hundred pounds and aren't quite five feet tall, ingenuity is critical to running a grape farm. Farmers (and tiny women) often take shortcuts and use innovative practices to save money and time. That is one of the reasons farming is such a dangerous occupation.

When I had finished setting the posts and stapling the wire to them, I climbed back up on the tractor, and the out-of-towners applauded. Then they pointed to my ugly sign and said, "We'd like to do the free tasting."

After Mr. New Zealand had continued on his way, I had invested in a box of plastic spoons and put a few bottles of syrup in the shed, which was still as cold as the inside of my refrigerator. I wanted to be prepared just in case I had another visitor in another isolated incident. We all moved to the shed and held the tasting, and they bought one bottle of each kind of syrup. I was flabbergasted. Then they asked me for directions to Niagara Falls. I told them to follow the Seaway Trail and explained that they would not only have a scenic route but would run right into Niagara Falls State Park. I shoved the money in my pocket with one hand while I waved good-bye with the other.

It was my first grape tour and my second attempt at providing tourist information. I had no inkling that I would spend the next eighteen years doing that routine over and over again. I went into the house to finish my milk and have some cookies, and Mirror mocked me, saying, "Isolated incident, huh?"

I still didn't want to give in and call Stan and his wife. I hadn't even told them that the sign was up and the shelves were stocked. I hated to admit that maybe they'd been right.

By the end of the first week, all fifty bottles were gone, and I was busy making more syrup every night. Someone asked me if I had any gift bags; they were buying the syrups for presents. I didn't. I was busy trying to get my trellis work completed and couldn't stop to go to town for bags. One evening after dark, I decided to see if I could make some fabric bags from the scraps in my sewing room. I made six and sold six the next day.

Throughout the summer, I picked all the fresh fruit I could find, processed it, made syrup, collected used juice bottles and recycled them, made bags, waited on customers between the vineyard chores, and got really tired. I likened the way I felt to Disney's sorcerer's apprentice, with his brooms and buckets; the more I did, the more there was to do.

I realized that these visitors were coming from all over the world, and they were stopping because of my homemade sign. I got a United States map, a world map, and some stick-on stars, and tourists enjoyed marking their hometowns with the stars. I also got a guest book.

Then, to my amazement, I started getting thank-you cards and letters from visitors, telling me that I had made a difference in their vacations. They appreciated me, which was a change from how the local population felt about me. They shared wonderful stories about their lives.

One couple in particular stand out in my memory. The woman was originally from Holland, and I asked her how she happened to be in the United States. She told me her story: "I was one of eleven children and lived on my father's peat farm. We had piles of peat drying in the fields. One day, I was playing hide-and-seek with my sisters, and a train taking Jews to Auschwitz stopped in our pasture, because the townspeople had blown up the railroad bridge over a river. They were trying to stop the Germans from taking the Jews to Auschwitz. We wondered who was on the train, so we all ran down to the pasture fence. We saw cattle cars with slats, and we could see inside. The railroad cars were packed with people, and between the slats, little children's hands and arms stuck out. People were packed in like animals, suffocating in the heat, and some of the children waved to us." Tears formed in her eyes, even though this event had happened fifty years earlier. She continued, "My parents hated what the Germans were doing, so they hid Jews in their ceilings and in fake closets and peat piles. German soldiers searched our farmhouse regularly, but we were never caught."

"How long have you been in the United States?" I asked.

"Since I was fifteen." She paused, and then continued her story. "One day after the war, a man came to our door and thanked my father for saving his family. He said he was a well-to-do American and wanted to repay us for our lifesaving kindness. He told my father that he would take one of his children to America and give that child the best education possible. I was that child," she said. "I became a surgical nurse in Florida, and I still work in that profession."

At the end of the story she seemed almost angry. "You know," she said, leaning forward and pointing a finger at my nose, "you Americans complain too much. You complain about your roads and your cars. You complain about the cost of your food and about your medical care. You complain about your politicians and doctors and lawyers. You complain about everything. Don't you know you're free?"

I was taken aback for a minute, but when I recovered, I said, "We're free *because* we complain and question and demand truth and excellence from our lives and our government." I don't think she had thought about it that way before. We shared a wonderful hug, and she said she would be back.

Another day, a carload of two young couples and their elderly parents, who were celebrating their sixty-fifth wedding anniversary, drove in. The older woman, nearly ninety years old, was fascinated by some wildflowers at the edge of the woods. She asked, "What are these flowers? What else grows in the woods? I don't know what poison ivy looks like. Does it grow here?"

"Would you like to take my arm and walk into the woods, to the edge of Lake Erie?" I asked. She agreed, and what a wealth of knowledge she was. She identified more wild plants than I even knew were there. We found poison ivy and got close enough for her to memorize its features.

"Thank you for the tour," she said. "You can be certain that I'll always know what poison ivy looks like, and I'll keep my distance from it." She wrote to me several times over the years from a nursing home as she approached one hundred, and she always thanked me for her last walk in the woods.

It was my first "Woods Walk to the High Bluff Cliffs of Lake Erie" tour. It seemed that the more I gave, the more I received in return. Instead of being mean, nasty, and hateful, I was genuinely happy and thought of myself as blessed. I sure wasn't going to admit that to Stan and his wife—even in the spirit of Christian brotherhood.

On Labor Day, I decided I had to close the door and end the first season of operation. I had a grape harvest to run for my own vineyard, which was more than a full-time job on its own. I also still owned and operated a picking business, which obligated me to harvest twenty-one farms and deliver their crops to the processing plants. I put up a "Closed" sign for the first time. Over the summer, I had entertained visitors from every state and twenty-three foreign countries. I had collected over five hundred signatures in my guest book, and that was with just one person signing per carload. I had money in the bank and a smile on my face.

I finally called Stan and his wife, surprising them when I said, "Thank you for your genuine friendship and positive advice. You guys were right. I'm glad I finally listened, because now I'm smiling; I have a positive outlook on life, I feel appreciated, and I have a fledgling new business. Your spirit of Christian brotherhood is truly amazing, and I will try to pay the favor forward by helping others like you've helped me. I'm planning a new sign and some advertising for next summer. Let's keep in touch."

I missed the people who'd visited every day from everywhere, but I was extremely busy. As I greased the tractors and went over the equipment, I recalled how I had gotten into the harvesting business in the first place. I was sure that the grape business was all part of some super-being's master plan for my life. My Christian-brotherhood friends would say that super-being was God, and, in my heart, I knew that was the truth.

It was time to concentrate on grape harvesting. I knew it would give me lots of time to reminisce and plan the direction my life would take; after all, I would be waiting in line for hours for my trucks to be unloaded at the grape-processing plants. I had undertaken a long, complicated journey: from being born and brought up on a mink ranch; to being one of the first women to own and operate a grape farm and harvesting business; to creating fruit syrups to sell at my farm gift shop. I thought about how the road to my successful business ventures was littered with potholes of abuse and challenging relationships with difficult men. I needed quiet time in the unloading line to look at the roadmap of how I'd gotten to this point and to map out my future path.

When I put up the Sugar Shack's "Closed" sign on Labor Day, I realized it had been a busy, lucrative and surprising summer. It had been a learning experience equal to a 101 course in business development and customer service.

As I pushed my tired body through my front door, Mirror said pointedly, "Well, did you learn anything? What'll you do with your newfound knowledge? The Sugar Shack is the vehicle." Mirror made me realize that the Sugar Shack would bring people to me and that I could multiply their visits by sending them on into my community. Tourism in our pristine town was the perfect alternative to industrial development.

While walking from the gift shop to the house, I'd heard the heavy traffic on Interstate 90, just a quarter mile south and directly parallel to Route 5. I thought about the five hundred carloads of people who'd traveled down my driveway and paid me a visit. Each of them had told me that they happened to be in my neighborhood because they were traveling to or from Niagara Falls. Maybe the paper-mill fight and the creation of the Sugar Shack were meant to encourage our political leaders to pursue tourism.

Mirror ordered, "Get a pen and paper and write this down before you forget it."

I began a list: "Ten things we could do to move our town forward." I included such things as listing all the reasons our town was special; amenities; educational opportunities; our proximity to large urban centers; the climate; nature, including endangered plants, forests, and streams; the infrastructure, especially highways, rail, and airports; existing tourist infrastructure; and recreational opportunities. The list took the form of an outline as I filled in details, and I realized that a business environment ripe for entrepreneurs was already in place. I typed up my list on the computer, revised it, and came out with a sketchy but reasonable marketing plan for developing the tourism industry and enticing clean economic developers.

I sat back in my desk chair, a cold cup of coffee on the desk, and marveled at the work in front of me. I thought the paper was brilliant—even Mirror didn't argue. I called Stan and his wife to brainstorm my new passion. As I dialed, I envisioned taking the plan to the next chamber of commerce meeting in my town.

Stan brought me back down to earth and reminded me I might be suffering from delusions of grandeur. "Gail, have you considered that the folks at the chamber meeting can't get any credit or kickbacks or back-scratching deals out of your plan? I opened my business with no grants, favors, or input from the government, and you did the same. What's in such a plan for them? They'll fight you all the way if they don't get something out of it for themselves. Think about it. They want control and credit, at least. They'll never buy it," he concluded.

Mirror said, "He's full of crap. Your plan is good." I polished up the plan, made a call, found out the chamber meeting would take place that afternoon, and prepared to present my plan.

I was pumped.

I walked in just as the meeting was called to order.

The president demanded in an unfriendly tone, "What do *you* want?"

"I want to give you some ideas I came up with following my first season in the tourism business," I replied, standing just inside the door.

"You don't belong to the chamber, and we aren't interested in any of your ideas. We heard enough of 'em over the last four years during Containerboard. You're an economic-development terrorist, and you aren't welcome here," I recall him saying.

"But—"

"No buts about it. Just leave. We don't want you here," he growled.

I was inwardly furious and shaking with anger. I managed to drive home and slam the front door good and hard when I went in for another coffee. As I drank, I realized Stan had a point. Mirror was too scared by the reflection of my anger to even comment.

Over the next two weeks, I wrote draft after draft of my development plan and list. When the next meeting convened, I was ready. I arrived at the meeting half an hour after it started and did not knock. I just stomped right into the middle of the group. I was prepared with a couple dozen copies of my plan. I interrupted the speaker by saying, "Hi, everybody. I'm here this morning to give you a gift—a gift from my mind to yours. You may do anything with it that you like. You can throw it in the trash can. You can read it. You can apply it. You can put someone else's name on it. You can use it as a springboard to move our town forward. Or, as I said, you can just shit-can it."

As I spoke, I walked around the table, distributing the copies of my plan. When I finished, not a sound could be heard in the room. Some of the members were reading the one-page presentation, on which I'd highlighted key points in bold font. As I opened the door to leave, I heard one man say, "This is really, really good."

"Thank you for your time," I said as I closed the door quietly behind me.

I felt good; I thought I had planted a seed in their minds, just like I planted seeds on my farm. I hoped and prayed they would water the seed. I already knew they were fertilizing it with their crappy attitude. Now they were in control.

Six months later, a couple of months into the Sugar Shack's second year of operation, I looked at the local paper and saw a headline that read, "Ten Things We Can Do to Market Our Town

More Effectively." It was my development/marketing plan, and I was elated. Then I saw the byline: it was the name of one of the politicians who had been most opposed, closed-minded, and nasty over every fact our Containerboard group had disclosed to the public. He was also a leader in the group I believed had originated my nickname of "economic-development terrorist."

I screamed at Mirror, "That bastard stole my ideas, and here they are on the front page of the county paper with his byline."

Mirror said, "You told the chamber that the plan was a gift to do with as they wished; you even said they had the option of changing the author's name. It doesn't matter who gets the credit, as long as the job gets done. You gave them control, like Stan suggested."

A grin replaced my anger. It had taken six months from the time I planted the seed for this meager result to appear.

My customer base exploded. My mailbox was active with many letters from visitors who wanted to say thank-you; often they shared some personal information or pictures. I called these pieces of correspondence my love letters and collected them in a scrapbook.

During the year I bottled maple syrup, transformed rhubarb into ice-cream syrup, picked and processed wild berries and made the apples, pears, peaches, cherries, and quinces into fruit spreads to sell in my shop . Somehow I completed the grape work on time, too. Soon it was picking season all over again. After some experimenting, I had added wild-elderberry syrup and pumpkin spice to my list of flavors for sale. I continued to stop whatever chore I was doing to wait on customers and take them for nature walks to the edge of the high cliffs that bordered my farm on Lake Erie. I made many new friends, including a couple from Kentucky who sent me a jug of sorghum syrup and directions on how to make it. Another Kentucky couple was instrumental in having me named a Kentucky colonel for my hospitality. They sent me a bottle of Kentucky White Lightning.

One fall afternoon, when I was in the midst of the grape harvest and had put up a sign that said "Open only by appointment or chance," I was home refilling my coffee thermos when I heard a car drive in. I ran out to wait on the visitors. An extremely tall, handsome man and a tiny, pretty woman were climbing out of a shiny black Mercedes. I greeted them and asked where they were from. The woman said, "Pittsburgh, Pennsylvania."

"What brings you here?" I asked.

"I'm doing genealogy research in some little towns around here," she replied. "I told my friend that this was a gorgeous fall weekend and the foliage would be great; plus, I wanted to show him a unique, rustic little shop I'd found. We drove out early this morning, and I was afraid you might not be here."

I was intrigued by the genealogy comment, as my ancestors had lived in the county for ten generations. "What towns are you searching?" I asked. "I take it you've been here before, and I'd like to know when."

"Last fall I brought my cousin here to visit her mother's grave and help me with the research," she said. "We stopped here, and you took us on a tour. On our way past your front porch, we noticed some huge apples, and you gave us each one to eat. I told my friend he just had to see this place."

"What's the family name you're researching? I've been here all my life and know a lot of people."

She pulled out a copy of a newspaper obituary notice from her handbag. and handed it to me. I glanced at it as she said, "The old funeral director gave me this copy. He told me this was the last man in the family alive in this county, but he died about five years ago."

When I looked at the obituary, my knees buckled, and I couldn't catch my breath. I sat down on the old log chair in my rustic shop. I pointed to the second column and said, "See that name? That's me. This is my dad's obituary. I must be related to you."

It was her turn to be shocked. "The funeral director said nobody was left in the family." We stared at each other. Then she said, "The lady who was with me last fall is your relative, too. Her mother and my mother married young, moved West, and didn't come back, but they're buried here."

After several hours of unraveling the family history, we discovered that we were distant cousins. This serendipitous visit was the beginning of family reunions with more cousins and loving friendships all around. The Sugar Shack was only two years old, and the surprises were endless, unbelievable, and a lot of fun.

My grape-harvesting business was intense, successful, lucrative, and also fun. As I pulled wrenches and greased the grape harvester, I marveled at how I'd gotten to the current stage of my life. I interrupted my vineyard work constantly to wait on new customers, many of whom became friends. All of them provided positive feedback, which erased my bitter attitude completely. "Stan was a genius," I told myself more than once as I worked. "His Christian-brotherhood attitude was right on. But the stuff I have to do to make it all work sure makes me tired."

Over 1,500 carloads of people had visited my business. My youngest son was graduating from high school in the class of 1995, and I was replacing the little gravel-floored shack with a permanent twenty-by-twenty-foot store, which included insulation and a wonderful rustic woodstove to keep it warm all winter. The new building even had a wide, covered front porch with a swing hanging between the support posts. Antique school benches flanked the entrance so that husbands could wait comfortably while their wives shopped. I made curtains for all the windows and real shelves to hold my growing line of syrups. I added fruit butters and some jellies. With the added space, and directions from a customer, I made corn-tassel wreaths and my own variety of cornhusk dolls for Christmas-tree ornaments.

In the fall, I fired up my chainsaw and wood splitter and worked at cleaning up the sugar bush and building up my wood pile for the wood stove. The shop took on a lovely country atmosphere. I began advertising to the tourist industry, and my beautiful new sign helped.

To my surprise, a lovely young girl asked to interview me for an article for our local paper. It was the first of dozens of newspaper and magazine articles about my unique endeavor over the years. These news items were unsolicited, free advertising.

I continually found ways to sandwich the Sugar Shack work between the grape-labor seasons. Working eighteen-hour days and the loss of Robert's help as he left for college in the fall of 1995 made me really tired. However, the Sugar Shack kept me occupied with planning, advertising, and record keeping during the long, cold, dark winter.

Still, I missed having a companion. The words "married," "divorced," "widowed," "annulled," "significant other," and "business partnership" all ran through my mind as I worked. I wondered how my friends could celebrate twenty-fifth wedding anniversaries and more. How did they do it?

Twenty years had raced by at lightning speed while I struggled along with Robert through his school years, and Bob had passed through my life as he reaped his fortune from my labor. Struggling against Containerboard had consumed four of those years. My dad and Freddie passed away as the rollercoaster of my life hurtled up and down the steep inclines. The constant, calming security of my agricultural life, where I could count on one season simply following another, kept me sane and gave me purpose. Even though farming was filled with circumstances I couldn't control, like weather and markets, it was fulfilling and offered enough fresh air and exercise to let me sleep soundly at night. It was an honest way to make a living. It was challenging mentally as well as physically. Chores rotated annually, and there were many hours of solitary work, so I could ponder where I had been and the paths I had followed.

As I worked, I wondered if this was progress. Here I was, working alone, with too much time to think. It used to be that I just farmed and picked the grapes. Then the Sugar Shack evolved, and now I had to think about all the other crops, too. I had developed many varieties of fruit syrups and worked to produce pure maple syrup, maple candy, maple spread, and maple sugar. None of this came without hard, long hours of work.

I thought about the chronological sequence of nature and the effect it had on my work schedule. It seemed like only seconds between making maple syrup and the ripening of rhubarb, strawberries, and then wild raspberries. I was always busy.

Gathering wild berries was a different challenge. I had to get up before the first light and be in the woods, searching and clearing paths through the brush, so that I could beat the Amish and the birds. Poison ivy and poison oak, wild brambles that sometimes grow up and over tree limbs, and groundhog holes and foxholes were just some of the hazards of wild-berry picking.

Wild rosebushes were the worst. They snatched my hat, tore at my canvas coveralls, and ripped my flesh to bloody shreds. Tiny hitchhiker sticktights covered the tops of my socks where they were turned down over my barn boots. The barn boots protect my ankles and calves from being torn by thorns and bruised by limbs and logs hidden in the underbrush. I had to stay alert and listen for changes in birdsong to avoid being surprised by native animals that might be carrying rabies or be upset by my presence in their habitat.

The places I went to pick luscious, flavor-intensive wild black raspberries, blackberries, black currants, elderberries, and crab apples were remote. When I first entered the wild environment, the sounds of birdsong and rabbits scurrying through the brush made me so thankful for the opportunity to experience nature. While I filled my basket with succulent berries, I realized that only God and I had touched the berries. "This is better than organic," I said to the birds.

A typical day was filled with warm sunshine and soft breezes that caressed my face and soothed the brush scratches as the hours slipped by. When my baskets were full, I would close and lock the pruning shears, gather the baskets, and leave the woods, following the path I had made when I entered the berry patch. However, I had to be very careful as I walked with my precious, handpicked, over flowing baskets because it was easy to trip on hidden obstacles under the brush.

With the sun fully overhead, the June heat was intense. Wild berries deteriorated quickly and had be sorted or looked over and processed as soon as possible. I was drenched in sweat by the time I reached my pickup truck.

The berries were always sweet, succulent, and tangy-tart. Even now, as I write this, I salivate with the memory of the handfuls I crammed into my mouth as I drove to the next berry patch.

Once I heard a coyote just out of sight in the undergrowth as I invaded their world. Their sharp yap was distinctive, but I wasn't concerned, so I kept picking. When the bottom of the basket was nicely covered and my taste buds were content, I heard the yapping again. This time it was just a bit to the right of the first yap. Suddenly I heard another bark, and then another, and then several at the same time. Terror crept up my spine, and my hands began to shake. The coyotes were making a circle around me, and it was nearly closed. I had gone quite deep into the brush, and the path out wasn't clear. I had neglected to bring my pruning shears and handgun into the woods, as I had planned to pick just the berries on the edge; somehow I had gotten carried away. I turned around and couldn't see the truck; I was too far into the patch.

Meanwhile, the coyotes were yapping and yipping and closing a circle around me. From my observations of kill sites and carcasses in the woods, I knew that coyotes circle their prey and attack in groups. This was especially true when they had young pups to feed—and it was June, that time of year. Their pups would be hungry. The older coyotes would be teaching them to surround and kill their food.

I surveyed my escape route, estimated the distance back to the truck, and took off, crashing through the brush, leaving my partially filled basket behind. I yelled and made as much noise as I could to let the coyotes know I was formidable and unafraid, but I was really terrified. Only a few days before, I had encountered a deer carcass along a wooded path, and it was a brutal kill site. The flesh—what was left of it on the scattered bones—was still red. The skeleton was dismembered and covered a hundred feet of the trail. The jawbone had been dislodged and torn from the skull. The kill was so fresh that the flies had not yet attacked it, and not enough meat was left for a decent meal for ants.

I ran like my life depended on it, which it did. The yapping stopped. The birds were silent. The only sound was my feet snapping twigs and my clothing being scratched by the brush. I could hear the coyotes behind me. Just then, I pushed through some high wild elderberry bushes and wild grapevines, and there was the truck. One mad dash and I was in it.

The coyotes stopped when I slammed the door and blew the horn. And, of course, there was my handgun on the seat, fully loaded and ready to protect me while it was safely locked in the truck. I decided I could do without that patch of wild berries unless I had someone with me and we each had a gun.

Many times, my customers wanted to know if I really picked the fruit myself. The day I survived the coyotes, I arrived home to find a carload of tourists waiting for me to open my shop at one o'clock. I pulled the truck up beside them, opened the door, and slid out. What a sight I was. My hair was stuck together with burdocks; my face had a long scratch with dried blood; my coveralls were torn from the rapid escape from the coyotes; and my boots were covered with mud from the shortcut I'd taken through a creek.

The tourists watched me uneasily. I could tell they were debating whether to come into the shop or run as I unlocked the door and switched on the lights and air conditioning. I said, "Excuse me. I have to bring in the berries I just picked," and I went back to get my baskets.

When I set the four eight-quart baskets of wild black raspberries on the counter, the woman exclaimed, "You really do pick the fruit yourself, don't you?" They marveled at the sweet black jewels, and I offered them a taste.

"They're so fresh. They're so tart and sweet and juicy," the young boy said, filling his mouth.

"Yikes! There are bugs and leaves in them. Yuck! I won't eat them," the teenage girl exclaimed as she examined the fruit more closely. "Where did you get these?" she demanded.

"I pick all the wild berries for my syrups in the woods. They're better than organic, because only God and I touch them. They have to be sorted, washed, and processed. The picking is only a small part of the work. Would you like to see some growing in the woods?" I asked.

"Sure. What happened to your face, and what's in your hair?" the girl asked.

"I pick the berries in the woods and fields and places where most folks don't ever go. This is how I look when I finish. A hot bath and shampoo will fix me up again, except for the bites from mosquitoes and other bugs. I spray myself with insect repellant so I don't get many bites," I replied.

"Why do you pick wild berries when you can just buy them or grow them?" the mother inquired as we walked down my trail to the edge of Lake Erie.

"The flavor is more intense, for one thing," I answered. "For another, I love nature, and I love being able to offer a taste of its true and unbelievable nectar to people like you, who would otherwise never have that opportunity. It's a gift to be able to find and pick the wild fruit and a gift to offer it to you as a syrup for your ice cream, pancakes, and more," I said. I pointed out the wild raspberries, elderberries, currants, and blackberries along my nature trail.

Later, as I processed the day's harvest, I felt thankful for my life, which was so simple yet so rewarding.

Mirror said, "You were right when you said the syrups were a gift. This whole show is a gift, and it's good to share it with folks who have evolved so far from their food source. Somewhere in their chain of ancestors, their predecessors had to pick wild food to survive. I bet they never think of that."

Summer progressed, and in between customers I processed half a ton of cherries. That's the pits, literally. I had to invent a process for pitting the little buggers quicker than one cherry at a time. After many trials and errors, I had my efficient system.

Wild dew berries ripened next and picking them required me to crawl on the ground and pluck them from beneath their trailing vines. Most of my visitors had never tasted their unique flavor. Poison ivy and snakes were the hazards in harvesting dew berries. As soon as I finished with them, the wild blackberries were ripening. I got up early again to find them before others got there. There was a patch of great big ones just on the other side of the woods behind the Sugar Shack. It was delightful, as I could walk to them and still see my shop. I put my cell-phone number on a sign in the window. When customers came by, I didn't miss them.

One morning, when the bushes were still wet with dew, I arrived at the edge of the woods. It was easiest to drop down onto my hands and knees and crawl into the patch from the woods side. I wore my coveralls, boots, gloves, and a hat tied down over my ears, which protected me from getting scratched. As I crawled into the berries, I noticed they hung in large, black, shiny clumps just over my head. I settled onto my heels and began to fill my basket a handful at a time. It wasn't going to take long with that heavy crop of gorgeous, moist berries. I was in heaven. The sun was warm, the birds were singing, breezes were gently drying the foliage, and then—*rustle, crash, thump*, and I was ten inches away from the biggest, scariest, most threatening whitetail buck I had ever seen. What a set of antlers. He was a twelve-point at least. He was also snorting, angry, and pawing the ground.

I dropped the basket. The angry buck swung those horns back and forth, knocking blackberries all over the ground right in front of my eyes. He was close enough to touch, but I was angry, too. He was destroying the best picking I'd ever seen. He was pawing the ground and squashing the berries. I yelled, "Get the hell out of here, you bastard! You're smashing my berries."

The deer swung his head again and stomped once more in my direction as I waved my arms, knocking more blackberries off the bushes. I was on my feet now, screaming obscenities and stomping my own feet. We were advancing on each other. I was so infuriated that I forgot to consider what I intended to do. Suddenly, the buck turned, threw up his white flag of a tail, and disappeared into the brush.

I sat back down, salvaged what berries I could from the ground, and picked the rest of the patch. There were so many I had to make two trips through the woods to get them all home. As I carried my buckets of berries to the Sugar Shack, I muttered, "Good thing it wasn't hunting season, or that buck would have been headed for my stewpot. I guess I spoiled his nap and his berry-delicious lunch, anyway. It sure is funny how I have to beat the birds, the Amish, the deer, and all the other critters to get the berries I need. We need to have an agreement. If the deer are going to eat my crops, I'm going to eat one of them in the winter.

I loved to pick wild berries early on Sunday mornings after we opened the pancake restaurant in the Sugar Shack, when the tables were filled with tourists and city folks enjoying our pure maple syrup and my berry syrups on their waffles and pancakes. It was delightful to see their surprise when I walked in, covered with scratches and wearing torn old clothes, a basket of wild berries in each hand and burdocks in my hair. The customers were there in their Sunday go-to-meetin' clothing, and shock jumped all over their faces when I tromped through the restaurant in my farm boots with two baskets of whatever I had just picked. I would offer them a berry or two to taste, and then everyone in the restaurant would laugh as they shared the berries' unique flavor. Most of them ignored a bug or two, a leaf, a piece of bramble briar, a sticktight, and my appearance. Word of mouth brought lots more business to me, the old lady who really does go out into the woods to get the fruit.

As my customer base increased, so did the demand for my wild-berry syrups. I needed a much larger volume of fruit and more time to cover additional ground in search of berry patches in the wild.

Wild-elderberry syrup was one of my fastest-growing flavors. The tiny, bittersweet, dark purple berry grows along road ditches, in hedgerows, and at the outer edges of the woods. The flowers are white and resemble Queen Anne's lace, but on a bush up to ten feet high.

I drove the country roads in the springtime, searching for clumps of elderberry bushes, and then marked the spots on a map so I could find them again when they were ripe.

My maple-syrup–making friend, Peggy, twelve years my senior, volunteered to go elderberry picking with me. Because she was a bit older, I worried about her climbing down through ditches and along steep creek banks, so I selected a picking site in an old pasture.

I marked the bushes on my map and called on the farm owner to ask permission to pick them. He told me he had no use for elderberries and that I could have all of them. I said, "I'll stop and tell you each time I come to pick them."

"No, no, no. I work nights, and I don't want to be bothered. Just go in there and pick them when they're ready, but don't bother me," he said.

The white blossoms turned to green berries and then to ripe fruit the size of BBs. I had previously honed the method I use to this day: I pick a whole cluster of them at once by snipping off the stem just below the flat flower head, which is up to six inches across. Then I take them home and look them over by taking them off the stems. The stems of elderberries are poisonous, while, ironically, you eat the stems of the rhubarb plant but the leaves of it are poisonous.

Late in August, the elderberries were ripe. Peggy and I set off to spend the morning picking. We took two-and-a-half-gallon buckets so that any berries that fell off the clusters would be contained in the pail. They are such tiny berries, and mostly seeds, that we didn't want to waste even one.

We drove the country road to the farm with the overgrown pasture full of elderberry bushes. I parked along the roadside by the owner's driveway, in front of his barn, and we unloaded our pails. We put on long-sleeved shirts to protect us from poison ivy and a plant called cutweed, which lacerates your skin if it rakes across it. The brush and weeds were as tall as we were. We sprayed each other with insect repellant, stuck our scissors in our pockets, and set off. We waded across a creek, climbed over a barbwire fence, and fought our way through tall plants that stuck in our hair and clothes. Finally, we made it to the bushes, which held clusters of elderberries as big as saucers, so heavy with juice they bent the branches to the ground.

"What a crop. I guess we can get most of what we need right here," I said to Peggy.

"You said this was an easy place to pick, Gail. I think you lied to me," Peggy said with a chuckle. "How many old ladies past sixty-five do you think would crawl and fight their way in here for these miserable things?"

"At least we don't have to hang over the edge of a cliff and a creek to pick them. Did I ever tell you about the time I was picking elderberries at daylight up in Amish country?" I asked.

"No, you didn't. It couldn't have been any harder to get there than it was to get in here."

"Peggy, I got to the patch of berries just as it was daylight. It was already hot, and I had my little dog, Kanigo, with me. I was worried about her having to wait in the hot truck, and I didn't want her to bark and alert the Amish that I was in their neighborhood, picking their local wild berries so I left the truck running, with the air conditioner on and the windows up. I slid down a fifteen-foot embankment to a creek that wound under the road several times in a mile. I had just started to pick when I heard gravel crunching. I looked up, and the truck was rolling slowly down the gravel road."

"What did you do? How did it get started?" Peggy asked.

"I dropped my bucket and scissors and I scrambled and struggled and climbed back up the steep bank. Each step I took, the truck moved down the road above me faster. Finally I got to the top of the bank and ran as fast as I could. I got the door open and pulled myself in just as the right front tire started tilting off the road at the next culvert where the creek went under the road. I slammed my foot on the brake in the nick of time. Kanigo had bumped the shifting lever and knocked it out of park. Another second and the truck would have pitched over the creek embankment and landed on its nose in ten feet of water. It was a close call and the last time I ever took Kanigo with me to pick berries."

"I already have one pail full. Do you want me to leave it here or move it over by the fence where we came in?" Peggy asked.

"We can set them here in a cluster, and then we won't forget any. I have a pail full, too," I said.

While we picked, we traded news about our kids, neighbors, and community. Soon we had eight buckets full, all sitting in a cluster. Just as I put the last one I'd picked down with the others someone whistled, sharp and shrill. I looked up. Across the pasture, the barbwire fence, the creek, and a couple of acres of cutweed, an angry-looking man stood with his hands on his hips and his feet wide apart. He put one hand up to shade his eyes and yelled, "Hey, you! What are you doing down there?"

"We're picking these elderberries. Do you need something?" I asked innocently.

"Hell, yes. I need you to get out of there right now. And I mean *now*," he screamed. "Who told you that you could just walk in there and pick all my elderberries?" He waved his arms around wildly.

"The man who owns them and lives over there told us to just pick them and not bother him because he works nights," I hollered, pointing to the owner's house.

"Well, he doesn't fuckin' own 'em anymore. I do. Least you dumbasses could do is ask permission. Now get the hell out of there and off my land. Who told you to park by my driveway? Listen up, old lady, don't you dare set one foot on my lawn. You go over to that creek and get off my land that way, you hear?" he screamed.

"Oh, my God, Gail, he's really mad. I hope he doesn't have a gun or something. How are we gonna get out of here? I've never been thrown out of anywhere before. I'm past eighty years old, and this is a first. What are we going to do?" Peggy sputtered nervously.

I hollered back at the angry man, "Look, we didn't know the land had been sold. I'll give you all the berries. You can have them, and you won't have to pick them. I'm so sorry. We'll leave right now."

"Not so fast, old girl. I don't want them damn berries. If you'd asked, I'd have told you to pick 'em, but you didn't. Now you get out, and just leave them there."

"Are you going to leave ten pails of berries, Gail? What are we going to do? I don't think I can make it back through all that brush to the creek and then wade across the creek and up that steep bank." Peggy whispered, almost in tears.

I whispered back, "We won't leave a berry for that SOB. Put as many of the buckets on your belt and in your hands as you can, and stuff your scissors in your pocket. You can probably get three or four of the pails, and I'll carry the rest. Here's the plan. Look at him. He's heading for the house. We'll follow our path back through the cutweed and fence and cross the creek while he isn't looking. When we get to the edge of his lawn, we'll run as fast as we can to the truck," I explained.

When the man got to his porch, he turned toward us and yelled, "Not one foot on my lawn, understand? I'm going in to call the cops."

Peggy had already fastened a bucket to her belt and had one in each hand. That left seven for me. I undid my belt and strung one on each hip and one in the front and refastened the belt. Then I put one on each elbow and one in each hand,

and we headed back through the tall, terrible grass the way we came in.

Just as we got to the edge of the forbidden lawn, the mean guy appeared and started to yell again, "I told you to stay off my lawn..."

"Run, Peggy, run!" I yelled. We did the best we could with the buckets of elderberries hanging from our bodies and we were nearly at the truck when I heard sirens. "Hurry, Peggy. Just get in. Don't worry about spilling the berries." We got the doors open and managed to get in.

"The police are coming. I heard the sirens," Peg said.

"Don't worry. I'll have this thing down the road in a second," I said, trying to reassure her. She was trembling and really scared.

The awful man was running toward us. I wheeled the truck around on his lawn, and we headed down the road the way we came. We met a fire truck coming at us full speed ahead, but no cops.

"We left four empty buckets in the berry patch," Peggy said, as if she expected me to go back after them.

"To hell with the empty buckets. It's these full ones we need to rearrange," I said as I pulled over.

We got Peggy out of her belt and buckets and me out of mine and decided we had done enough picking for one day.

I chuckled as I finally finished my work for the day. Reminiscing had made my work time fly by.

Chapter Twenty-Two: Synergy and Accolades, 1996-2000

WHEN THE SNOW BEGAN to fall, it was time to plan for another year of Sugar Shack operation. Wild berries were in limited supply on my farms, and there wasn't a sufficient amount to keep up with the growth rate of the business. The solution was to plant berry bushes and fruit trees of all kinds. The problem was that the time from planting to the first full harvest was five years.

I ordered the stock from nurseries far and wide. I planned the delivery dates according to the unique microclimate in the five-mile strip of temperate weather along the shoreline of Lake Erie. The weather in this microclimate usually supports a five- to six-month growing season, as opposed to a three-month growing season just over the escarpment and five miles inland. Because it takes water longer to warm up in the springtime and to cool down in the fall, the thirty-five-mile width and two-hundred-foot depth of the water in Lake Erie create perfect conditions for forming a microclimate along the shoreline, that supports the largest juice-grape—growing region in the world.

I decided that the rational way to handle the Sugar Shack workload added to the grape -farm workload was to list all the chores in chronological order, estimate the time for each, and create a budget for my time.

My sons had observed my early business practices. Concerned, they had installed a QuickBooks program on a new computer for me, saying, "The tax guys will get you. You have to do this, like it or not."

That winter, I learned about laws, restrictions, licenses, and permits in the business world. I wanted to scream, "Help!" Instead, I called my local community college and asked for their help. They referred me to the Small Business Development Center on their campus.

The appointment made me think long and hard about the nuts and bolts of the operation. I had to reconcile my expenditures and sales to find out if I was operating in the black. I had just been having a grand time with the tourists. I felt wonderful about making them happy and getting their thank-you notes and letters of appreciation. The business stuff and records for the government were hard work.

Mirror spoke up in its know-it-all way. "You're just mentally lazy. It'll do you good to keep records and file reports."

I seriously considered quitting. I had enough records to keep for grape farming; I had spray schools to attend and chemical records to keep. Keeping labor records and meeting filing deadlines took up a huge amount of my time. How could I possibly do all the work of growing, picking, processing, manufacturing, bottling, labeling, stocking, waiting on people, maintaining the grape businesses, and comply with still more government regulations and record keeping?

I rearranged my life and work and added education, planning, and complaining to my off-season list.

The Small Business Development Center researched the permits I needed, got applications, and helped me file all the legal stuff. I got a business license and a sales-tax number. Larry converted the old bedroom that had been the Containerboard war room into a business office; he installed desks, computers, printers, and filing cabinets.

I spent that winter learning new computer skills from Andy, including how to use a credit-card machine, and packing and shipping intricacies.

One day, soon after Larry retired from the military, he asked me to ride to the New York State employment office in the next town so he could look for work. About three miles from my farm, he noticed a man putting up a sign in his yard. It said, "HOME WITH LAKEFRONT FOR SALE BY OWNER."

Larry said, "Did you see that sign? Turn around and go back. We'll take a look."

"No, Larry. I already have lakefront. I don't need anymore."

"But, Mom, you should at least look. You never know what he has."

He kept on insisting for the next twelve miles. Finally, I agreed to go back and take a look, just as a comparison for the value of my own lakefront land. As we pulled into his driveway, the man was putting his tools away, the sign securely pounded into his front yard.

"Hi," I said when I'd rolled down the truck window. "What do you have here?"

"I've got eighteen acres of beautiful Lake Erie lakefront, plus the house, and I want to sell it. Let me take you out back to the lake and show you," he said proudly.

Larry moved over; John, the old man, got in; and we drove about two thousand feet to the back of his property. We drove through open fields full of fall wildflowers and then into a shaded lane of hard maples. We rolled through locusts and hornbeam and oak and ash trees, and suddenly the forest opened onto a perfectly manicured picnic area. At the end of the clearing were the high bluff cliffs at the edge of the lake. On one side was a manmade access road, heading straight down the forty feet to a gorgeous three-hundred-foot beach. The frontage was approximately a thousand feet. The beauty took my breath away.

"What's the house like?" I asked.

"I built it myself back in the early sixties. It's solid as a rock. I built it right, because I built it for myself. Drive back up, and I'll show you." He added, "I never expected to have anybody stop to see it so soon. My wife divorced me after forty-five years of marriage, because she thought I cheated on her the first year we were married. Now I'm not in such good health, and I don't want to be here alone anymore."

We followed John into the attached garage and then up a few steps into the kitchen. It was out of date, but it was large and nicely finished. Then he showed us the bedrooms, living room, eating area, and bathroom. "I have one room finished in the cellar. The cellar looks out at ground level. In other words, you can just walk right out into the backyard. There's electric heat, and I have a woodstove. You can see there's plenty of wood to cut for the wood stove," he continued as we made our way to the basement. The finished room was full of old tires. The rest of the basement was full of firewood and an antique woodstove. It was dirty, but the foundation was poured concrete, and the floor joists were even, straight, and drilled for plumbing and wiring. It was a professional job.

When we returned to the kitchen table, I was thinking there was no way I was going to buy this messy place. It would take me two years and a drum of Mr. Clean just to get it livable. I asked what he wanted for it, and he said, "$125,000, as you see it. I wasn't expecting to sell it for a long time. It usually takes time to sell a home place."

I distinctly heard myself say, "I'll take it." I jumped at the sound of my voice. Larry was grinning from ear to ear. "I'll go get my checkbook and give you a down payment, hand money, you know, to hold the deal."

"Oh no, Mrs. Black, I know who you are." I hadn't introduced myself, and I was surprised that he knew me. "We'll just shake hands. I don't want to sell it right now—thought it would take awhile, you know. I need to find a place near my son and the VA hospital in Buffalo, and I don't want to sell 'till I get that done. We'll just shake hands."

"I don't want to buy it right now, either," I said. "Just let me give you some money to bind our agreement."

"Nope, won't have it. A handshake is all I need." He stuck out his hand, and we shook.

Our shaky deal lasted for almost two years. Every once in a while, he would drive in, roll the window down, and say, "You ain't changed your mind, have ya?" I would reassure him that I hadn't and ask if he wanted money. He always replied that the handshake was all that was necessary.

I was convinced that I would never see the day that the deal was final. He took the sign down two hours after he put it up. In those two hours, every real-estate salesperson in the state of New York must have driven by. They heckled him continuously, telling him it was worth twice what he'd agreed to sell it for. They begged him to tell them who he'd sold it to, and he refused. I didn't tell anyone, either. The longer the deal dragged on, the more I really wanted the place.

One day, he drove in and said, "I'm ready. I have a place in Buffalo, and I'm ready to go. I know you'll take good care of her and not develop her, and I know you'll keep her mowed and the woods clean. I have no regrets about selling her to you."

I paid him and then faced all the angry next-door neighbors who had also tried to buy that land. Larry asked what I was going to do with it, and I honestly didn't know. He suggested that I make it a bed-and-breakfast; I already had a great tourist-based business, and it would be such a compatible addition. "Synergy," I think he called it.

After closing the deal, I worked all winter to clean, remodel, and furnish the house. I bought books on how to run a B and B. I went back to the Small Business Development Center and enlisted their help. Finally, I had my first customer. What I hadn't realized was that the closest neighbor—only a couple hundred feet through some trees—ran a daycare. Somehow, when I wrote the sketchy business plan for the B and B, I had forgotten to survey the neighborhood. These neighbors also had several chickens and a rooster that crowed at dawn. A couple of big, snorting, rooting, smelly pigs lived in a muddy, garbage-infested pen, but they were a few hundred feet away. I had never been to the house at dawn, and I worked on the house and yard in the evenings, when the daycare was closed. The pigs weren't a problem until the summer grew hot and humid and the wind blew from the northeast.

Even with this undesirable neighborhood circus next door, I was able to rent enough rooms at the B and B to cover the cost of taxes and utilities. However, when I failed to get repeat customers I realize that the neighbors were definitely a problem. Drastic measures were in order. I went to the young couple next door and offered to cook a rooster dinner—using their rooster. I offered to butcher their hogs and cure the ham and bacon for them. I offered to move the daycare fence to the other side of their house. They would have none of it. I persisted for several years.

Finally, the husband said, "If we could just find somebody who would buy it, we'd sell it."

The bed-and-breakfast section of my tourist-based business doubled when I bought their little farm, and so did my workload.

This second piece of property bordered the east side of my originally purchased one, stretching all the way to Lake Erie and nearly doubling the lakefront. As I finalized the paperwork, I discovered that the ten acres were covered with abandoned, deteriorating farm equipment, discarded furniture, old appliances, and more. The fields could not be mowed, and cutting the fallen trees in the woods was a problem because of metal staples, barbwire fencing, and maple-syrup taps that had grown into the tree trunks. Hitting even one piece of metal with a chainsaw would ruin the blade or perhaps cause the saw to buck, injuring the operator. Cleaning up the ten acres took the better part of a year. The inside of the house needed to be updated, as did the furnace. I eliminated the old water system and replaced it with a state-of-the-art one that chlorinated and softened the water and delivered an abundant supply to both houses. Eventually, I had a newly painted, updated, furnished second house to use as additional bed-and-breakfast accommodations.

Chapter Twenty-Three: Self-Propelled Business, 2000-2010

In the master plan over which I had no control and no privilege of insight, my youngest son went to college and specialized in general agriculture. When he received his degree, he informed me that he had always wanted a first-class maple-syrup–production business and a pancake house where he could serve the syrup.

He was a great kid, and, like his brothers, he had worked hard all his life in the grape vineyard, gotten his tractor certification as soon as he was old enough, and learned to tie knots before he went to school by tying grapevines to the bottom trellis wire— the only one he could reach at the time. However, he had no business experience and had been absent or preoccupied with growing up during most of my business-expansion years. I had several businesses going that demanded my full attention and all my resources worked to expand them. I said, "Okay, Robert, you get a job selling tractors at one of the local farm-equipment businesses, show me your abilities, and I'll think about it." He sold so many lawn tractors that the farm-equipment store had to restock. He built a customer base that followed him to his maple business and became loyal customers.

One day, Rob announced to me that I had never taken him on any vacations when he was a kid. I said, "Damn straight I didn't take you on many vacations. I had to work the farms and support you. I had to put your brothers and you through college. There wasn't any money or time. What do you want me to do about it now?"

"I was about to tell you that since I have my commercial driver's license, I thought I would get a job driving a tour bus," he said.

He went to work for Coach USA, and, again, it ended up being a part of the master plan we never could have fathomed. He drove both local and long-distance trips for school groups, seniors, and sports teams. He traveled everywhere and honed his tourism skills. He was really proving himself to me. He had sold more tractors and lawn mowers in a difficult farm economy than anyone else had in a long time. His bus-driving job went wonderfully well; he was seeing all the hot tourist spots while getting paid and enjoying the passengers.

One day he called me and said, "Mom, I'm three hours east of you with a busload of senior citizens, near Corning, New York. We just arrived at a business where there's a gift shop and a restaurant. We had reservations, but the place is closed down; the door is locked, and nobody's here. The old folks are mad as hell, and I thought maybe I could bring them to your shop as an alternative on my way back to Erie. What do you think?" He sounded completely stressed. I could hear the angry passengers' voices in the background. Like every mother I know, I wanted to do everything possible to help him.

I said, "Bring them. I'll do some free tastings over ice cream. I'll give them a grape-farm tour and a nature walk in the woods, too."

He called his home office and talked to his boss, and they started on their way. It was the first bus tour to visit the Sugar

Shack, and I am convinced that it was all part of the bigger picture, over which I had no control.

By the time they arrived, I had pots of coffee made, ice cream and fruit-syrup samples prepared, the gift shop rearranged to accommodate a busload of people, and my nerves calmed down.

Meanwhile, as the bus moved steadily toward me and my business, my son told his senior passengers jokes, explained what the Sugar Shack was all about, and prepared his clients for a fun stop. His boss had suggested he stop at the nearest McDonald's and treat everyone, which gave me a bit of additional preparation time.

Robert soon drove the bus right up to the Sugar Shack porch, where he made it kneel. The door swung open, and he invited me onboard and handed me a microphone. I had no idea what to say, but managed to welcome the seniors, told them what our game plan was, and invited them in. I was pleasantly surprised to hear the questions and witness the interest they had in my farming enterprise. Many of them later returned on their own with family and friends.

One small, innovative kindness, and I was in the bus-tour business. My businesses just kept advancing without any conscious effort on my part. I realized that I was prepared for this predestined, high-energy business thanks to my multitasking experiences involving illness, farming, abuse, community, school involvement, and various part-time jobs in my past. Now all those experiences seemed to be coming together like a jigsaw puzzle.

I was mowing the lawn one afternoon when a car drove slowly down my driveway. As usual, I stopped the riding mower, jumped off, and greeted the couple. They were from the Cleveland, Ohio, area and had seen my sign. I learned that when the gentleman saw my sign, he said, "I'm going to drive in here and see this place."

Esther, his wife, said, "You can't drive in there. It's a private driveway."

"There's a sign by the road that says Sugar Shack. It's not a private driveway," he insisted as he made his way down the long gravel driveway between my vineyards.

They tasted and took my tour through the woods. We walked and talked, and as we meandered through the hardwood maple trees, with the blue tubing strung from one to another, I explained the sap-gathering process. We passed wildflowers, endangered plants, and various berries growing along the trail. I was identifying some wild black-currant bushes as we passed my old mailbox, which was still riddled with the bullet holes that dated back to the Containerboard fight.

I had installed the mailbox along the trail near the edge of the cliffs so that people would be curious and ask me what it was doing there. Sure enough, they asked, just as I'd suspected folks would.

"What's the mailbox doing here?" Esther asked.

"Well, a $210 million paper mill tried to locate here a few years ago, and I got embroiled in a bitter battle with local developers, politicians, and the paper-mill company," I answered.

"Did it locate here?" the gentleman, Carl, asked.

"No. It was a long three-and-a-half-year battle, but it went away. My mailbox was up by the road where you turned in. Someone thought they could intimidate me by shooting it with a .45 caliber hand gun. It made me mad instead of frightening me, so I loaded my own handgun and took advantage of my permit to carry. For years after that, I never left the house without the revolver in my pocket. Eventually, after many bitter battles, our small group of concerned citizens sued the town to ensure full disclosure of the project. We won, and the plant was never built."

I continued, "It would have drained polluted, untreated wastewater down this beautiful little creek here beside us. The creek would have dumped that dirty paper-mill waste right here into Lake Erie, into some of the best bass-breeding grounds in the world. We felt that it would damage our pristine grape-growing region and even eliminate it completely. Cornell University's grape specialist found that a 19.4 percent reduction in the productivity of Concord grapes would occur. No grape farmer here works on a 19.4 percent profit margin, so grapes for a ten-mile radius would have been eliminated."

"Anyway," I continued as the mailbox with the bullet hole enabled me to, "our group found many other environmental problems with air quality close to the school and hospital windows. We found what we felt were disastrous financial implications for the citizens of our community and county, including the paper mill's free use of our county-owned landfill and its projected diminished life before it was filled. There would have been no cost to the paper mill; our taxpayers would have paid the price."

"The mailbox and all the other intimidating threats against me only made me more dedicated to keeping that paper mill out of here. It wasn't a pretty fight, and it cost me a lot of personal time and money, but now I have the opportunity to tell other people to watch their backs, their environment, and their politicians, with possible personal agendas, who may cut deals and spend taxpayers' money in the name of environmentally unsound economic development."

By now, we had walked the trail to its end and had arrived at the pond, fruit trees, berry bushes, and vineyard. I explained the climate along Lake Erie, its effect on the grape industry, and how the grape business worked. We were looking at the circa

1832 house I lived in. They were so interested and attentive that the tour just went on and on.

Not long after they signed my guest book, marked their home with a star on my wall map, and returned to Cleveland, Ohio, they called to book a bus tour for Esther's fellow city-hall workers. The booking was to include a pancake meal, a woods walk, and a talk including everything she and her husband had heard.

The bus tour arrived on a hot summer day, and the group enjoyed their experience so much that they returned each summer for about ten years. We look forward to their visit, and so do they. Over the years, they have watched the business grow and the pancake restaurant develop.

Bus groups have become regular events, and I've found that I can design a tour to suit the interests of each. They come from Alabama; New Jersey; Pennsylvania; the Niagara frontier; Rochester, New York; Ohio; and many other places.

My sons kept encouraging me to do more and more. The master planner kept dumping more responsibility and new experiences onto my farm. Thank goodness it happened gradually. The woman who had forgotten about the arrival of the bus tour near Corning had lost a great opportunity. However, I had gained another avenue to connect with tourism, tell my stories, and promote other businesses in my area.

It became habit to get back on each bus and thank the people for coming, invite them back, and bid them farewell with a joke or story to make them laugh. I discovered that most people loved to be entertained, and I perfected my storytelling abilities.

Many customers from the first five years come to mind when I explore the journey leading to the success of the Sugar Shack. As people visited my business and I interacted with them, I found that my former life experiences were a basis and a bond with them. Often, it seemed as though they had come down my driveway just to entertain me with their lifelong experiences that held a whole range of human emotion. Other times, my own experiences were germane to the conversation. Sometimes their visits were just random, but they were always fun.

Occasionally, folks wandered in who needed uplifting or inspiration for overcoming a difficulty. Sometimes people just needed a bathroom, but they all bought something, which reinforced my theory that you should never put up a sign that says, "No bathroom here; no telephone here; no food served here; no shoes, no shirt...," because the whole point of the endeavor is to get them in the door.

One time, five women from Minneapolis, Minnesota, drove in. When I asked them how they'd happened to stop at the Sugar Shack, they all started to laugh hysterically.

"We saw your sign, and we just *had* to stop," one woman, apparently the oldest, said. She was clearly the spokeswoman for the group. "We're on our last sisters' vacation. We're all past eighty-year-old and decided that we wanted to travel along some of the Great Lakes shoreline, and here we are."

Around that time, a big, burly, robust man entered the shop. Because we were already engaged in the tasting experience, I offered him a dish of ice cream and included him in our conversation. He told us he was a heavy-equipment salesman and wanted to know if I would like a catalogue of his brand of farm tractors. I declined, but one of the ladies said, "I don't want a tractor, but I'd love to have a picture with you."

She asked if I would take a picture of them with this guy in the middle. She wanted it taken under the Sugar Shack sign over the door. The salesman good-naturedly agreed.

It wasn't necessary to ask them to smile, as they were laughing uncontrollably. I asked them to share the fun, and the spokeswoman said, "Back in Minneapolis, Minnesota, a sugar shack is a male strip joint. We want a picture of all of us with this handsome man so we can tell our bridge club that this is what we found at a sugar shack in New York State."

Lots of customers arrived and departed who tasted, bought products, and received tourist pamphlets and information, and a trend began. Sometimes folks would say, "Hi. Remember us? We were here last summer." At first I would say that I didn't remember them, and they always seemed surprised. But there were hundreds of them and only one of me.

Whenever I stepped off my front porch to cross the yard and greet another carload of customers, I never knew what to expect. The experiences were varied and provided great conversations with other tourist vendors as I sent my guests to their businesses, multiplying the benefit of tourism in our community.

The Sugar Shack became famous, and unsolicited news articles and positive reviews appeared in local newspapers. The caption under my picture in one such story called me "Chautauqua County woman"; another caption was, "Following the golden rule." These new tags were big improvements over my former nickname of "economic-development terrorist."

I was asked to be a panelist at a cooperative extension workshop on agritourism in Auburn, New York, and then participated as a speaker at a statewide event in Buffalo. My business was used as a case study for New York Sea Grant. Within the first few years, I became a positive influence and leader in the fledgling agritourism industry in New York State.

As I thought about the progress, I remembered that in 1996, the third year in business, I'd seen an article in my local paper announcing a contest for the national scenic highway called the Seaway Trail, a national scenic byway, which was New York State Route 5, the road in front of my farm, which also followed the Lake Erie shoreline. An award was being offered for the best business use of the Seaway Trail, and there was a specific prize for the western section from Niagara Falls to the New York/

Pennsylvania state line. I wrote a letter, got an application, and sent it in. The application asked for supporting letters from an applicant's community. *Fat chance of that*, I thought.

As I thought about the support I needed, I remembered my old friend, the mayor, who had been such a positive part of my years in Westfield before the paper-mill controversy. I had been his campaign manager before he became one of the legislators who were angry that I opposed the paper mill's arrival in our community. Our families had been such good friends, sharing children's birthdays, confirmations, graduations, challenges, and successes. But due to our political differences over development, we had become bitter enemies and did not even speak.

I felt sad and held a deep sense of loss over this rift; I missed my old friend. The controversy was over. I wondered what would happen if I made the first move—offered the olive branch, so to say, to rebuild the relationship. After all, our feud had been caused by a difference of opinion over an issue, which wasn't something that should kill a longtime friendship. I picked up the phone, dialed the old number from memory, and my friend answered.

"This is Gail. I miss you and your family in my life. Is there any way we can put the Containerboard issue aside and go on with our friendship?" I asked.

Without any hesitation, my old friend said, "Put the teakettle on, and I'll be right there for a cup of tea." The friendship was healed, but discussion of the paper mill was still a no-no. When I told the mayor about the Seaway Trail award and what the publicity would do for our town and county and how I perceived that it would help, he offered to write the supporting letter. I won the award and a lovely plaque, which I hung permanently in my gift shop.

The award was formally given at a statewide Seaway Trail luncheon, which was held in our county. News articles about the event appeared in papers across the state, and I eventually was asked to sit on the Seaway Trail board of directors. Through this position, I was able to directly impact several aspects of growing and publicizing tourism in Chautauqua County. First, I was able to organize a group that included our new chamber of commerce president, our Westfield development director, our county executive, my legislator friend, and me to travel to the new Seaway Trail Discovery Center north of Syracuse, at Sackets Harbor, New York. There, we designed and installed the first display the public sees when they enter the Discovery Center. We built an actual grape arbor in the museum, and provided information about Westfield and Chautauqua County, the largest juice-grape–growing area in the world. The added publicity for our county heightened interest in developing a tourism industry as an alternative to paper mills and other heavy industrial development. A new emphasis on visitor-friendly businesses led people passing through our area on the main highways to spend time and money here, which helped our local economy. Perhaps a greater power than me wanted to see tourism development instead of industrial development.

Many others visited my business, and the memories grew. So did my file of "love letters." Sometimes gifts appeared, and lots of Christmas cards stuffed my mailbox. Keeping up with the fan mail was a time-consuming chore. I started to file the letters and pictures in thick three-ring binders.

One day, an older pickup truck interrupted a tasting session, beeping its horn loudly. I excused myself and stepped out the door. The truck window came down, and the man and woman inside held out a brown paper bag and said, "You probably don't remember us, but we're from Kentucky. We sent you some of our own sorghum syrup. We thought you must be out by now, so we came around this way on our trip to Maine. Here's another quart. Thanks again for a great time a few years ago."

Before I could do more than say "Thanks," they were gone.

Another day, a car with Georgia plates drove slowly down the driveway, and I was across the lawn before they got out. The old couple had difficulty getting their stiff bones and muscles to stand up and my first thought was that they might be lost. Then the woman, whose name was Margaret and who turned out to be celebrating her ninetieth birthday, said, "We finally found you." Speaking to the gentleman, whose name was Charlie, she said, "Get her prize out of the trunk, and give it to her."

Charlie shuffled to the rear of the car, fumbled with the key as he steadied his hand to get it into the lock, and then withdrew a large cardboard box from the trunk. I could see something wooden inside. He took his treasure out of the box, held it up for me to see, and said, "You win the prize, sweetheart."

Margaret said, "Charlie worked for almost a year to make this sconce for you. He has a wood-working shop in our garage. We'd have been here last year, but he had a heart attack and open-heart surgery, and we couldn't travel. We'd have been here last spring, but I had to have a hip replacement, so this is the first we could come to give you your award."

I was completely overwhelmed and confused. "What award are you talking about?"

Charlie grinned and said, "Girly, you won our hospitality award. This wall sconce is your prize so you won't forget us. We had to sneak away, because our kids didn't think we should drive from Georgia to here. We thought we could just come straight to you and your Sugar Shack, but we was wrong. We didn't remember quite as good as we thought we did. We ended up east of here, near Corning. We drove all around and couldn't seem to find you, so we stopped at an information booth on Interstate 86. The lady there looked pretty puzzled at first, but then she said, 'Does she make fruit syrups along with maple?'

"We said yes and told her that you lived by a large body of water. As luck would have it, she had been here, too, and she told us just how to find you." He turned to his wife of sixty-nine years and said, "Margaret, get the rest of this darned thing."

She reached in the back seat and brought out the glass chimney for the sconce. Then she said, "Charlie, get her the rest of your gift."

Charlie rummaged around in the trunk again and came out with a paper bag containing a bottle of homemade Concord-grape wine. "Get the rest of it, Charlie," she urged, waggling her finger at the car. He pulled two jars of grape jelly from the backseat and handed them to me.

"I'm flabbergasted," I said. "I don't know what I ever did to deserve these delightful gifts and your award, but thank you from the bottom of my heart. I'm so thankful and humbled that you'd make such an effort to come and see me again. Whatever did I do to earn this?"

"You were kind to a couple of old folks three years ago. We drove down that driveway at five after five in the afternoon. Your 'closed' sign was in the window, and you were just stepping onto your front porch. You turned around and came back to your shop. We thought you were going to tell us you were closed, but you said you'd open the door for us. We asked to use your bathroom, and you said to come right in, that you had added two new ones when you started the pancake restaurant. You offered us some samples and gave us a bit of ice cream.

"We were really tired, in our late eighties and, frankly, just exhausted. You asked us if we'd like to sit on the porch in front of your gift shop. Then you let us eat our sandwiches there. To top it off, you told us we could go out by the lake to a picnic table if we wanted to. You brought us each a glass of grape juice, too.

"We couldn't think of a time when anyone had been so hospitable when we just needed a bathroom. So you won our hospitality award. We bought some grapes from your you-pick operation, but you said we looked tired and that you'd pick them for us while we rested by the lake. We made the wine and jelly out of those grapes and brought some to share with you."

I was so moved that tears ran down my face. It was a humbling reaffirmation that the more I gave of myself and the gifts with which I had been blessed, the more I would receive in thoughtfulness and friendship.

Before the season finished that year, I had another visitor who will always hold a place in my memory. An expensive Mercedes roared down my driveway and slammed to a stop in a cloud of dust. The door flew open, and a stylish middle-aged woman stepped out, threw up her hands, and said, "I don't have a clue why I drove in here. What is this place, anyway? Is it a farm or a gift shop of some kind? I don't know why I'm here. I don't have any money, not a cent, not a nickel, not enough to buy a cup of coffee. I was driving by and just felt compelled to turn around and drive in here. That's crazy, I know. So you tell me why I'm here."

I heard myself say, "Well, no matter the reason, come on in. Let me give you some ice cream with fruit syrup on it, and we'll talk about it."

"I told you, I don't have any money. I can't buy ice cream. I have one tank of gas, and that's all. I don't have any grocery money. I've only got what food is in the cupboard. That bastard left me here—broke, flat broke. And he won't be back for a week."

"That's okay," I said. "The tasting is free, and so is the listening. Please tell me what's wrong. Maybe I can help."

The woman started to cry and then to sob hysterically. "He shoved me. He broke my favorite coffee mug. He told me he was leaving, that he'd be back when he was good and ready," she said between the tears.

I suggested that we walk out to the edge of Lake Erie, sit at the picnic table, listen to the waves crashing against the cliffs and rocks, and she could tell me all about it. I took her arm, and we went into the woods to the table. It turned out that she was the wife of a famous, wealthy surgeon from a neighboring city. They'd had a fight, one of many in their thirty years of marriage, and she was sure he was leaving her at their condo so he could carry on with a girlfriend. After she had shed her tears, vented her anger, and dealt with the blow to her self-esteem, we talked about the options she had and actions she could take. Forty-five minutes later, she apologized for her distress. I told her that no apology was necessary, and she went on her way. I questioned what that was all about, shrugged my shoulders and said to Mirror in my front hall, "Can't figure some of 'em out."

Mirror, who had been quiet for a long, long time, replied, "You probably haven't heard the last of her. Next time, you'd better tell her about the abuse you endured."

I didn't need to listen to that damned mirror on the wall. I didn't need to think about the abuse I had endured. It was all in the past. What could my stories possibly do for that stranger? Nothing. I went on with my work.

A few weeks later, that black Mercedes again screamed down my driveway in a cloud of dust. As I walked through the front hall, Mirror said, "She's back. Remember what I said." A cold shiver ran through my body, and I shook it off.

The "woman from *Vogue*" stepped into my gift shop. Her eyes were swollen, and she was slumped forward in defeat. I said, "How are you today? Good to see you again."

"Nothing's changed. He's gone again and left me no money or food and only half a tank of gas. The only place I wanted to go was here to see you."

"Do you want to go out by the lake again?" I asked.

"No. I just came by to say thank-you for listening to me a few weeks ago. I thought maybe I was wrong about him, but this time, he pushed me and slapped me and ..." She began to sob again.

We sat down on the porch. I asked, "Do you have any friends or family in the area?"

She replied slowly, "He won't let me have any friends. We're in and out so much that I'm never at the condo long enough to make friends. Every time I meet a potential friend, he insists we leave. You know, I haven't told him about you. I hope we can be friends." She looked at me for a moment. "Why are you so kind to me?"

I hadn't realized I had been. I was just concerned about a fellow human being in distress.

Mirror screamed across the summer breeze at me as we sat on the porch of the Sugar Shack. It said, "You know what you have to do! Tell her you understand and why you understand and that she can survive no matter what he does or what happens. Tell her, you coward."

Talking about my abusive marriage and its tragic end was heartrending, devastating, emotionally draining, humiliating, and probably in bad taste at my place of business, which was designed for my customers' enjoyment and entertainment. No. I was not going to subject myself or her to that debilitating dialogue.

Mirror, loud and clear, on the summer breeze, simply yelled, "*Now.*" I watched myself, as if from above, struggle with the decision.

I took the lovely lady's hands, eased her onto the porch swing, and said, "Let me tell you what happened to me. Maybe there are things to be learned from my experience, maybe not. No matter. I need to tell you, because I totally understand what you're experiencing." Slowly, painfully, dredging up courage, questioning my sanity for listening to Mirror, I began.

She didn't interrupt me from the time I started to recount my horrible, abusive marriage until I finished.

My customer was sitting on the edge of the porch swing, she was extremely attentive; several times, she nodded and said, "That's it, exactly. Just like me. I'm not the only one. I thought I was the only one." By now, I was crying with the memories.

Finally, I said, "I think that's enough for now."

She hugged me. I hugged her.

She asked, "How did you survive?"

"Someday I'll finish the story, but for now you need to know that you're not alone. Please, please, call the hotline for abused women."

She agreed to do that, and I didn't see her for a couple of years.

It surprised me that my whole accounting of the terrible events took two hours. It also surprised me that I had had no interruptions—no customers, no phone calls, nothing. It was unusual.

Two years later, the *Vogue* lady brought her abusive husband to my shop. When I saw her drive in with him in the passenger seat, I wondered if they had tried counseling and if it had been successful. She came into my shop, and we laughed and talked while her husband sat on the porch.

At last, she bought a bottle of maple syrup, and we went out on the porch. She said to her husband, "See, I *told* you I had a friend." I knew then that he had not changed and neither had her situation. I felt sad and lucky at the same time and hoped that the friendship I offered was helpful to her.

The day-to-day operation of the Sugar Shack demanded all my attention all year long as I greeted and treated all customers—rich or poor—equally. In January, I needed to take a complete inventory of the Sugar Shack; update charts with sales information; and order stock for both the shop and the manufacturing kitchen. That meant counting all the bottles, caps, labels, and ingredients on hand. Addressing income-taxes was also on the agenda. Once maple sap began to flow from the trees, I had no rest. I had to create all the craft items as well. Winter was not a time of rest, although the tourist traffic diminished significantly. As soon as the peepers started to chirp in the spring, we knew maple-syrup season was over, and it was time to clean, sterilize, and put away all the equipment again.

Several craft and sports shows invited me to display and sell my wares during the winter months. That meant I had to pack up all the stock, including crafts and decorations for the display; I also had to prepare sales-record sheets, tasting supplies, and signage. Participating in these shows took time: three days to pack and travel to the shows; three or four days of intense selling at the shows; and then three days to travel home, unpack, sort, and store all the inventory and equipment. Licenses had to be renewed; decisions about advertising had to be made; and, of course, the B and B needed to be booked for the summer season.

By mid-April, I was ready to check on the rhubarb crop again, fertilize the rest of the crops, and check to make sure I hadn't forgotten to prune any trees or berry bushes. And I always tilled up a good-sized garden for my own eating and canning.

My black and white cocker spaniel worked as hard as I did at the Sugar Shack. Wannago, Kanigo's successor, would bark every time someone drove down our driveway. I had a buzzer in my cellar's commercial-cook kitchen, one in my office, and one in my sewing room. Wannago would sound her own alarm, and then the buzzer would go off. She would always beat me to the gift shop and keep the customers occupied with her dancing, prancing, jumping, and wonderful smile, an actual grin of welcome. She had several different barks, and I learned to differentiate among them. She had one voice for the tractor trailer full of restaurant supplies; one for the UPS man, who carried a treat for her; one for customers; and one for raccoons, squirrels, rabbits, or deer that ventured into our yard. She also had a special voice for the Amish when they came to sell me their baskets and leather goods at wholesale for my shop. They arrived in a horse-and–buggy, and Wannago thought the horse was there to play with her.

One day, an Amish man named Maylon and his horse-and-buggy came down the driveway with a *clippity-clop*, and he tied his horse-and-buggy to a telephone pole. Wannago beat me out the door just as Maylon was lifting a box of wonderful homemade leather doorbells out of the buggy. I made my selection for resale, and then I grinned and said facetiously, "Maylon, if I put gasoline in this rig, what would you charge me for a little ride in this buggy?"

Maylon stroked his beard and thought about the joke for a moment. When he understood the humor in my question, he said, "Well, Gail, I don't think it would be right to charge you. Just climb in. Where would you like to go?"

"Just around the grape vineyard would be fine. I've always wanted to know how it felt to ride in one of your Amish buggies."

He untied the horse, and I put Wannago in the house, much to her disgust. Off we went, slowly rocking from side to side a trifle with the horse's gait. The ground was soft and a little muddy, and the new leaves of spring were just softening the starkness of winter.

Quiet and peacefulness prevailed as the rhythmic *clip clop* of the horse took us past my pond and woods and along the end of the vineyard. We turned the corner, and there was my neighbor Mary's house straight ahead.

Mary was another angel in my life. She was old enough to be my mother, and her family had owned the land I lived on long before I did. Apples, chickens, and grapes had kept the wolf from their door and provided them with a good life.

Mary and her husband were Italian immigrants with a proud history of becoming productive Americans. She gifted me with wonderful Italian delicacies and dinners; she taught me about wildflowers and added to my knowledge of gardening. She gave me asparagus from her garden every spring, and I gave her rhubarb. Mary was tiny, only about 4'10", a bit shorter than I am. She would walk from her house to mine and pick wildflower bouquets for me. Whenever she knocked on my door, I'd put the kettle on. We enjoyed tea and a walk in the woods on nice days.

The day Maylon and I took our buggy ride was her birthday. She had white hair now; her husband had died, and her sons lived far away. Mary's life was her church, religion, and prayers. She called on the sick and prayed for others daily. She was a dear, sweet, loving person. She was a treasure as neighbors go.

I had a wild inspiration. "Maylon," I joked, "if I put more gasoline in this rig and paid you money for an oil change, what would you charge me to take my neighbor for a ride? It's her eighty-eighth birthday, and I can't imagine how an Amish buggy ride would delight her."

Maylon laughed as he pulled on the reins and stopped the horse. "She's eighty-eight? Where does she live?"

"Right across the road, there." I pointed.

"Okay. I'll circle the house and pull up by the kitchen door," he said. He cracked the reins, and the horse crossed New York State Highway 5. The sharp *click click* of the horse's hoofs on the pavement was so different from the soft *clip clop* they'd made in the mud surrounding my grapes.

I hopped down from the buggy and felt the springs give way a bit as I did. Up the steps to Mary's door I trotted. She had seen me coming and opened the door immediately.

"Mary, I have your birthday present here for you. It's an Amish buggy ride. Are you interested?"

Mary threw her tiny hands in the air and exclaimed, "Lord a mercy. I'd love to have a ride. Just help me get this apron off."

We struggled to get her old-fashioned bib apron untied and over her head and then found that she was too little to step up into the high buggy. Maylon took care of that. He just picked her tiny frame up and set her on the seat like a little doll.

Off we went down the side of the highway, with her grinning and hanging on and yelling, "Lord a mercy," over and over. We rode a mile along Lake Erie to Barcelona Harbor. Maylon turned down the driveway to the pier and let her enjoy the soft spring breeze and beautiful blue water that stretched as far as the eye could see.

On the way back, the slow, rhythmic *click click* of the horse was interrupted only when a tractor trailer zoomed by, billowing its diesel smoke. "Maylon, would it cost me extra to have you put this rig in overdrive?" I giggled. He was sitting backward in front of us, and the horse was slowly walking along.

"You want to see overdrive?" he asked.

"Yup."

"Hang on," he said. He turned around, cracked his whip, and the horse took off at a gallop. The buggy lurched and swayed, and the springs squeaked. Mary squealed, and the wheels whined; the spokes looked like they were turning backward with the speed. I hung onto her and the buggy for survival. The wheels seemed to be loose and made a constant grinding sound on the pavement as we sped along toward Mary's house. When we turned into her driveway, I thought we would tip over, but the buggy springs kept us upright.

Mary was on her feet, waiting to be lifted down, the minute we stopped at her kitchen door. "Wait, Maylon, wait right here," she demanded as she wiggled her finger at him. She dashed into her kitchen and returned seconds later with a fresh rhubarb pie. "Here you go. Warm from the oven, just for you. I had a wonderful time."

304

Maylon said in his broken German accent, "What will I tell my wife, bringing another woman's pie home?"

"Just tell her you were out riding around the countryside with a couple of old women past seventy," I said. I guess that worked, because Maylon didn't return the pie.

Nearly every week, fairs and vending opportunities presented themselves. I just couldn't pass them up, and they added to my busy schedule. I was busy all year long with customers, people bringing me stock to sell in my gift shop, and folks selling advertising. Someone was always coming in to stock the brochure racks with flyers. Providing tourist information was a large part of giving back to the community, and I kept several racks full for that purpose.

Not long after Mirror had encouraged me to share some of my abusive experiences with customers, a tall, distinguished, handsome young man came to my gift shop. Much like the *Vogue* woman, he announced that he had turned around to come and see my gift shop. He said he "felt compelled" to do so and that it was the strangest, most overpowering experience he had ever had. Puzzled, he paused, pulled out his handkerchief, and wiped his eyes and blew his nose. Then he said, "It was a strange feeling, and I knew I had to turn around, but it really wasn't as overpowering as the death of my son."

He couldn't continue speaking for a few seconds. When he did, he asked me, "Do *you* have any idea why it's so important for me to come here?"

I was speechless. I thought I was going to faint, and I was short of breath. I managed to ask him if he was all right, and he told me he wasn't. Words tumbled forth as he described how he had found his son hanging in the garage—something that just wasn't supposed to happen to people like them. He tried to wipe the tears from his face, but it was a losing battle.

My conversation with the *Vogue* woman was still fresh in my mind. I didn't plan what I said; the words just flowed forth.

"This is as surreal to me as it is to you, sir," I began. "You're not the first person to come into my gift shop and tell me these things. Yes, I think I know why you're here. You see, my second husband committed suicide. I nearly lost my mind. I was completely incapacitated and had to quit a great job because I couldn't stop crying over the replays of the tragedy in my head."

"You seem fine now," the man said as he shrugged his shoulders. "I'd think you've never had a problem in your life. How did you survive? There are days when I think my wife will self-destruct and I will just disintegrate. I can't think straight. I can't talk. All I want to do is get in the car and try to drive away from the pain, and I can't."

"I understand. You seem more worried about your wife than anything. What are her interests?"

"She likes to paint. She's artistic. She used to spend hours painting country scenes. Now she's covered up her paint supplies and locked her studio door. She just sits and stares. I just drive around," he continued. "We both had counseling—came home completely wiped out. We just couldn't do it anymore. What happened to you? How did your husband kill himself?"

He sat down in one of my restaurant chairs, and I got him a cup of tea. Then I began to recount what had happened so long ago. It always made me cry, made me tremble, and made me sad. I dreaded the telling, but if there was a chance that it would help, I would do it.

Mirror had said, "There are seasons of fruit, and there are seasons of pain. Your fruit syrups are the reason they drive in. Your experiences can help the folks who seem compelled to visit your shop. It's the purpose of your business and your existence. You and I both know this was predestined to happen." In my heart, I knew Mirror was right.

I began by telling him about the years and years—thirteen of them—of abuse I had suffered.

When I finished, I told him, "I was at the deepest, darkest, blackest point of my life. The day that started with my friend's abortion ended with my husband's suicide. I should have lost my mind," I said. The young professional man sat motionless, listening. Our hands were clasped together, and his tear-filled eyes never left mine. I had lost track of time, and the afternoon had slipped away. Like the other time I'd shared my painful story, no customers had stopped at my gift shop that afternoon.

"You survived. How did you do it? Please help me; help us," he pleaded.

"I had a wonderful group of friends. I had been isolated during the abuse, but friends who are sincere are always ready to jump right back into your life and support you. My family and friends were worried and in constant communication with me. I also had God."

"But what if you don't have that kind of friendship available? What if you live a long distance from your family and friends? We're so isolated and alone," he said sadly.

"The other thing that helped me was my work, and I kept at it. I found that physical work was the best, and I worked until I was so tired there was no question about sleep. However, I did have to quit my real-estate sales job, because I was having mental replays of the trauma. I also sought counseling. It helped me discover that I, myself, had to decide that it wasn't my fault that my husband killed himself. I did not pull that trigger. He did."

My guest said, "Our son was depressed over a girl. We'd talked to him, taken him on a vacation, and explained that there would be other girls, but it didn't help. We didn't say the right words. We didn't know the right words. We can't forgive ourselves." His voice crumbled until he couldn't speak anymore.

"I can't say any magic words to fix your broken hearts. I can only tell you that hard work and my determination to go on with my life and raise my little boy made me slowly get better. I will never get over what happened. Guilt is insidious. It sneaks up and invades your mind in your sleep and at odd times, whenever you aren't fighting it," I told him.

Then I asked him to tell me again about his wife's interests and passions before their son died. He mentioned her art.

I asked, "Could you have your wife bring her drawings of local nature over so I can look at them?"

"I'll tell her about our conversation. Thank you. I'll never forget this afternoon, and I wish you well."

I gave him a hug. It had been an intensely emotional afternoon. I wondered if I would ever hear from him or meet his wife. I wondered if sharing my grief had helped him at all.

Two days later, the man's wife walked into my shop with her artwork. "My husband insisted that I bring these," she said softly. "I argued with him, and then he told me your heartbreaking story. It's a lot like ours. He said he stopped here just because he felt compelled to." She spread her work over on my counter. Her watercolors were delightful. "I don't know why you want to see these drawings; they're just for my own enjoyment. My son loved them," she added.

I told her I believed that healing started with hard work and a compelling interest in something besides one's troubles. I suggested she make her drawings into note cards.

"I have no idea how to do that or where to start," she said.

"You start by investigating the things you need to do, such as making copies and getting paper stock. Make a list, and then check off the chores until you come up with a plan. Come back and see me every few days and let me know how the plan is progressing. Your art could be a memorial to your son. The work will keep your mind busy. The new drawings and paintings you'll need to do will get you out into the sunshine. I've found that sunshine heals and lifts your spirits. You'll have purpose—and I'll have another locally made product to offer my customers. You'll have a new little source of income, and we'll have a reason to stay in touch. The great part of it is I think we'll become friends."

"I suppose I could try it," she said. "It beats staying in the house with the curtains drawn. I sit for hours with my hands over my eyes, trying to block out the memory of my son's ..." Her voice trailed off, and tears kept her from finishing her thought. She gathered her things and left. I wondered if she would listen to an old woman who'd given her such simple suggestions.

A week later, she knocked tentatively on my house's front door, holding a little box in her hand. In the box were a dozen note cards, all individually drawn and lovely. I'm no artist, so I couldn't imagine their value. Mirror on the wall behind me whispered just loudly enough for me to hear, "The price you put on the cards doesn't mean a thing. Just tell her how beautiful they are and that you'll sell them for her. Get her started. Once begun, half done, you know."

I took the first twelve cards. Within three months, she was producing copies, packaging them in cellophane, and selling them in half a dozen gift shops besides mine. She was so involved in growing her line of cards, marketing them, and getting to know her suppliers and customers that she was actually smiling each time I saw her. She returned to her regular job before her leave of absence was up. We became friends, a great bonus for both of us. She wrote a short autobiography to display with the cards and made a sign saying, "In loving memory of my son."

Fruit ripened and was processed, bottled, and stocked on the Sugar Shack shelves. Customers came and bought and left. The sun came up and went down. Days and weeks and months passed, and the cards sold. Another local woman was inspired to bring cards she had made during her chemotherapy. I sold those, too.

Suddenly, I had local crafts and gift items from senior citizens who needed to augment their incomes, from people who had lost their jobs and were looking for a new direction, and from other gift-shop owners who wanted to enlarge the audience for their particular creations. My rustic little shop was filled with homemade birdhouses, doilies, pot holders, wreaths, stained-glass suncatchers, fancy brick doorstops, handcrafted bird mobiles, and antiques and collectibles hand-painted with appropriate scenes. I even carried a line of hand-dipped chocolates made by a gal I was able to mentor through the maze of entrepreneurism.

I was so thankful for the opportunity to use my tragedy to help others and to create something useful. I noticed that the variety of customers mirrored events from my life: some happy, and some tragic.

The workload, however, was nearly unbearable, and my personal life was desperately lonely. A parade of suitors (as Mirror called them) marched regularly down my driveway, but there were no keepers. My workload scared most of them away; if that didn't, my past did.

CHAPTER TWENTY-FOUR: ON THE ROAD AND POPULAR, 2000-2010

FEATURE WRITERS FREQUENTLY INTERVIEWED me and took pictures of my gift shop. I thought about advertising, insurance, and bookkeeping. The increasing demand for wild black raspberries had me constantly hiking and searching the woods; I also sought wild elderberries and blackberries. Another angel, a female farmer in the next township, offered to let me pick all the wild berries on her hundred-acre farm, and the supply was enough for my needs. Customers suggested new flavor combinations and offered jelly recipes from their grandmothers. A steady flow of love letters arrived from folks who had stopped in for a tasting and a visit.

I was pleasantly surprised by a feature article in an adjacent town's large newspaper, which was entitled, "Following the Golden Rule." It explained my feelings about sharing the wealth. The article mentioned a couple from Indiana who had received a free tasting and a free farm and lakefront tour and who had enjoyed this friendly interlude on their vacation. The couple had written a thank-you note to me and sent their friends and relatives to my shop the next year.

This article snowballed into invitations to participate in statewide workshops as a presenter. I received invitations to participate in women-only shows, large craft shows, and sports shows. These appearances generated invitations to speak at service clubs and school groups. I worked harder, picking and processing more and more fruit to supply these new venues. The shows, in turn, led to more day-tripping customers from nearby cities, along with carloads and busloads of senior citizens, college business classes, school groups, and more. My old friends Peggy, Carol, and the mayor found ways to help. My older boys took over the grapes, managed the website, and made a new line of jellies. Robert made the maple syrup and managed the pancake enterprise.

The first time I was invited to display my wares at the hunting-and-fishing exposition in Buffalo, I felt out of place. I was the only vendor at the show selling food products. The fishermen and hunters were decidedly unfriendly and obviously did not want me to be part of their gig, but I was there to create an activity for the women attending. As the guys passed my display, they'd look disdainfully at my little cruets filled with twenty flavors of syrup. I offered them free tastings on little spoons, but they tossed their heads, scowled, and walked on. The atmosphere was cold; they ignored me and made me feel uncomfortable and out of place. I was determined to make an impression on them and win them over. Standing alone in my booth, I had lots of time to hatch up a plan, because I was not busy and finally, I figured out the solution.

One of my earliest entrepreneurial pursuits was a fishing-worm business I started in 1982 to help Robert and me stay busy during our period of grief. My farm was only a mile from the Lake Erie harbor that was closest to the best bass fishing in the world. I had noticed the large number of fishermen there all summer, and I had also noticed that there was no place to buy worms. I tacked a board that said "Worms" on a grape post by the road. The little enterprise taught Robert about hard work and how to make change, and it helped keep us both sane and busy for years immediately following the chief's suicide.

Years later, after the Sugar Shack was established, it was open all the time since it was right next to my house, so I continued to go out on rainy nights and pick up night crawlers instead of watching TV. The sign for worms brought even more folks down my driveway and, unbelievably, they bought syrup when they came in for night crawlers. I had cut down a grape-harvesting crate and filled it with the right materials for keeping the worms healthy. Early in the spring, I started stocking up on fresh night crawlers to sell to fishermen. By mid-April, the beginning of the fishing season, I had built up a great supply and kept replacing those I sold. I had been selling fishing worms for twelve years before the Sugar Shack was even imagined.

Now, at the hunting-and-fishing expo, I recognized many of the guys who wouldn't speak to me. They had been worm customers for my "dollar a dozen" night crawlers for years. I set my tasting supplies away from my display window and walked through the show until I found a booth with a sign identifying them as a local fishing association. I marched right up and said, "Hello, guys. I'm the jelly lady over near the restrooms. You all walk by and don't speak to me or taste my syrups, so I came over here to introduce myself and tell you about my other business."

They were stunned. I continued with a question: "Do you fish for bass or walleyes with night crawlers?" They nodded, but nobody spoke. "Where do you buy your worms?"

One rough-looking, bewhiskered fellow in bib overalls grunted, "Get 'em in Buffalo. Why?"

That was the opening I needed. "Because I sell worms just a mile from Barcelona Harbor, down near Westfield," I said. "And mine are better than what you can get in Buffalo."

The salty old fisherman pushed his worn, stained cap back on his head and said, "Worms is worms. None is better than another. Worms is worms."

"Sir, I beg to differ," I argued. "Mine are completely different—and better. I fish, too, so let me tell you why you should wait to get your worms until you get to Barcelona and then buy them from me. You see, I pick them fresh and keep them in a natural environment. The fish recognize that and bite more often."

They all laughed, just like I knew they would. The old guy with the stained cap hooked his thumbs under his overall straps and said, "That's a crock. Worms is worms. The fish don't give a damn where they come from." All his buddies laughed, but they were paying attention now.

"Well, you see, I treat my worms as soon as I pick them." They stopped laughing and looked puzzled. I had their full attention now. "I love to fish, too," I continued. "I particularly love to fish for walleyes. I use worm harnesses—you know, the device where you hook the worm up so it appears to be swimming through the water. When the walleye bites, one of the hooks in the worm catches the fish." They looked skeptical and suspicious, like I was talking down to them. I was, and it was on purpose. "I know that you know how important it is to get the worm hooked up with the head in front and the tail in back. Trouble is, some guys can't tell which end of a night crawler is the head and which is the tail."

They nodded their heads and leaned forward.

"That's why I pick them and treat them myself. I'm short, and it's easy for me to pick worms on my grape farm on the humps under the trellis wire. I wear a miner's hat with a red light on it. I tie an ice-cream bucket on my belt, and I can pick three thousand night crawlers on just one rainy night."

They nodded again. The guy with the bib overalls snapped his straps and showed me his every-other-tooth smile.

"I take those worms into the house, put tin foil on my kitchen table, and dump two cups of regular household flour on the foil. Then I dump the worms into the flour. I gently lift them up and move them around until they're all coated with flour." I moved my fingers to demonstrate. "I have a black marker there, and when the worms fart, I mark which end is the head and which end is the tail."

Noise throughout the expo space stopped as the men erupted in raucous laughter.

When it got quiet again, I said, "That, gentlemen, was not one of your fish stories. It was a worm story, and that's why you should stop at my booth and visit my farm for worms."

The crusty old geezer with the stained cap said, "Boys, this here lady's got a good idea, and she made us all laugh. Let's make it a rule that our new members have to visit the Sugar Shack and buy a dozen worms. Let's write it into the initiation rules that they have to ask her why her worms are better than anybody else's and then report back to us at the next meeting with a coupon or something."

I walked back to my booth. My homemade joke was perfectly, and I sold lots of syrup to their families. At the end of the three-day show, the group's president gave me a stack of coupons to give to new members when they visited me.

I had a whole new clientele. I also discovered that mixing humor into my product presentation and tasting experience was a great motivator for more sales.

I had been doing the off-site shows with a little pine shed made of four walls held together with eight screws. The boards were only half an inch thick, and the shed was easy to assemble. The shelving was antique wooden grape-picking crates that screwed to the framework. The roof was a piece of tapestry stretched over a copper pipe at the peak of the roofline. It was unique, eye-catching, and quick to set up and tear down.

One day, I saw an Amish shed about the same eight-by-ten-foot size. I visited the man who'd made it and hired him to make one to my specifications. A friend of mine welded a frame with wheels for the shed to sit on. It had a trailer hitch on one end, so all I had to do was back my pickup truck up to it and hook it on, and away I could go with no help. I started doing shows not only in convention centers but in parks as well. In between events, I occasionally used the shed on the roadside by the Sugar Shack.

The news media loved the mobile Sugar Shack shed, and my business was showcased in newspapers and on TV because of it. Another benefit of the mobile mini-store was that it was exempt from property taxes.

Robert had proven his sales ability and polished his tourism skills in the jobs he'd had since graduating from college. He was ready to start producing first-class maple-syrup and launch the pancake house of his dreams. We poured more concrete, ordered a state-of-the-art maple-syrup evaporator and the accompanying equipment, counted our sugar-maple trees, and leased enough additional trees to support the expansion.

The three sons I couldn't protect from abuse, who had suffered beside me, had all become successful young men who each worked full-time jobs yet still found time to help and support me on the farm. I was so blessed and thankful for them.

Chapter Twenty-Five: More Forks in the Road, 2000-2010

I CONSIDERED EXPANDING MY Sugar Shack enterprise even more and wondered what I needed to do to grow the business. As I worked I planned an advertising campaign and put notes about it by the telephone. I decided to put my fishing-worm sign back up by the highway. I knew I could fill my long, lonely evenings with picking night crawlers. I had to make gift bags for my shop, and I could expand that idea into table runners and plastic-bag holders. Friends would call, people would come by, and I would be okay—not quite so lonely.

Again the rhubarb grew tall and red and luscious, and the routine of the familiar harvesting seasons progressed. One day, I had hundreds of quarts of fresh strawberries all picked and lined up outside my processing kitchen when a news reporter/ photographer drove in to buy a bottle of maple syrup. He saw me, Wannago, and the strawberries, the morning sun shining on their red ripeness.

He asked, "May I take a picture?"

I agreed and stepped out of his way.

He said, "I want you and your dog in the picture, too." That photograph ended up on the AP wireless and was printed in papers all over the Northeast.

Old customers saw it in faraway places, clipped it, and sent it to me. Potential customers clipped it and put it and the accompanying article in their glove boxes. Local folks came by to see what the Sugar Shack was all about.

Mirror said, "See? You didn't need any man around here to get that publicity, did you? There's a master plan, and don't you forget it."

I replied, "Predestination, maybe, but where's the next reptile-in-waiting? I need someone to share the highs."

I was invited to participate in another cooperative-extension panel on agriculture, tourism, and something billed as sustainable agriculture. My business fit those profiles, because I added value to my crops and then sold them to the tourist trade as customers visited my farm. I continued to speak about my successful agritourism business at local entrepreneurial gatherings, seminars, women's church meetings, and service organizations like Kiwanis.

Presenters at the university-sponsored seminars were usually college professors who used the opportunity to sell their books instead of offering free information on business startups. Their speeches were based on "book learnin'," as my dad called it, not on actual experience. After one presentation, questions were allowed; the sponsoring school provided and paid the moderator. An entrepreneurial attendee, who had paid $50 to attend the conference, asked a question; instead of an answer, he was referred to a book that cost $16 and had been written by a presenter who had already been paid by the conference sponsor in addition to his professor's salary. I raised my hand to offer specific information on the topic and to direct the questioner to free help in his own community, but the monitor refused to recognize me.

Finally, the questioner stood up and shouted, "I don't want your canned replies telling me to buy your damn books. I paid to come to this conference, and I want to hear from the lady who has been there, actually done it, and succeeded. I want Mrs. Black to tell us how she addressed this problem."

The monitor made a fake bow in my direction and announced that the question period was over; he said that if anyone had questions for Mrs. Black, they could see her privately. I stood behind the speakers' table for over thirty minutes that day, giving out free information and directing potential entrepreneurs to small-business development centers at their local community colleges. I figured my speaking career was over, but it wasn't finished yet.

Once again, I was asked to be a presenter by an independent, statewide farm group at a seminar that was now billed as an agritourism event. Over five hundred registrants from around the state came to Buffalo to participate. I was asked to write an introduction that would be given before I spoke. This was going to be the largest audience I had ever faced. The conference was being held at a convention center, and I had to use a podium and microphone. I was terrified.

At home, I paced and worried about writing my introduction. I was mumbling to myself about my lack of credentials, lack of a college degree, and lack of experience at writing introductions when Mirror said, "Get their attention. Don't take yourself so seriously. Tell them how you started your worm business. It'll break the ice."

"Mirror, you're brilliant," I said, grabbing a pen and paper. I sat right down on the floor in front of Mirror, and this is what I wrote for someone else to read:

Ladies and gentlemen,
Today it is my pleasure to introduce a pioneer in agritourism entrepreneurialism. Your speaker has created and continues

to operate several agritourism and sustainable agricultural businesses. She is currently pursuing her master's degree in business at the University of HK. Please welcome Gail Black of Vinewood Acres Maple Grape Farms, located just sixty miles west of Buffalo, on the shoreline of Lake Erie.

At that moment, I opened the rear door of the auditorium and ran down the aisle, loudly shouting, "Welcome to Planning Your Own Business 101." As planned, the house lights came up. Every head turned as the light from the open door drew their attention. There I was in my stained yellow rain suit and barn boots, the light on my red helmet attracting every eye as I ran down the aisle. The outfit was complete with a battery pack and an ice-cream bucket hanging from a belt around my waist.

Thunderous applause welcomed me to the podium, and I owned the audience from that moment on.

"Ladies and gentlemen, please let me explain my attire this morning," I said. "One of my first businesses was worm picking. I believe that there are opportunities all around us. I believe that all we have to do is open our eyes and ears and let our imaginations take over as we examine the possibilities of those opportunities. Returning from shopping one day, I noticed that trucks and boat trailers were lined up at a local grocery store, where bait was available. A sign offered live bait for $2 a dozen. This immediately caught my attention. I had a grape farm, and I picked my own night crawlers when I wanted to go fishing. I knew it was easy to get a couple dozen in a few minutes, and I wasn't even that experienced. I only picked them up when I fished, and, with a grape farm to run, that wasn't often. I knew I could become more efficient.

"That day I made a sign that said 'Worms $1.00 per dozen.' I couldn't wait until dark. I was lucky—it was raining, and the worms are known to make love in the rain. If you're fast, you can get two at a time, because they don't seem to notice the light from a flashlight when they're so engrossed in copulating. I filled a gallon ice-cream bucket just like this one in a little over an hour." I undid the belt and removed the bucket, setting it on the podium.

"It wasn't necessary to purchase a helmet for the worm business. I had a helmet, complete with a red light, for hunting coyotes and foxes at night. I pulled it out the next evening, charged it up, and attached the battery pack at my waist." I took it off and added it to the things on the podium. "I found my rain suit and boots," I continued, slipping out of my worm-picking uniform. "With the addition of my grape-tying gloves with three fingers cut out so I could still use my fingers, the uniform was complete. I was able to stay warm and dry while I picked up the copulating worms, two at a time."

Now I stood before my audience in a business suit. "Does anyone have any questions so far?" I asked when they stopped laughing.

A hand shot up. "Did you learn all this in your college courses, or in your graduate work? And where is the University of HK?"

I had to quiet everyone down, because they were laughing again. I answered, "I learned all this in regular courses, and I'm refining the knowledge now in my graduate work. UHK stands for the University of Hard Knocks, and the most important business tidbit I learned there was to write a business plan. At UHK, I learned that worms that aren't kept in the proper environment rot and smell bad. I learned that a marketing plan would have been beneficial, since it would have eliminated the need to store the worms for long periods of time. I found that the more information and thought you put into your business plan, the fewer problems you'll encounter during business operation."

The audience roared with laughter. The back doors kept opening, and the empty seats filled up. Several people were standing in the back.

"At this time, I'd like you to stand up if you have a specific entrepreneurial business idea. We'll take a few minutes for each of you to state your name and your idea."

There was a lot of shuffling, and about a quarter of those seated stood up. Many unique, brilliant, strange, and unusual ideas were mentioned from people all the way across the state.

"What a treasure we have in New York State," I said. "If all your ideas were brought to fruition, we'd have no unemployment here. I'd like to tell you about my primary business, the Sugar Shack. It's a sustainable farm business, because I grow, pick, process, and sell fruit syrups right on my farm. That enables me to get a higher financial return on my produce, and it helps to pay my taxes.

"When I started the Sugar Shack, I had to have a sign by the highway. It was a homemade sign at first. I put it next to the sign that said, 'Worms $1.00,' until someone pointed out that as they drove by they saw, 'Sugar Shack, free tasting, worms.' Sometimes you overlook small but important things in your business plan."

Again the audience burst into laughter. The doors at the back swung open, and the speaker from the next section stomped down the aisle. "Could you just tone it down an octave?" she demanded angrily. "All my people have walked out and come over here. They hear the laughing. Just quiet it down," she shouted as she left.

I finished my presentation by assuring my audience that the services offered by small-business development centers at community colleges were free. Those services included a mentor, research on permits and licensing requirements, help with finding competitive businesses in order to complete a marketing plan, and suggestions for finding financial backing, including low-interest loans. I answered questions for a long time and invited those with interest to visit my farm.

Most conference attendees were packed into my section and didn't want me to leave. Many of them later appeared at my farm for encouragement.

The positive outcome is that a local dairy farmer in the audience started a riding stable that has flourished. It has become the main income generator on that farm, and it draws thousands of people to our area, where they spend money on food, fuel, accommodations, and more. Another maple-sugar producer drove for over an hour to ask me questions about the newest extension of my business, the pancake restaurant. He now has a full-service restaurant that serves his own maple products and his own turkey, beef, and buffalo meats. When asked why I would help another maple business, I say it's "co-opi-tition"—cooperating with the competition for the betterment of the whole industry. I am humbled to have had a tiny part in encouraging these businesses.

My sons were all active in my life and supplied me with nine delightful grandchildren. A day seldom passed without a visit from one of my descendants. My life was full of work, friends, family, and satisfaction. I felt successful and accomplished and happy.

I reasoned that some women have problems with their kids, some with their health, some with finances, and many with other problems. My problems were with men. An honest, permanent relationship just wasn't meant to be. I felt that I had finally learned how to be alone, and it was really great.

The speaking engagements ended, but the bus tours expanded and more and more product was needed, so I got up earlier and went to bed more tired. I enjoyed the company of several long-term romantic companions, but none of them lasted more than a few months or years. I gave up completely on romance after I thought I had found the love of my life, only to lose him to cancer.

The experiences of life tangle with one another like an endless field of mixed wild berries waiting to be picked. In my life, a lot of special angels appeared at various times to assist with filling the empty or discarded baskets.

That is exactly what happened when a couple of wonderful women rode down my driveway on their bicycles. Alice and Bobbi were crossing America by bicycle to fulfill one of their dreams. They rode past my sign and decided to turn around and visit. We spent some quality time together before they rode on toward their destination. They wrote a book about their experiences and told me they had included the Sugar Shack in it. I had mentioned my dream of writing a book of my own, but I didn't have time for such a huge undertaking. They encouraged me to just write down random stories in case I found time to put it all together someday.

During my long, hard years of labor, friends and family would ask me how long I thought I could keep up the physical work that enabled my business to exist. I always had a plan, and I would say, "When my body is used up and can't continue, my mind will still be in virgin condition. That's when I'll write my book."

The events in my life have shown me that my "plan" may not have been entirely of my own making. I am sure that the way my life turned out was predestined. How else could all of those angels have shown up when I truly needed them to lead me out of despair and into a successful and happy life?

THE END
or
THE BEGINNING OF THE NEXT CHAPTER
Predestination will decide.

Epilogue:
Never Too Old to Hope

ONE JUNE EVENING NOT too long ago, my friend Betty, a B and B owner, suggested we both needed to take a break. She drove us to a club, where we enjoyed the dinner and danced to a band that was playing lively country tunes. When we returned to the table with our current dance partners, we noticed a man sitting alone at a table near the door. Single, lonely, senior women always notice a man sitting alone.

We knew that tomorrow would be another brutally busy day, and we walked past that cute guy as we headed for the door. The man reached out and firmly grabbed my wrist. His hand was warm and so was the twinkle in his blue eyes as he held on to me.

"You're not leaving, are you? My name is Bruce," he said.

"Yes, my friend drove, and she wants to go home now," I said. But I hesitated, curious about why this guy, who was obviously drinking alone, had stopped me.

"Please don't go yet. I want to dance with you," he said.

"My friend is leaving, and I rode with her. Sorry."

"Just give me five minutes of your time and a dance, and I'll tell you anything about me that you want to know. Tell her to go on, and I'll take you home." Bruce kept his hold on my wrist. Betty stopped a few feet away and stared.

Betty is a great-looking, stylish dresser with long legs and a saucy hairdo. She smiles easily and makes friends quickly. Usually she never sits out a lively tune, but on this night she had danced only a couple of times, and she was ready to go home.

I pulled my hand free just as the band began a slow song. I said, "Dance with her," and nodded in Betty's direction. He dropped my wrist and held out his hand to Betty, and they moved to the dance floor.

I said under my breath to no one in particular, "That was pretty stupid. He's really cute, even if he probably is a drunk." I returned to my group of friends and danced with my former partner.

I noticed that the cute guy was dancing with Betty but looking at me.

When the dance was over, Bruce took my wrist again and said, "I have two tickets to the Jersey Boys concert tomorrow night. Would you go with me?"

"I don't know you," I said. "I'm not going anywhere with you. If you're serious, please show up at my place of business tomorrow afternoon between one and three, and we'll discuss it then. I own the Sugar Shack on Route 5, a mile east of Barcelona Harbor." I was sure I would never, ever see him there. As he held my wrist tightly, I thought of him as "Mister Man," because he was really cute with his curly red hair and sparkly blue eyes.

He continued, "Would it impress you if I told you I owned two junkyards and another business in Texas?"

With a long, dragged-out "No," I halfheartedly tried to pull away.

"Would it impress you if I told you I was a retired airline pilot?"

That got my attention, but my pride and fear were still in the way, so I said, "Fly boy, playboy? I don't think so."

I pulled my wrist free and left. All the way home, Betty said repeatedly, "I don't get it. You walk in there with your cowboy boots on and walk out with a guy asking for a date."

I shrugged it off. "He's probably a married drunk looking for a quick pickup. Or maybe he's a needy guy looking for a nurse or a purse. I'm experienced at this, and you can't be too careful." At home, I kicked off my cowboy boots, took a long, hot shower, and went to bed on my side of the king-sized bed.

Saturdays in tourist season at the farm gift shop were busy with carloads of tourists stopping in for free tasting of some of the fruit syrups or maple products on ice cream. I kept looking at the door as groups waited for me to have a free moment to guide them on my nature trail or ring up their purchases.

I reminded myself that cute Mister Man, Bruce somebody, would never show up on his white horse to take me anywhere. I knew better than to think it would be any different. Lonely was my lot in life but I continued to be an optimist whenever I met a new guy. My age, the odds and the competition were stacked up against me.

Then there he was, handsome, curly-haired, smiling Bruce, with no wedding ring on his finger and two tickets in his hand. He wandered right into my crowded gift shop. My heart leaped right to the tip of my tongue and tied it in a double bow knot. My face flushed, and I embarrassed myself by ringing up a sale wrong. My hands were sweaty and trembling. The line of customers was endless. I had people wanting everything. If only they would all go away before he walked out, I thought desperately.

Bruce hung back, watching the chaotic scene. Then one of my customers put a tiny sample cup of ice cream and a spoon in his hand. Before he could voice his firm decision *not* to participate in the tasting, there was a spoonful of ice cream

329

covered with wild currant raspberry syrup tickling his taste buds and making them scream for more. Pumpkin spice and Apple Cinnamon made their way quickly to his tongue. He had not spoken and neither had I, but our eyes met and an instant connection sizzled.

It seemed like hours before there was an empty space before me at the counter. Then Mister Bruce filled that space beautifully as his presence seemed to suck all the air out of my lungs.

"You're so busy I'll just pick you up at six," he said quickly.

"No, no. I don't know you, so I'll meet you at the concert, near the gate. I'll drive myself," I replied. At least I could escape if the evening didn't work out.

"Okay, then. I'll see you there at seven sharp so we can get a good seat." He winked at me as he vanished through the door with a crowd of people. He told me later that he thought I must have a staff of elves hidden somewhere. No way did he believe I did all that work alone, like I'd told the other customers.

Finally it was five o'clock. I put the "Closed" sign in the window and locked the door. All I had to do was make it across the parking lot to my old farmhouse before another customer drove in. Then I could remake myself, find decent clothes, iron them, and drive to the concert. With my luck, I thought he'd just stand me up at the gate.

Six outfits and three hairdos later, I drove up the driveway and was off for an evening of adventure. It was just a date, after all, but maybe, just maybe, it could become a great summer romance. Nothing ventured, nothing gained. I buzzed along in my little red Smart car with the Sugar Shack business logo on the sides.

"So much for incognito," I laughed. "This guy will see me coming for a mile, but the parking-lot attendant will find me half a parking space close to the gate if I smile at him right." I was pumped, excited and praying that I wasn't setting myself up for disappointment if he wasn't waiting for me. I reminded myself that I was seventy-one, not seventeen.

As I approached the gate, I saw Bruce with the tickets in his hand and a huge smile on his face. He took my arm, handed the tickets to the gatekeeper, and then said, "Now hold my hand and tell me how many kids you have, how old they are, and what they do. We're meeting some of my friends here, and I don't want them to think I just picked you up at the gate."

I stopped walking and said, "But you did just pick me up at the gate, and you tried to pick me up in the bar last night."

"Okay, okay. But I'd like to introduce you, and I need to know something about you," he explained.

He softened; he was a gentleman and worried about appearances. I thought he must be a nice guy, or he wouldn't care. When we joined his friends, introductions were made. I discovered that some of his friends were business associates of mine, and others were mutual acquaintances. I relaxed, feeling a little foolish for not letting him pick me up at home. He held my hand and helped me put a jacket on when the evening breeze cooled the air. He let his arm linger on my shoulders, and when I shivered, he pulled me close and kept me protected and warm against his body.

At the end of the concert, he explained that he had arrived by boat with some friends and that he would love for me to accompany him a few miles down the lake to where his car was parked. Then he would return me to my car. Other people were along, and he was such a gentleman, so I accepted. The summer romance was off and running.

Moonlight drew a map to our destination and sparkled on the water as the cabin cruiser raced along over the small waves on the lake's surface. Bruce stood behind my seat with his warm hand on my cool shoulder and set that shoulder on fire. Soft classical music was playing on the boat's radio.

"The Jersey Boys were never better," someone said.

"Chautauqua Institution is such a wonderful cultural center for the arts. The programs are outstanding this year," someone else commented. The hum of voices blended with the music and the waves lapping at the side of the boat.

I heard the hum, but only in the distance. My head became heavy. For some reason, I just wanted to drop it back on Mister Bruce's chest, with the curly red hair sticking out by his shirt collar. I looked at the moon lighting up the lake and forced myself to resist.

The ride was lovely and surreal and made seventy-one seem exactly like seventeen. It was over too soon, as was the tour of Bruce's houseboat, which was docked in front of the most prestigious hotel in town. The car ride back to my Smart car was also too fast. When we found my car in the lot, he pulled up beside it. Then, to my delight, he hopped out, opened my door, and took my hand. When I hit the remote and unlocked my own car door, he quickly and smoothly stepped around me, lifted my chin, and kissed me.

I was dizzy. I had to grab the car door to steady myself. Air was sucked into my lungs like a tornado. I amazed myself when I reached my arm up and encircled his neck. Instantly his arms were around me, pulling me into another long, inflaming kiss.

"I'll see you tomorrow morning around ten o'clock, so reserve me a seat at your Sunday pancake restaurant," he whispered. "I hope you're not too busy to join me." Then he slipped into his car.

I was so flustered that I turned the wrong way in the huge maze of the parking lot. "Oh, my God," I said. "I can't find my way out of this place."

I made several turns, and then there was Bruce, laughing and ready to escort me to the exit. How embarrassing. That damn kiss had caused this. *No fool like an old fool*, I thought. I was shivering, and it wasn't from the cold when I turned left and he turned right. I was way too old to feel so giddy. I got myself home and into bed and fell asleep with fantasies of a long summer romance in my head. To hell with nurses and purses. A long, hot summer romance would fit the bill for a seventy-one-year-old young lady.

On Sunday morning, no empty tables could be found at the Sugar Shack pancake restaurant. I saw Mister Bruce come in and look around at the noisy, crowded confusion, obviously looking for me, but I was frantically ringing up bills for the waitresses so we could turn over more tables. People were shopping, waiting in line, visiting with friends and relatives, and listening to the three-piece bluegrass group playing lively music in the midst of my gift shop.

Finally, I caught Bruce's attention, and he moved through the crowd to my counter. A waitress came to pick up her slips, and I ordered two pancake meals to be served while I worked. We stood while we ate. His visit lasted all day, because I couldn't find time to do more than smile at him.

Finally I put the "Closed" sign up. We sat on my front porch, had a sandwich, and watched the sunset. Just before he left, he asked, "Do you have a passport?"

"Heavens, no," I answered. "Why? Do you want to go to Canada?"

"I suppose I could take you there, but I had a couple of extra tickets for something else. Would you like to get a passport?"

"I don't even have the enhanced driver's license you can get instead of a passport. I never leave the farm, let alone go to Canada, especially since they now require a passport, even though it's only an hour and a half away."

Bruce said, "I'll be back in the morning if you'd like to go to the post office and apply for a passport."

I agreed. "I've needed one for a while. It wouldn't hurt anything, and now is a good time—I read that the price is going up."

"Good night, sweetie," he said as he got into his car.

Later, as I drifted off to sleep, I remembered that he'd called me "sweetie." Even though I really could use a passport, I had sure sounded anxious to comply with Bruce's suggestion. I reminded myself not to read too much into the situation and not to seem needy and overly anxious.

The next day, on the way home from the post office, I asked Bruce, "Why are you so anxious for me to get a passport?" His answer took my breath away.

He said, "I'm having so much fun with you that I'd love to have you come back to Texas with me. I have two tickets to fly from Austin, Texas, to Washington, DC, and then to Rome, Italy, for a few weeks."

I decided that I had to tell my kids and friends that I had applied for a passport and that the reason was a two-week cruise in the Mediterranean, with a tour of Italy—yes, Italy. My three sons looked at me with incredulous disbelief.

"He was just a date five days ago," one of my sons yelled.

"What the hell is wrong with you?" another exploded.

"You don't know this guy from a lizard by the pond," the third pointed out.

With a smile as wide as Lake Erie, and one I could control about as much as the white caps on that lake, I stood my ground. "When you're old, you have to move fast. There might not be much time left. There's nothing wrong with me; I'm having a summer romance. He and I discussed it, and that's all there is to it for either one of us, because he's going back to his home in Texas this fall. And I'm not going to give up on my dreams so easily. He just might be a handsome prince disguised as a frog by my pond. Who knows?"

"Mom," all three shouted, "get real. You're seventy-one. How old is this guy?"

"He'll be seventy in a month. That makes me a cougar." I laughed at the thought and at the stark horror and disbelief on the faces of my three conservative sons, who seemed to have forgotten the lonely dating years.

At the end of August, just sixty days after Bruce picked me up in a bar beside a lake in New York State, he put a stunning two-carat diamond ring on my finger. Still worried about what other people would think, he told me, "This is not an engagement ring, but it would look better on the cruise if you appear to be my fiancée. Will you accept it?"

I agreed with that mind set and bought new luggage. I had never seen Texas and never dreamed of visiting Europe. I wondered if this would be like all my other romantic escapades, a total disappointment, and if I was once again on a wild goose chase. Would my dream of frogs and princes turn into a nightmare?

The day of our departure arrived. I was climbing into my pickup truck to leave for the airport when a car drove down my driveway. A woman jumped out, saying, "Don't get in that truck. Remember me? I'm Bobbi, and I have a copy of our book, *Across America by Bicycle*, for you. You're in it! I wanted to deliver it in person and say hello. Alice says hello, too."

I was delighted. This was the angel who had encouraged me to write down the stories of my life, which I had been doing. The writing had eased the long, lonely winter nights when the only sounds were howling wind, crackling fires, and recorded fiddle tunes.

We hugged and sat on my front porch. I told her I had been following her advice, and I asked her to take a look at a story or two on my computer. She quickly read them. "These need some work, but they're really good, Gail. Keep writing," she said.

I confided that my plan was to spend the winter in Texas and devote most of my time to refining my writing. She offered me two valuable gifts. First, she offered the gift of friendship; second, she offered to review my writing and guide me through the process. Because Bobbi Montgomery was a retired English teacher, the offer of her professional counsel was a godsend. Her encouragement and direction enabled me to embrace this project.

I had attempted book writing for several years. Interruptions and work, however, had always taken precedence. Bruce entered my life unexpectedly and offered me an environment where I had time to write; he even created an office for me in his home.

Later that day, after Bobbi left, I drove away from my family, my farm, my Sugar Shack business, and life as I knew it to explore Europe and the fourth career of my life, writing.

Our concerned families and friends keep asking us when the wedding will take place. Bruce just smiles and says, "When she gets pregnant and has the baby, I'll make an honest woman out of her."

After a six month vacation in Europe and Texas, our "summer romance" evolved into a serious relationship. We spend winters in Georgetown Texas and summers operating the Sugar Shack, along the Seaway Trail in western New York.

THE END